The World of
House Plants
&
Flower
Arranging

The World of
House Plants
& Flower
Arranging

Leslie Johns
&
Violet Stevenson

Peter Lowe

The colour of the poinsettia Euphorbia pulcherrima *comes from bracts or modified leaves, not from its small, bud-like flowers.*

Contents

Introduction

It is not difficult to see why house plants are so popular throughout the world. They are decorative in the home, office, showroom and factory. They are relatively inexpensive and easy to obtain. With only moderate care, they are long lasting and so economical. They are available in a wide range of shapes, sizes, colours and types. Their care is a matter of both natural and acquired skills and sensitivities and their use as decoration is an exercise of taste and personality. Anyone who looks after a plant indoors for a period of time cannot fail to become interested in its development, in each new leaf that unfurls and each new flower that opens.

Strictly speaking, a house plant is one which is grown indoors under normal living conditions for periods of a year or more (through all the seasons) for the beauty or interest of its shape, its colour, its growing habit, its foliage or its texture. There are many plants, however, which will live for shorter periods in the home or office and which have become accepted as house plants although technically they do not conform to the rule.

Because some of the botanical names of house plants are long and difficult to pronounce, many plants have been given popular names. Unfortunately these are both inaccurate and imprecise. For example, when we call a plant a daisy we invite misunderstanding because we do not specify which of the 400 or so species of daisy we mean.

Common names are not only duplicated, but they differ from country to country – even from region to region. It is for this reason that we have used the correct, botanical names in preference to popular names. To take one example, the plant called 'bow string hemp' in the United States is known as 'mother-in-law's tongue' in the United Kingdom.

From its common names, it seems like two different plants. But if we call it by its botanical name, *Sansevieria trifasciata laurentii*, anyone – Japanese and German, English and Egyptian – will know at once which plant is meant.

The International Committee on Horticultural Nomenclature agrees all names and has adopted a simple foolproof system. All names are in Latin. All plants are classified under four headings: family, genus, species and variety. The family need not concern us here, for it is not included in the name but is used for technical classification.

We can make this clearer by using a person as an example. To identify a person so that there is no possibility of a mistake, we say that he belongs to the family Man, that his genus is Smith, his species John and his variety 10 High Road, Blanktown. He is thus completely identified: there is no other such person in existence. Plants are not quite as individual as people, but the comparison shows the purpose of the different parts of a botanical name. *Sansevieria*, for example, belongs to the family *Liliacea*, the genus *Sansevieria*, the species *trifasciata* and the variety *laurentii*. If there was such a thing as a special golden cultivar (cultivated variety) this could also be specified as *Sansevieria trifasciata laurentii* 'Aureus'.

A botanical name is always written in italics. The first part of the name, the genus, begins with a capital letter but the species and variety names do not. If the first part of the name is used alone it is no longer written in italics and does not need a capital letter at the beginning. When a botanical name has been used several times, so that the reader knows which plant is being discussed, the name is abbreviated, for example to *S.t.laurentii*.

As house plants are not national but international, this universal and logical method of naming is very important. One of the reasons why house plants are so international is that they live in the artificial climate of the home and the office. Outdoor climates and conditions differ widely in different parts of the world and outdoor plants vary with the climate. But indoors we all like to live and work in very similar conditions of temperature, light, humidity and cleanliness. As a result the same plant will grow well in a brightly-lit and well-warmed Scandinavian home and in a cooled, air-conditioned South American office.

Another reason for the international nature of house plants is that the nurserymen and plant breeders who produce new plants are constantly seeking to improve varieties, looking always for greater toleration of poor conditions or mishandling, for stronger colours, longer life, a wider range of temperature and light requirements. 'New' plants are constantly being introduced after long trials and no plant is ever considered incapable of improvement.

Many people who are interested in growing pot plants will also enjoy using cut flowers as decoration in the home, though with these the situation is rather different. Though the practice of decorating the house with cut flowers is far more ancient than growing plants indoors for this purpose, the flowers themselves have a shorter life. This is one reason why they have been linked with house plants in the mixed *pot et fleur* (literally pot and flower) style.

In spite of air freight and refrigeration, it is not always possible to obtain the same flowers in the southern hemisphere as the northern. And, because of the artificial way in which our houses and offices are warmed or cooled, cut flowers rarely last for very long. Nevertheless, they are so important and irreplaceable that they retain a place in the home and their artistic arrangement has become an international pastime of considerable importance. Flower arranging societies, clubs and groups have millions of members throughout the world, experimenting continually with the different kinds of material available to them. If a plant illustrated in a particular arrangement does not grow in their part of the world, there is always an equally, perhaps more attractive substitute to be found.

In these mechanized and impersonal days, handling plants and flowers brings us closer to nature. It is at once a delight and a duty to treat them in a way that will prolong their healthy lives and they will repay such care many times over.

Leslie Johns
Violet Stevenson

What is a Plant?

A plant is a living organism capable of living wholly on inorganic substances and having neither power of locomotion nor special organs of sensation or digestion, a member of the vegetable kingdom.

CONCISE OXFORD DICTIONARY

Everything we grow indoors is a plant, though it is not necessarily a house plant in the strict sense. These are mainly evergreen, long lasting, tolerant of poor light, demanding of even temperatures and of course decorative, slow growing, pest and disease resistant and undemanding of attention. Some house plants have attractive, even exotic flowers, but as flowers are essentially ephemeral, these are grown either on a short term basis for the blooms alone, or are better known for their foliage.

Among the families of house plants there are a few giants – ivies, philodendrons, bromeliads, figs – which between them probably produce at least one-third of the total of several hundred individual species or varieties. Indoors all of these are slow growing, but they are attractive at all stages of development. They come from many different parts of the world, from tropical South America to the Himalayas, but all adapt well to indoor life, far from their natural habitats.

House plants can survive for long periods in confined conditions, their roots enclosed in astonishingly tiny pots. Indeed, to a certain extent their restricted growth is due to this confinement of root. If they were planted in open ground many would grow larger, quicker and might even flower and fruit, which some never do indoors, however carefully they are cared for.

Because they are grown under artificial conditions, they are subjected to extremes which they would not normally find in nature. Their surroundings can become too cold or too hot. They may receive an excess or a deficiency of water, food or light. Their stomata can be clogged with dust, their roots self-strangled in overgrown concentration, their cells choked with polluted air from gas fires or city fumes.

In particular, house plants are dependent on intelligent watering. Only turgid stems can carry vital foods and liquids throughout the plant and the ability to remain for long periods without water, or to regain turgidity quickly when watered after a period of drought must be an essential characteristic of a good house plant.

Many, but not all of these leaf shapes are found among house plants. In general, plants in arid regions have evolved smaller leaves, so that there is far less surface for evaporation. Many of the plants in tropical rain forests have pointed 'drip tips' to prevent water from collecting. Prickly or spiky leaves may have developed as a protection against damage by grazing animals.

Stem structures vary from plant to plant but all consist basically of a mass of cells, divided into three zones: the cortex, the vascular bundles and the pith. The cortex is the outer, protective skin. In trees it is a hard, woody bark but in smaller plants it is softer. One of its main functions is to prevent evaporation and it also protects the other tissues inside. The vascular bundles are the 'vein' system of a plant. They are made up of closed tubes, tapering at each end. Water and minerals absorbed by the roots, and food manufactured by the leaves, pass from one to another, gradually reaching all parts of the plant. Different types of 'vein' carry different substances. Some carry the water and minerals, others sugar. In some plants the vascular bundles are arranged in a distinct pattern among the surrounding cells.

The roots of a plant fix it firmly in the ground. They also absorb moisture from the soil, sucking it upward through minute pores or stomata in the root hairs. The moisture contains plant food as a solution of chemical salts and minerals.

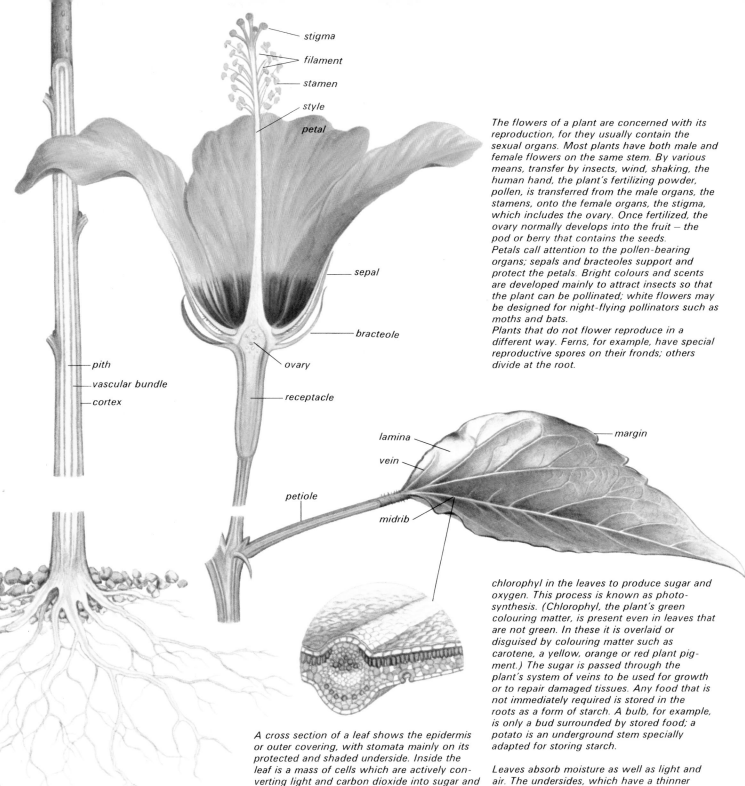

stigma

filament

stamen

style

petal

The flowers of a plant are concerned with its reproduction, for they usually contain the sexual organs. Most plants have both male and female flowers on the same stem. By various means, transfer by insects, wind, shaking, the human hand, the plant's fertilizing powder, pollen, is transferred from the male organs, the stamens, onto the female organs, the stigma, which includes the ovary. Once fertilized, the ovary normally develops into the fruit — the pod or berry that contains the seeds.

Petals call attention to the pollen-bearing organs; sepals and bracteoles support and protect the petals. Bright colours and scents are developed mainly to attract insects so that the plant can be pollinated; white flowers may be designed for night-flying pollinators such as moths and bats.

Plants that do not flower reproduce in a different way. Ferns, for example, have special reproductive spores on their fronds; others divide at the root.

sepal

bracteole

ovary

pith

vascular bundle

cortex

receptacle

lamina

margin

vein

petiole

midrib

chlorophyl in the leaves to produce sugar and oxygen. This process is known as photo-synthesis. (Chlorophyl, the plant's green colouring matter, is present even in leaves that are not green. In these it is overlaid or disguised by colouring matter such as carotene, a yellow, orange or red plant pig-ment.) The sugar is passed through the plant's system of veins to be used for growth or to repair damaged tissues. Any food that is not immediately required is stored in the roots as a form of starch. A bulb, for example, is only a bud surrounded by stored food; a potato is an underground stem specially adapted for storing starch.

Leaves absorb moisture as well as light and air. The undersides, which have a thinner outer skin and more pores or stomata, absorb this more quickly than the tough upper surfaces.

Leaves give out oxygen, produced by photosynthesis, and water vapour. Moisture evaporating from the leaves acts like a siphon, drawing water absorbed by the roots up through the stem to other parts of the plant. In dry countries some leaves are specially adapted to prevent this evaporation. Some succulents have thick outer skins with few stomata; others have fine hairs which stand erect to absorb moisture but lie flat in times of drought to prevent fluid from escaping. Some actually store water in thick, fleshy leaves.

root hairs

growing tip

A cross section of a leaf shows the epidermis or outer covering, with stomata mainly on its protected and shaded underside. Inside the leaf is a mass of cells which are actively con-verting light and carbon dioxide into sugar and oxygen. The veins are part of the plant's vascular system, used for transporting food and water throughout the plant. The branching network of leaf veins shows that this plant belongs to the Dicotyledon group.

Roots grow at their tips, which are covered in fine hairs to absorb fluid more quickly. Root development keeps pace with stem growth, but if the root ends are damaged, the plant may not be able to absorb enough food and will not grow properly.

The leaves of a plant (or the stems in the case of cacti, which have no leaves) absorb energy in the form of light and carbon dioxide. They grow on the stem in such a way that they receive as much light and air as possible, usually growing out from the stem on a thin stalk or petiole. Sunlight and carbon dioxide from the atmosphere act on the green

Choosing your House Plants

NAME OF PLANT	SIZE Climber **C** Trailer **T** up to 4ft (122cm) Varies with species **V** Approx height in inches cms		FLOWERING SEASON Spring **Sp** Summer **Su** Autumn **A** Winter **W** (No flowers) **NF**	CARE Easy **E** Medium **M** Difficult **D**	TEMPERATURE Cool up to 60°F **C** Medium 50°–60° **M** Warm 65°–75° **W**
Acidanthera	10–18	25–46	W	E	C
Adiantum cuneatum	8–24	20–61	NF	M	M
Aechmea rhodocyanea	8–18	20–46	Su–A	E	C–M
Aglaonema	18	46	S	M	M–W
Ananas	12–24	30–61	NF	E	M–W
Anthurium	6–18	15–46	S	M	M–W
Aphelandra	10–20	25–50	S	M	M–W
Aralia elegantissima	12–40	30–102	NF	M	M
Araucaria	6–24	15–61	NF	E	C–M
Asparagus plumosus	C		NF	M	C–M
Aspidistra	12–24	30–61	S	E	M
Asplenium	6–30	15–76	NF	M	M
Azalea	6–24	15–61	W	D	C
Begonia	6–24	15–61	Su or W	M	M–W
Begonia rex	3–18	8–46	NF	E	M
Beloperone	5–15	13–38	Su, A	M	W
Bletia or Blettilla	3–6	8–15	Sp & Su	E	M–W
Bougainvillea	C		Su	D	M–W
Billbergia	9–24	23–61	Su	E	M
Caladium	9–24	23–61	NF	D	M
Calathea	8–14	20–36	NF	D	M–W
Chlorophytum	6–18	15–46	NF	E	M
Chrysanthemum	6–15	15–38	Sp, Su, A, W	E	C–M
Cineraria	10–20	25–50	W, Sp, Su	M	C–M
Cissus	C		NF	E	M
Citrus	12–20	30–50	Sp, Su	D	M
Clivia	12–18	30–46	Sp, Su	M	M
Codiaeum	9–24	23–61	NF	M	M
Colchicum	3–9	8–23	A	E	M
Coleus	12–24	30–61	NF	M	M
Columnea	T		Sp, Su	M	M–W
Convallaria	5–10	12–25	Sp, Su, A, W	E	M
Cordyline	12–24	30–61	NF	M	C–M
Crocus	3–6	8–15	W	E	C
Cryptanthus	3–9	8–23	NF	E	M
Cyclamen	6–12	15–30	W	M	C
Cymbidium	24–36	61–91	Sp, Su, A, W	D	C–W
Cyperus	12–30	30–76	NF	E	M
Cypripedium	15–30	38–76	W	D	C–W
Dieffenbachia	10–20	25–50	NF	M	M
Dizygotheca	10–30	25–76	NF	M	M
Dracaena	12–30	30–76	NF	M	M
Epiphyllum	3–15	8–38	Sp, Su, A, W	E	M
Erica	2–6	5–15	W	D	C–M
Eucomis	10–20	25–50	S	M	C–M
Euonymus	4–12	10–30	NF	E	C–M
Euphorbia pulcherrima	12–30	30–76	W	M	C–M
Euphorbia milii	6–30	15–76	Sp, Su, A, W	E	M
Fatshedera	6–60	15–152	NF	E	C–M
Fatsia japonica	12–48	30–122	NF	E	M
Ficus	V		NF	E	M
Fittonia	8–15	20–38	NF	M	M–W
Fuchsia	10–30	25–76	Su	D	C–M
Galanthus	3–8	8–20	W, Sp	M	C

LIGHT	HUMIDITY	WATER	FOOD	ATMOSPHERE	SOIL

 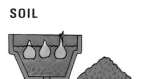  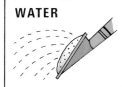

LIGHT		HUMIDITY		WATER		FOOD		ATMOSPHERE		SOIL	
Full sun	**S**	Humid above 70°F	**H**	Damp soil at all times	**D**	Never feed	**N**	Must have clean air	**C**	Open, well drained	**O**
Light shade	**L**	Slightly humid above 60°	**S**	Water only when soil is dry	**O**	Feed lightly, summer months only	**L**	Can tolerate some pollution	**P**	Peaty, water retentive	**P**
Deeper shade	**D**	Relatively dry above 50°	**D**	Moist in summer but not in winter	**SW**	Feed regularly when in flower, or growing fast	**R**				

LIGHT	HUMIDITY	WATER	FOOD	ATMOSPHERE	SOIL
L	S	SW	R	C	O
L	S	SW	L	C	P
L	D	In 'vase'	L	P	P
D	S	SW	L	C	P
S or L	D	SW	L	P	P
L	S	SW	L	C	O
L	H–S	SW	L	C	P
L	S	O	L	C	O
S or L	D	SW	L	C	O
L	H–S	SW	L	C	P
L or D	D	O	L	P	O or P
L	S	D	L	C	P
L	S	D	R	C	P
L	S	SW	L	C	P
L	S	D	L	P	P
L	S	D	L	C	P
L	S	D	L	C	P
L	S	D	L	C	P
L	D	In 'vase'	L	P	O
L	S	D	L	C	P
L	S–H	D	L	C	P
L	S	D	L	P	O
L	S	O	L	P	O
L	S	O	L	C	O
L	S	O	L	P	O
L	S	O	L	C	O
L	S	D	L	P	O
L	S–H	D	L	C	O
L	S	O	L	P	O
L	S–H	D	L	C	O
L	S–H	O	L	C	O
L	S–H	D	L	C	O
L	S	SW	L	P	O
L	S	D	L	C	O
L	S	SW	L	P	O
L	S	D	L	C	O
L	S	SW	L	C	special
L	S	D	L	P	P
L	S	SW	L	C	special
L	S	SW	L	C	O
L	S	SW	L	C	O
S–L	D	O	L	P	O
L	H	D	L	C	P
L	S	SW	L	C	O
L	S	SW	L	P	O
L	S	D	L	C	O
S–L	S	SW	L	P	O
L	S	SW	L	P	O
L	S	SW	L	P	O
L–D	H–S	SW	L	P	O
L	H–S	SW	L	C	O
L	H–S	SW	L	C	O
L	S	D	L	C	O

NAME OF PLANT	SIZE  Climber **C** Trailer **T** up to 4ft (122cm) **TV** Varies with species **V** Approx height in inches cms	FLOWERING SEASON  Spring **Sp** Summer **Su** Autumn **A** Winter **W** (No flowers) **NF**	CARE  Easy **E** Medium **M** Difficult **D**	TEMPERATURE  Cool up to 60°F **C** Medium 50°–60° **M** Warm 65°–75° **W**
Gardenia	24–48 61–122	Sp, Su	D	C–M
Haemanthus	10–15 25–38	Sp, Su, A, W	M	M
Hedera	C	NF	E	C–M
Helxine	2–3 5–8	NF	M	M
Hibiscus	15–30 38–76	Sp, Su	D	M
Hippeastrum	20–30 50–76	Sp, Su	E	M
Hoya	C	Sp, Su	E	M
Hyacinth	6–12 15–30	W, Sp	E	M
Hydrangea	15–50 38–127	Su	M	C–M
Hymenocallis	10–20 25–50	Sp	M	M
Hypocyrta	6–18 15–46	Su	E	M
Impatiens	8–20 20–50	Sp, Su	E	M
Kentia	15–150 38–381	NF	M	M
Lilium	10–30 25–76	Su	M	C–M
Maranta	6–10 15–25	NF	M	M
Monstera	C	NF	M	M
Narcissus	9–15 23–38	Sp	E	C–M
Neanthe	12–24 30–61	NF	M	M
Nephrolepis	10–20 25–50	NF	E	C–M
Nerine	12–24 30–61	Su, A	M	M
Nidularium	9–15 23–38	NF	E	M
Odontoglossum	10–40 25–102	Sp, Su	M	M–W
Oxalis	2–12 5–30	Sp, Su, W	E	M
Paphiopedilum	10–40 25–102	Sp, Su	M	M–W
Pelargonium	V	Sp, Su, A	E	C–M–W
Peperomia	3–8 8–20	NF	E	M
Philodendron	C	NF	E	M
Phoenix	12–36 30–91	NF	M	M
Pilea	9–15 23–38	NF	E	M–W
Platycerium	6–12 15–30	NF	E	M
Plectranthus	T	NF	E	M
Pleione	6–12 15–30	W, Sp, Su	E	M
Primula	6–12 15–30	W, Sp	M	M
Pteris	6–12 15–30	NF	M	M
Rhoeo	6–12 15–30	NF	D	M–W
Rhoicissus	C	NF	E	M
Saintpaulia	3–9 8–23	Sp, Su, A, W	M	M
Sansevieria	12–36 30–91	NF	E	M
Saxifraga	9–12 23–30	Su	E	M
Schefflera	12–60 30–152	NF	E	M
Schlumbergera	6–15 15–38	Sp	E	M
Scilla	3–12 8–30	Sp	M	M
Scindapsus	C	NF	M	M
Senecio	C	NF	E	M
Sprekelia	12–24 30–61	Sp, Su	M	M
Syngonium	C	NF	M	M
Tetrastigma	C	NF	M	M
Tradescantia	T	NF	E	M
Tulipa	9–15 23–38	Sp	E	M
Vallota	24–36 61–91	Su	M	C–M
Veltheimia	12–18 30–46	W–Sp	M	C–M
Vriesia	9–24 23–61	Su	E	M
Zebrina	T	NF	E	M
Zygocactus	6–12 15–30	W, Sp	E	M

LIGHT	HUMIDITY	WATER	FOOD	ATMOSPHERE	SOIL

Full sun **S** Light shade **L** Deeper shade **D**	Humid above 70°F **H** Slightly humid above 60° **S** Relatively dry above 50° **D**	Damp soil at all times **D** Water only when soil is dry **O** Moist in summer but not in winter **SW**	Never feed **N** Feed lightly, summer months only **L** Feed regularly when in flower, or growing fast **R**	Must have clean air **C** Can tolerate some pollution **P**	Open, well drained **O** Peaty, water retentive **P**
L	S	SW	L	C	P
L	S	D	L	C	O
S–L	S	O	L	P	O
L	H–S	D	L	C	P
L	S	D	L	C	O
L	S	D	L	C	O
L	S	O	L	P	O
L	S	D	L	P	O
L	S	D	L	C	O
L	S	D	L	C	P
L	S	D	L	P	O
L	S	D	L	C	P
L	S	SW	L	P	O
L	S	D	L	C	O
L	S	D	L	C	O
L–D	S	O	L	P	O
L	S	D	L	C	O
L	S	O	L	P	O
L–D	S	D	L	C	O
L	S	D	L	C	O
L	S	In 'vase'	L	P	O
L	H–S	D	L	C	Special
L	S	D	R	C	P
L	H–S	D	L	C	Special
L	S	SW	L	P	O
L	S	SW	L	P	O
L–D	S	O	L	P	O
L	S	O	L	C	O
L	S–H	D	L	C	P
L	S	O	L	P	O
L	S	D	L	P	P
L	S	D	L	C	P
L	S	D	L	C	P
L–D	S	D	L	C	P
L	S–H	D	L	C	P
L	S	O	L	P	O
L	S–H	D	L	C	P
L–S	S–D	SW	L	P	O
L	S	D	L	P	P
L	S	O	L	P	O
L	S	SW	L	C	P
L	S	D	L	C	P
L	S	O	L	C	O
L	S	O	L	P	O
L	S	D	L	C	O
L	S	D	L	C	O
L	S	O	L	P	O
L	S	O	L	P	O
L	S	D	L	C	O
L	S	D	L	C	O
L	S	D	L	C	O
L	S	In 'vase'	L	P	O
L	S	O	L	P	O
L	S	SW	L	P	O

Flowering House Plants

There are surprisingly few flowering house plants. The reason for this is simply that few plants which flower fit into the strict definition of a house plant – a plant which is grown indoors under normal living conditions for periods of a year or more, for the beauty or interest of its shape, its flowers, its foliage or its texture. Flowers are very much temporary ornaments on a plant so, strictly speaking, flowering plants are not house plants.

There are, however, considerable numbers of flowering plants which will decorate the home, the office, the store or the showroom for periods from a few days to several months and are thus well worth considering here. Like all house plants, the secret of their popularity lies in the fact that they can be kept close at hand and examined in detail at every stage. But as well as shape, colour and texture they have the very special attraction of flowers whose form and colour are more vivid and striking than any foliage.

The flowers on a plant are basically designed to attract attention to the sex organs so that reproduction can take place. Almost every plant has flowers, though sometimes these are so insignificant that they are almost unnoticeable. The flower of the aspidistra, for example, is a small, insignificant, fleshy pod which appears on the surface of the soil and is seldom noticed until actually looked for.

The main requirement of a flowering plant as opposed to one grown mainly for its foliage, is that it needs a greater degree of light in order to flower freely and produce well-coloured blooms. Flowers appear according to light and temperature at different times of the year, although in their natural habitat the original species are more regular in their habits. A plant in flower is using a greater quantity of its energies than at other times and it is therefore helpful to see that it gets a little more food and, possibly, water. The principle of all feeding should be that half the recommended dose applied twice as often is better than the other way around. It is seldom that any plant will require feeding more than once a week and fortnightly or monthly applications are the general rule.

Many flowering plants have been specially bred for indoor culture. Some are short and bushy, with long-lasting flowers, while others are so prolific with their blooms, producing not only a great number but a constant succession, that they appear to be continuously in flower. Examples of these two types are the chrysanthemums, with comparatively large blooms of several colours, long-lasting, bushy, stocky and sturdy and the smaller, daintier saintpaulia or African violet. The saintpaulia's flowers may not last so long but they appear

Aeschynanthus speciosus, *generally known as* Trichosporum lobbianum, *is a straggling trailer which grows to about 2ft (60cm) long. Its striking and beautiful flowers are seldom seen in temperate climates for the plant is difficult to obtain. Originally from Java, it needs more warmth and humidity than can normally be provided.*

with such regularity over so many months of the year that the plant seems to be in constant bloom.

The best flowering house plants are those that produce beautiful, unusual, striking or delicate flowers, yet which have such interesting or colourful foliage that after the flowers have gone, the plants still retain their charm. Perhaps the best known of these are classed among the room pines or bromeliads. *Vriesia splendens* is an obvious example. The flower – quick-growing and dramatic – appears in the shape of a sword, slim and blade-like, increasing in colour until it is a fiery orange-red. It then gradually dies to a not unattractive tan colour and can be cut away at the base. Yet all this time the banded green and chocolate leaves, growing outward in a rosette from the central cup from which the flower springs, are sufficiently attractive in themselves to justify having the plant in the house.

The so-called 'flower' of the vriesia is in fact a series of overlapping bracts, technically modified leaves tightly sheathed together. The quite insignificant and comparatively few tubes that appear at intervals through the bracts are the actual flowers. This is common among house plants. The vivid scarlet, pink or white 'flowers' of the poinsettia are bracts and the flowers are the small, berry-like items at the top of the stems. The yellow cockscomb at the top of a stem of an aphelandra, with its zebra-striped foliage, is really a series of bracts concealing and protecting the little flowers within. Bracts are almost always much longer lived than the flowers they contain or protect, and thus they considerably extend the decorative life of the plant.

Another type of flowering plant which will be examined in greater detail later is grown from bulbs and depends for its charm almost entirely on the flowers it produces. These flowers are fairly short lived, but the fascination of watching them grow, open, develop and then gradually fade makes up for their temporary nature. Cacti and succulents, on the other hand, are generally grown for their unusual shape and any flowers which appear are in the form of a bonus.

The list of flowering plants which follows is made up of the most useful, most attractive, most easily cared for and easily obtained plants. One or two may be rarities, but on the whole they should be readily available.

Aechmea rhodocyanea, also known as *A. fasciata* and popularly called the Grecian vase plant, is one of the best and easiest of all house plants. It has 3in (7·6cm) wide leaves up to 2ft (60cm) or so long, curving out from a central vase or cup, banded horizontally with tones of grey and green. From the centre of the cup rises a flower stem bearing a spiky pink scape, flower-like and attrac-

tive, which is studded with small lavender, blue and white flowers. Although the flowers themselves last only for a day or two, they are many in number and when they have all faded the scape remains for as long as six months. It should then be cut away. Each plant will flower only once but as the flower dies, a new plant will appear growing from the soil beside the main one. This can either be left to grow where it is or it can be cut away and repotted separately (see Chapter 8).

The aechmea makes few demands, preferring good light but tolerating some shade, accepting a dry atmosphere, living for years in a surprisingly small pot. The central vase or cup should be kept filled with water at all times and the sparse, tightly-packed roots can be fed with a liquid feed perhaps once a month, though they should not be kept constantly moist. It will grow well in a wide range of temperatures, showing little difference at 45°F (7°C) or 75°F (23°C).

Bromeliads or room pines usually have a central cup, formed by foliage, which should be kept filled with water at all times. Aechmea rhodocyanea *(left)* is known as the Grecian vase plant because of the shape of its grey-green leaves. It is easy to grow and produces a single pink, prickly scape with dozens of small blue, pink and white flowers. These fade quickly but the scape remains attractive for several months. Neoregelia carolinae tricolor *(below)* also has small flowers but the leaf bases turn a vivid scarlet when the blooms appear.

The aechmea is a bromeliad or room pine, which grows as an epiphyte in its natural habitat in South America. All cultivated bromeliads grown as house plants have leaves which arch outwards from the centre and these are always toothed or spined to varying degrees. Although it is a large family, only half a dozen or so species are grown as house plants.

The majority of the bromeliads available to us are similar to the aechmea in that they have a central cup or vase made by their leaves which should be kept filled with water at all times. The flowers differ according to species, some being magnificent and spectacular and others being insignificant. An example of the latter type is *Neoregelia carolinae tricolor*, which turns red when it is about to produce a flower. The interior of the cup or vase gradually changes colour from its normal dark green to a greenish red and finally to a brilliant scarlet. Then, in the centre of the cup and normally under water,

a small flower appears: it is so colourless, so unspectacular that it would not normally be noticed except for the vivid hue of the cup.

Another bromeliad which is slightly different from the aechmea is the pineapple itself, *Ananas comosus*. A special version, generally known as *Ananas bracteatus striatus* has been produced for indoor culture. This is a handsome plant with long, spiky, sharp-toothed leaves of a gorgeous golden yellow and green, delicately tinted with pink. It makes a taller and slimmer plant than most bromeliads and has little or no central vase. It must be watered through the soil. More details of its care will be found in Chapter 2.

Other members of the bromeliad family will be found in Chapter 2 under the names of cryptanthus, nidularium and vriesia. Not all produce spectacular flowers, but those that do are so theatrical in their appearance that they must deserve a place in this category.

Only the most striking or picturesque plants achieve common names and one which has received three must certainly be interesting. Piggy tail plant, flamingo flower and palette plant are all given to the anthurium because of its peculiar flower. The two species most frequently seen are *Anthurium andreanum* and *A. scherzerianum*. The first can have a red or a white flower, the second a red only, but in each case the colours are so vivid as to be almost unreal. The 'flower' is actually a large leaf or spathe, from which grows a short and sometimes curled spadix containing a large number of miniature flowers. It is the spadix which has produced the names piggy tail plant and flamingo flower and the shape of the spathe which has given rise to the name palette plant. The flower grows at the top of a long, naked stem and because it is extremely long lived – about a month – it is a favourite with flower arrangers. The leaves, usually spear-shaped, dark green and glossy, grow up to a foot (30cm) in length at the end of a short stalk.

Anthuriums enjoy normal room temperatures (around 60°F, 15°C), a moist soil and good light but not direct sun. They like a fairly humid atmosphere, which they get largely from the somewhat moist soil their roots prefer. They should receive a regular weekly or fortnightly feed of dilute fertilizer when they are in flower. The plant will not live long if conditions are too hot and dry and the leaves will in this case rapidly turn brown and crisp. Apart from their extraordinary flowers, anthuriums are not of great interest, but they are long lived, undemanding and are also fairly tolerant of poor conditions.

Less easy but equally striking and having the advantage of being interesting both when in flower and when not, is the Zebra plant, *Aphelandra squarrosa* 'louisae' which gets its common name from the vivid white horizontal stripes which decorate the dark green leaves. At the top of each stem, above the last pair of leaves, grows a bright yellow flower bract, like a cockscomb. The small yellow flowers which grow from this are hardly seen against the more vivid colour of the bract, which continues long after the flowers themselves, with a life of only a few days, have faded.

Because of the striking striped foliage, the aphelandra is always interesting and a more recent variety, *A. sq.* 'brockfeld' is even sold when it is not in flower, simply for the beauty of its foliage.

The aphelandra likes to be warm (60°–70°F, 15°–21°C) and if possible humid, or it may drop its lower leaves. Its soil should be kept moist at all times but never allowed to become wet. A light situation is necessary, as with all flowering plants, but direct sunlight will damage it. When the flowers open, the plant should be given light but regular applications of fertilizer.

The familiar florist's azalea, which is brought into so many homes in the northern hemisphere at about Christmas time, covered with masses of pink, red, white or orange blooms is a rhododendron hybrid and although called *Azalea indica* or *Rhododendron indicum*, it comes from Japan, not from India. This plant can be a lovely sight, but enjoy it while you can, for it is normally grown under highly artificial conditions especially for the gift trade and under normal home temperatures and aridity it is almost impossible to keep it in top form for more than a few weeks. It is, however, possible to plant it out in the garden when it has finished flowering and

Piggy tail plant, flamingo flower and palette plant are all common names for Anthurium andreanum *and* A. scherzerianum. *These attractive plants grow to between 1 and 2ft (30–60cm) in height. The flowers, which grow at the end of a long, naked stem, are tough, waxy and long lasting. This is* A. andreanum.

Below: Winter flowering begonias produce a constant succession of bright flowers if they are kept fed, moist and warm. Begonias do not thrive in polluted air. Fumes from gas fires or cookers, even ordinary city air, will affect both flowers and leaves. This is B. semperflorens.

there it can be kept until brought indoors again, preferably in late January or early February, to be forced once more into early flower.

To maintain flowering plants for as long as possible, try to keep them in a cool room rather than an overheated one, preferably in a temperature which does not rise higher than 60°F (15°C), and make sure that they never dry out. If they suffer from too lengthy a drought the flowers will brown and shrivel, the leaves will dry and fall, and the root ball will be almost impossible to moisten again. One way to tell if an azalea needs watering is to examine the main trunk of the plant just above the soil. If this is dark and damp-looking for a couple of inches (5cm) or so, the plant does not need water, so try to maintain this dark and damp lower trunk. A plant may need watering as often as twice a day in circumstances when temperatures are high and the air is dry. Because the plant is almost continuously in flower while it is in the house, it should receive good light, and regular feeding.

So far as we are concerned in this book, there are two main types of begonias, those grown for their flowers and those grown for their leaves. Of the former, which

are considered in this chapter, the fibrous-rooted types are unquestionably the most useful and with species and hybrids there are probably hundreds of different plants available. They are usually sold as named varieties.

Begonias are characterized by their lop-sided, heart-shaped leaves, which are often extremely handsome and colourful, even with the flowering types. Their flowers can be of many shapes, sizes and colours and with some plants, *B. semperflorens* for example, a succession of flowers will decorate the plant for periods of up to two months if conditions are suitable.

One thing begonias do not like is polluted air. If there is domestic gas in the atmosphere this is usually fatal and even the characteristic and inescapable atmosphere of large cities is sufficient to make some begonias difficult to grow well, causing their flowers to drop quickly and their leaves to droop, dry and turn brown. They like some warmth, between 55° and 65°F (12° and 18°C) but not hot and dry conditions and they prefer to be moist but not wet at the roots. When they are in full and luxuriant flower they need regular feeding and good light to keep them looking their best.

A curiosity that seems to attract greater interest than

it really warrants is the shrimp plant, *Beloperone guttata*, which gets its popular name from the form and colour of the reddish brown bracts which enclose the small white flowers. The plant is of no interest or beauty except for these bracts, so it is worth while making sure that they grow both large and vividly coloured. You can do this by taking care that it is never in too warm or dry a situation in the home and that it gets as much light as possible without actually subjecting it to direct and burning sun; ideal temperatures are between 55° and 65°F (12° and 18°C). Water shrimp plants thoroughly so that the soil is uniformly moist and then allow the roots to become almost dry before they are watered in the same way again. Dry plants will fail to set their flowers and the leaves will fall. To keep plants dwarf and bushy, pinch out the growing tips and feed them regularly during their growing period.

Bougainvillea is a climbing and flowering shrub that is best seen on a wall or a balcony outdoors, its vivid flowers colouring the entire area. It must be treated as a temporary plant indoors unless it can be given restorative treatment in the greenhouse once every month or so. The colours are tones of rosy red and once again it is the bracts that are spectacular while the flowers are less significant. The type usually grown indoors is *Bougainvillea glabra*. It is not really recommended as a house plant unless it can be grown in a conservatory or some place where uncomfortably high levels of humidity can be maintained for long periods. Conservatories today are rare but the special conditions they offer – high light intensity, humid atmosphere, comparatively high temperatures and staging and floors which can be thoroughly wetted – can be of great help in the cultivation of a large number of our more delicate house plants. If conditions in the house are not right for a bougainvillea it will fail to produce many flowers or will drop its flower buds before they fully open.

The modern house plant chrysanthemum is as much a product of science as of nature, for it is grown in artificial light and heat and usually treated with special chemicals which will not only keep it bushy and dwarf but which will maintain the flower heads at an even level. Pots of many different kinds and colours can be obtained and the strength of the plants, as well as the magnificence of the blooms, warrants a real tribute to the skills of the producers.

Buy plants with a future rather than a past, those with buds still to open. Make quite sure that the foliage is crisp and firm, that the blooms are free from browning at the edges. When you get them home give them a place in a cool room (preferably not hotter than 60°F, 15°C) where they get plenty of light. Keep the soil in the pot constantly moist – a dry or sickening plant will droop flowers and foliage quite unmistakeably. As the flowers fade remove them, both for the sake of appearance and to encourage continuity of bloom.

Because young plants are always grown in rich soil, they should require only the lightest of feeds even though they are in flower. A good plant should last at least two months in the home and when it has passed its best it can be planted in the garden. After a resting period, it will take its place among other garden plants but will not again be able to stand the rigours of indoor life.

Cinerarias can have flowers which are even more vivid than those of the chrysanthemum and they can be raised quite easily from seed. Plants will not live very long indoors – up to 2 or 3 months – but their colours of red, pink, white, blue, purple and mixtures of these make them cheerful additions to the indoor scene.

Cinerarias may require watering as often as once a day and will indicate their need by drooping their leaves. To keep them for long periods, do not leave them in too warm a temperature. 65°F (18°C) should

be the norm, though they will live happily but more briefly when the temperature is as high as 70°F (21°C). Keep them in a light position, out of the direct sun.

Cinerarias are 'dirty' plants, subject to attack by aphids and you should keep a very close watch on them and spray with insecticide at the first sign of trouble. It is sometimes sufficient to add a little systemic insecticide to the water which is applied to their roots. If you adopt this method, follow it from the time the plants first come into the house or when the seedlings are sufficiently developed for potting up.

A flowering house plant that is too seldom seen and can look magnificent when grown high in a room so that the long trails hang, vivid and dramatic, is the columnea. The best place for it is a tall, antique, oil lamp stand or a *torchère*. *Columnea banksii* will grow long trails covered with tubular scarlet flowers and *C. gloriosa* produces yellow flowers.

Good light helps flower production and the soil should be kept uniformly moist in the summer although rather drier in the winter. Temperatures can rise to 75°F (23°C) in the summer but may drop as low as 60°F (15°C) in winter, at which time watering should also be reduced. Individually the flowers may last no more than a week or so but a well-grown plant will be constantly covered with a succession of them during the flowering period. Try to keep the plant in as humid a situation as possible, even to the extent of giving it an occasional light spray with clean water. If a plant fails to flower or drops either buds or flowers prematurely, it is too cold, in too draughty a situation or dry at the roots.

Cyclamen are among the most popular of all indoor flowering plants and those people who fail to keep them for long are usually those who coddle them too much. For cyclamen do not like too warm a situation. The maximum temperature should be no higher than 60°F (15°C) and this should be maintained as evenly as possible for the cyclamen does not do well in draughts or fluctuating temperatures. They should be kept in good light, as far as possible from radiators or fires. Nor do they like stuffy atmospheres, domestic gas or polluted air. They are best watered through the base of the pot in case water gets into the top of the corm, where it will set up rot. The soil should be just moist, so it will need frequent, small amounts of water. Do not let water stand in the saucer holding the pot for more than a couple of hours or the plant will become saturated.

Feed it when it is in flower and when the flowers have faded, gradually reduce the watering until the soil is almost dry. Repot the corm in fresh soil at the end of the summer and begin the watering and feeding programme as the buds appear.

Euphorbias are a large genus of plants which include tender succulents, hardy herbaceous plants, trees and shrubs. The genus is characterized by almost all its species having a milky latex which is frequently poisonous. In the home, euphorbias provide us with two completely different but equally excellent types of house plant from the two thousand or so species known. The first is the graphically named crown of thorns, so called because of its large, vicious thorns and the many tiny, scarlet flowers which look like drops of blood. Most nursery men still use the botanical name *Euphorbia splendens* although the correct name is now agreed as *E. milii*. As we have so often seen, the tiny, vivid scarlet flowers are actually bracts which contain and protect the even smaller flowers. A variety, *E. splendens lutea*, is exactly the same except that the flowers are a pale lemon-yellow colour.

Both plants are extremely easy to grow, needing as much light as they can get, even direct sunlight, some warmth (they grow well in temperatures between 50° and 80°F, 10° and 26°C), plenty of water and regular feeding at the roots during the warm days with rather less in winter. Evergreens, they shed their flowers and foliage gradually rather than all at once. If the conditions do not suit them, the process is accelerated. *E. milii* is supposed to grow no more than about three feet (1m) tall but we have a specimen which we have had for some twenty years and not only is it taller than this, but it has never during this period been without some flower! These are interesting rather than beautiful plants, but their undemanding nature, striking appearance and extreme longevity make them bargains in the house plant world.

Another member of the euphorbia family, the poinsettia, *E. pulcherrima*, is an excellent house plant. Much work has been done on the poinsettia in the past few years, with the result that instead of being a remarkably short-lived plant, it will now live for many months in the home and hardly shed a single leaf. These new, long-lasting varieties are known as the Mikkelrochford strain after the Mikkelson and Rochford nurseries which bred them in the United States and England respectively.

The poinsettia is best known for its vivid scarlet bracts topped by the little green and gold berries that are the actual flowers and live for a shorter period. There are equally attractive pink and white forms which are just as long lasting as the more popular scarlet varieties.

Although they have achieved this new toughness it is nevertheless helpful to see that plants are not kept in too warm conditions and are not placed in a draught. They will last up to six months and sometimes longer where the temperatures do not exceed about 60°F (15°C). See that they get plenty of light and that the roots are not allowed to dry out. A light but regular feed should be given when the plants are growing well. The lower leaves will fall and the bracts will curl and dry if temperatures are too high or humidity is lacking.

There has also been some development of the dainty and charming fuchsia and it is now possible to grow certain hybrids indoors for longer periods than it was a few years ago. These special plants are usually available as named varieties, but they are not normally to be seen in great quantities nor in all parts of the world. Garden fuchsias can be brought indoors for brief periods of a week or two at a time and if they are given plenty of light and not too much heat they will suffer no real harm. Temperatures should preferably be no higher than 70°F (21°C) and this only for a short time. A restorative period in the garden or in the greenhouse, depending on outdoor conditions, will bring them to peak condition again. First indication that the plants are suffering will be the dropping of flowers and buds. Keep the soil moist at all times and feed regularly when the plants are in flower. Humidity can be provided by giving them a light spray with clean tepid water each morning, just enough to moisten the foliage and not enough to harm the furniture.

Even more difficult and recommended only for the calm and even-tempered is *Gardenia jasminoides*. This evergreen shrub, usually grown in the garden in warmer climates, or in the greenhouse, produces flowers of such delicate beauty and such glorious perfume that it is always worth trying to grow it indoors. Unfortunately the gardenia has an infuriating habit of dropping its flower buds just when they seem about to open. They will drop their buds if it is too warm for them or too cold, if the roots are too dry or too wet, if they are too light or too dark.

In general it needs plenty of light but not direct sun, a high degree of humidity, a temperature of between 65° and 80°F (18° and 26°C) and constant moisture at the roots. However, conditions vary so widely in different parts of the world and at different seasons that it is unwise to be dogmatic. It likes a rich soil, so feeding should be regular when plants are in flower. It should be remembered that these flowers are of a particularly delicate nature and so should be handled as little as

Hibiscus makes a striking and unusual pot plant, its large, vivid flowers standing out from dark, shining leaves. It needs a cool, well ventilated position but even in ideal conditions the flowers will not normally last for more than a few days.

Left: Tints, tones and shades of red predominate in this arrangement of dracaena (left), cordyline (right) and poinsettia, Euphorbia pulcherrima (foreground). The plants are still in their own pots but are grouped together inside a large copper pan.

possible. Almost any plant will suffer from handling.

The general view of hibiscus is that it is so exotic, so rare and oriental that it is only those fortunate enough to live in warm climates who can enjoy its large, languorous blooms. Yet *Hibiscus rosa-sinensis* makes an unexceptional pot plant and in some instances will even do better in the garden than indoors. It does not need high temperatures and humidity but rather an airy atmosphere and a freedom from over-coddling. It must have good light but will tolerate rooms warmed only to about 65°–70°F (18°–21°C) so long as the roots are kept constantly moist and fed once a fortnight or so. Flowers will not normally last more than a few days

indoors and if conditions are not right, they may drop even while they are still buds.

The huge flowers vary from white, yellow and orange to pink and red in colour but are always striking, trumpet shaped with a dominant, protruding set of stamens. There are a large number of named varieties of this hibiscus, some having single, others semi-double or double flowers.

The hibiscus is best kept in the garden in summer and brought indoors, ready pruned to shape, before it begins to bloom in the later summer. Where summer temperatures are normally high this process should be brought forward in the year by a couple of months.

Two of the easiest and least demanding climbers are *Hoya carnosa* and *Hoya bella*. They have thick, fleshy leaves, the variegated form being cream and white in colour. The leaves grow in pairs off a central climbing stem which, given only a little encouragement, travels upwards without further help. Every now and again in the summer *H. bella* will produce a cluster of pretty, fragrant, waxy white flowers with pink centres, not so dominant that they attract attention but a source of considerable pleasure when they are unexpectedly found. Because the flowers are uncertain but the plant is nevertheless worth growing for its foliage alone, it is discussed in greater detail in the section on foliage plants (Chapter 2).

More dominating is the rather heavy and somewhat Victorian hydrangea. This is really better for the garden than the house but it can be very useful for large interiors such as stores or showrooms and for special occasions such as weddings. The hydrangea's pink or blue flowers are too familiar to require description; to obtain the popular blue it is necessary to grow the plant in acid soil.

The hydrangea is a thirsty plant, sometimes requiring copious draughts of water twice a day. Those plants which are potted are best kept outdoors until or unless they are required for indoor decoration. When they are brought indoors for more than a few days they must be given as much light as possible, but never direct sunlight, and the roots must be kept constantly moist. If possible a light spray over the plants in the evening or morning will be greatly beneficial. They prefer a cool, airy location to one that is hot and stuffy and if possible temperatures of 70°F (21°C) or so should not be exceeded. Dropping leaves and dehydrated flowers will indicate that the plant is ailing and probably in need of water. Hydrangeas can be kept to reasonable shape by cutting down severely after the flowers have faded.

The hypocyrta or goldfish plant is so called because of the shape and appearance of the orange-red blooms on the short and wiry stems. *Hypocyrta glabra* makes a small plant, not more than a foot (30cm) or so tall and about as spreading, with almost as many pretty flowers on its stem as leaves. It likes to be moderately warm, between 55° and 70°F (12° and 21°C), given a light position out of the sun and to have its roots moist in summer and little drier in winter. When the plant is growing well, the flowers will stay on it for two weeks or so and will constantly be replaced by new ones. A light spray over the plant during the hotter months of the year will help to keep it fresh and while it is in flower it should be fed regularly. If it is being given the wrong

Pelargoniums or pot geraniums are among the most popular house plants. They are grown for foliage as well as flowers and can be climbers or trailers as well as bushes. Some have scented foliage and in some countries they grow both indoors and out.

treatment the flowers will disappear and whole stems at a time will droop, wither and die.

It sometimes seems that there can be few homes or offices anywhere in the world without a plant of busy lizzie growing somewhere. This is probably because it is such an easy and rewarding plant: it grows quickly regardless of the size of its pot or the type of its compost; it can be propagated without any trouble, in plain water alone even; and it is attractive to look at.

Busy lizzie may be *Impatiens holstii*, *I. sultanii* or, in its dusky, bronze-leaved form, *I. petersiana*. All are equally easy to grow, but this does not mean that they will not give even better value if they receive some attention. They need constant moisture at the roots and, if they are also fed regularly, they will grow into enormous bushes, always thick with flowers of pink, red, yellow, purple or white in many tints and shades. The flowers do not last long, but are constantly replaced.

Impatiens plants grow so quickly and so easily that they sometimes outstretch themselves. Their stems are thick and fleshy, hence brittle. An over-grown, lanky

Hydrangeas are too large for many houses and need to be given ample moisture at all times to prevent the leaves drooping and the flowers drying up. Here they are shown in a conservatory with other plants including lilies, bougainvillea and ivy.

impatiens is not only ugly, it is unnecessary, for a piece or two broken off and firmed into a pot of soil will grow roots and make a new plant very quickly. It will even grow roots in plain water. It is therefore much better to have a series of new plants always coming along than to keep one alone and let it grow old.

Moderate warmth (60°–70°F, 15°–21°C), plenty of slightly shaded light, copious water and an occasional feed is about all an impatiens needs but it will also appreciate some protection from cold draughts and from the direct warmth of any heating apparatus. Falling flowers and leaves or drooping stems are a sign that impatiens is not receiving the right care.

The pelargonium is a garden plant which is almost hardy. At the same time it is a greenhouse plant for colder climates which with only moderate special care will adapt itself to normal house condition. Its temperature range can be anywhere between 45° and 80°F (7° and 26°C). It can be grown for its flowers of several colours or for its almost equally colourful foliage – or both. It is easy to propagate, and it will make a small,

bushy plant, a considerable shrub or even a pillar-like climber. It can be trained and pruned. In short, the pelargonium is one of the most versatile, accommodating and useful plants to have. Pelargoniums like a fairly rich soil, though not so lush that they make leaf at the expense of flower. If you have a choice, try to use a fertilizer with a comparatively low nitrogen content and a higher than usual proportion of potash. It also helps if plants are allowed to starve a little during the winter and then are fed regularly when the warmer days arrive and the plants show obvious signs of growth. Plants that tend to lose their leaves and become leggy can be suffering from dryness at the roots, lack of sufficient light or they may have outgrown their strength. In this case if their growing tip is pinched out they will almost certainly quickly make new growth which will help to hide the bare patches.

They like plenty of water during the hotter months with regular feeding, and much less moisture and no food during the colder, darker days. They like plenty of light and will even accept direct sunlight where this is

Latest saintpaulia cultivars have brought greater strength and tolerance to these previously difficult plants. They are popular and widely grown, though while some people seem to do well with them, others have only failures. Clean air, some warmth, long periods of good light each day, even artificial light at times, are necessary to get the best from these plants,

Right: Primula obconica, *normally a garden plant, will last quite well indoors if it is kept in a cool and airy place and given plenty of water at its roots. A morning spray with tepid water will also help it to stay fresh.*

moderate instead of baking. They are remarkably trouble-free and pest-free.

It is not always possible to grow primulas as a house plant in all parts of the world and even in their natural territory they may survive only for brief periods. Nevertheless, they are worth bringing indoors if only for a few days at a time. *Primula vulgaris*, the simple primrose, *P. obconica* and the well known 'polyanthus' will all grow for brief periods in the home before being returned to the garden again. There are, in fact, something like five hundred species of primula, mainly from mountains as widely separated as the Caucasus and the Japanese Alps, the Alpes Maritimes and the Himalayas.

To keep them looking well in the home, their roots must never be allowed to dry out and they will benefit from a morning spray of tepid water. Keep them in as cool and airy a situation as possible, where the sun will not rest on them for more than a few minutes each day.

The saintpaulia or African violet has a reputation for being a difficult plant to grow. Fortunately plant hybridists are working hard to produce easier strains and today there are cultivars which are simpler. There are single saintpaulias, semi-double and double. They come in white, blue, pink and several tones of these colours. They can have hairy leaves or smooth. The flowers are not violets, of course, and it seems a pity that they ever received that label in the first place, but they are long lasting and some of the latest cultivars have bred into them such strength that the flowers hang onto the plants for weeks.

Some warmth, between 55° and 75°F (12° and 23°C), plenty of good light but no sun, some protection from draughts, clean air and regular watering and feeding are the main requirements of saintpaulias. Unfortunately a drop of water on a saintpaulia leaf can act as a burning glass if the sun strikes the plant even for a few minutes and, again unfortunately, water settling in the crown of the plant can lead to leaf and stem rot. For this reason it is wise, though perhaps not strictly necessary, to water from the base. Pour a little water into the saucer or other container in which the pot stands and allow an hour or two for the soil around the roots to absorb it. If the water has not disappeared after this time pour it away; otherwise the plant may drown.

There are many thousands of hybrid orchids. Many, like this cypripedium (above) are more curious than beautiful, yet they have a real fascination for the specialist enthusiast. Some orchids need extra care and cymbidiums (left) cannot normally be grown indoors without special conditions.

A light liquid feed can be administered at the same time as the water.

If the atmosphere in which it is kept, or the treatment it is receiving do not suit the saintpaulia, its flowers will wilt and die. No replacements will appear but the leaves will seem to contract and the entire plant will take on a miserable and shrunken appearance. The greatest enemy has always been atmospheric pollution, with which we nearly always get bad light. City dwellers in particular find saintpaulias difficult to grow well and it may be necessary to give them their own micro-climate inside a goldfish bowl or a terrarium. In the cleaner air of the country, saintpaulias grow like weeds and are seldom to be seen without masses of flowers.

ORCHIDS

One or two bulbous, soil-growing orchids are available at reasonable prices and are comparatively easy to grow. Several of the epiphytic orchids, which grow high on trees in their natural habitats can also be grown in a moderately warm home and in some countries they are, of course, a commonplace. If indoor temperatures can be maintained at between 60° and 80°F (15° and 26°C) and light is good, there is no reason why some of the most beautiful and exotic orchids should not be grown. However, some of them pose problems and the wise indoor gardener will make quite certain that he can provide the correct conditions and can carry out some of the rather complex operations that may be called for before he spends too much money on plants.

Suppliers usually sell plants which are just about to come into flower. There are many, many hybrids, some of which differ only slightly, but all are beautiful and the flowers are very long lasting. Useful plants to try are the terrestrial cypripedium, known as the lady's slipper orchid, and the cymbidium, particularly epiphytic varieties, which can have stems bearing as many as thirty flowers. There are also terrestrial or epiphytic varieties of paphiopedilums and probably hundreds of varieties of the epiphytic odontoglossum species. All of these are possible exotics for the home. The simpler, more easily grown orchids are discussed in greater detail in the chapter on bulb flowers (Chapter 4) and it may be wise for the enthusiast to begin with these.

Foliage House Plants

The whole beauty of foliage house plants is the tremendous variety and range of form of the leaves. They can differ in colour, shape, texture, size, number, uniformity, in their thickness and in the shape and regularity of their edges. They can differ in the way they grow from the plant and in the way they hang. Some house plant leaves can be as much as 2ft (60cm) across and others can be smaller than an inch (2·5cm). Many leaves begin life with one colour, one shape, one texture, one size and gradually develop and change as they grow so that by the time they are mature they are completely different. Some single leaves are astonishingly beautiful and others are uninteresting, even drab, until seen in the mass on a plant, which they clothe with dramatic effect.

Most foliage is long lived. It persists on the plant for weeks, months or possibly even years. This means that foliage plants have, on the whole, a much longer decorative life than flowering plants. Some can be used to decorate a room in much the same way and with much the same effect as a picture on the wall. The clever housewife or home decorator takes a hint from the main painting on her walls and chooses her furnishing colours to blend or contrast with the colours she finds there. In just the same way it is possible to look closely at the leaves of any plant and find there not just the basic overall colour but a number of different tones, tints and shades which can be picked up in the furnishings to the benefit of the appearance of the room as a whole.

The true value of house plants as furnishing material is discussed in later pages and here it will be well to have a look at those foliage plants generally available. Although there are natural variations according to climate and hemisphere, most popular house plants are almost standard products today, as available and as uniform as cornflakes.

As a general rule foliage plants are easier to grow in the house than those which flower. Some of the more delicate specimens have a comparatively short life but many of the hardier types will live almost indefinitely with no more than normal care under home conditions. Certain plants grown for their foliage produce flowers but as these are either insignificant or ephemeral, they are largely ignored. It is among foliage plants that we find the most useful examples of plants for interior decoration, for they are long lasting, easy to grow, tolerant of neglect, easily trained and make few demands on the grower. Seasons make little difference to them, although during the cooler and darker months rates of watering and feeding should be reduced to allow the plants their required rest period.

Although there are great numbers of ferns, many differing widely in appearance, they are not always easy to buy except from large centres or specialist growers. They like humidity, light shade and moist roots.

Adiantum cuneatum is the maidenhair fern, with little green segments on fronds supported by wiry black stems. It is not an easy fern to grow except under humid conditions, and may do best in company with other plants in a bowl or terrarium where the plants jostle each other and each creates a shared micro-climate. Like most ferns it prefers a situation of light shade and a cool, moist atmosphere. If possible temperatures should not rise to more than about 60°F (15°C) and the roots should be kept constantly moist. An occasional spray with tepid water is helpful, otherwise the little segmented fronds tend to dry out, become brown and drop. Only the lightest of feeds should be given to this fern, no more than once a month or so during the growing period.

Aglaonemas are more likely to be found today as named varieties or cultivars than as species. This is partly because of their awkward and not particularly attractive botanical name. The common names, silver spear plant, Chinese evergreen and others with similar visual connotations have a better chance of being remembered. Their spear-shaped leaves grow on short stalks; colours are mainly different tones of green marked with spots or slashes of cream, yellow, white or silver. To retain or indeed intensify these colours, the plants should be placed in a situation where they get plenty of light, but no direct sunlight. Keep aglaonemas warm (60°–70°F, 15°–21°C) and moist in summer months and still warm (60°–70°F, 15°–21°C) but very much

Coleus hybrids produce some of the most vivid leaf colours of any plants and no one leaf is exactly the same as another. Plants are easy to grow indoors from seed and will also do well in the garden so long as the sun is not too hot. They produce small, pretty flower spikes but to retain strength and colour in the leaves, these should be pinched out as soon as they appear.

drier in winter. A light feed when the plant is growing well will help young leaves to develop and replace those that are past their best. Too dry an atmosphere tends to make the leaves curl and shrivel. Polluted air, particularly with oil or gas fumes, will be fatal to these plants after a few days.

As with many other fruits and vegetables, it is possible to propagate a pineapple plant and even bring it to fruiting stage. The technique for doing this with the ordinary pineapple fruit, *Ananas comosus*, is discussed in Chapter 9. Apart from the interest and sense of achievement involved, it must be admitted that this familiar variety is not particularly decorative, certainly not nearly as attractive as *Ananas bracteatus striatus*, or ivory pineapple. Where the domestic fruit merely has an undistinguished tuft of grey-green leaves, small and stunted, the ivory species is much larger, with lance-shaped leaves, dramatically striped with cream and green. These leaves, however, are spitefully toothed with what are almost thorns, so it is wise to place the plant where family or visitors are unlikely to come into contact with it. Like all bromeliads, the ivory pineapple is easy to maintain, asking merely for a little warmth (anywhere between 50° and 70°F, 10° and 21°C), a little water and an occasional feed.

Because it is variegated, its colour is best maintained by placing it in a situation where it gets long periods of good light. It will even tolerate direct sunlight for short periods each day. This is a tough plant and little is likely to go wrong with it, although after it has been grown for some months the tips of some of the older leaves may become brown. If this happens the plant will look better if the tips are snipped off with a pair of scissors.

The toothed leaves of *Aralia elegantissima* are entirely different from the thorny leaves of the ivory pineapple, being smooth, soft and – as its name implies – elegant. The plant makes a little tree, up to 3 or 4ft (1 or 1·25m) tall, its branches standing out from the main trunk. The plant is topped with an umbrella cage of segmented leaves, dark green with an almost white midrib. Confusingly and inaccurately this aralia has been given the popular name of spider plant. Unless it is kept in a humid atmosphere it tends to lose its lower leaves after a time, but it remains attractive nevertheless.

Aralia elegantissima grows well in a wide range of temperatures, from 50° to 70°F (10° to 21°C) but when it is warm it is helpful to spray the leaves once or twice a week with clean, tepid water to enable the plant to retain them for as long as possible. It requires only the lightest of feeds and although the loss of its lower leaves is almost inevitable, the process is a gradual one which

The Norfolk Island pine, Araucaria excelsa *(above) is a plant for the heavy-handed and is almost impossible to kill. Though it has pine-like needles these do not drop if the plant gets dry, instead the whole plant tends to droop. Aglaonemas (below) are rather more difficult to grow. They need warmth and humidity, with good light to retain the colour of their leaves.*

allows the plant to remain decorative for many months at a time. It is a useful plant and though obviously it must not go in dark corners, it does not need a specially light situation.

Another good and attractive plant in the same family is sometimes called *Aralia japonica*, the castor oil plant. It is more correctly named *Fatsia japonica*, the false castor oil plant, and is discussed under that heading.

The Norfolk island pine *Araucaria excelsa* is quite different from any of the plants we have discussed so far. It is a perfectly genuine, though miniature pine tree, with glaucous green branches made up of pine-like needles. It is an easy plant to handle, tolerant of most conditions and needing no great warmth, humidity or light. Nevertheless it is worth growing well. It should have a lightly shaded situation with plenty of water at the roots during the summer months, less in winter, a temperature of between 50° and 70°F (10° and 21°C) and, during the summer, an occasional light feed and a gentle spray with tepid water. It does not drop its needles and if it has been allowed to become too dry the entire plant tends to droop rather than shed its foliage.

Asparagus plumosus, the asparagus fern, is a berry-bearing evergreen climber, not a fern at all. Its lacy 'fronds' have a certain charm and once it finds a position indoors which it likes, it will climb and trail for 10ft (3m) or more and give little or no trouble. Keep it out of sun and draughts, water freely in summer and less in winter.

A situation of light shade seems to suit it and although the soil around its roots should be kept moist, the long trails of fronds are more tolerant of dry atmospheres than one would imagine. The plant is also tolerant of a range of temperatures between about 50° and 70°F (10° and 21°C). An occasional feed during the lighter, warmer months will keep it growing well. If it is allowed to become too dry the fronds tend to break up and drop.

The parlour palm or cast iron plant achieved these names during its heyday in Victorian times, when it was to be seen in every parlour in spite of the fact that the room was heated (rarely) with smelly coal fires and lit (dimly) with gas mantles. During the inevitable period of reaction, *Aspidistra elatior* almost disappeared but it is now making a strong comeback. It is said that the aspidistra thrives on neglect, yet if it is given just a little care and attention it responds by becoming a real, glossy-leaved beauty. Its long, spear-like leaves grow on a short stalk to 2 feet (60cm) or so in length and there is a form *A.e. variegata* which is attractively striped with gold. Both are easy to grow and need no special attention, though the variegated form maintains its deep colour only when it is in a well-lit situation. A well-moistened and regularly-fed soil will keep the active rhizomes moving and sending up new young, glossy leaves. Temperatures for this plant can vary between 40° and 80°F (4·5° and 26°C) without affecting it and only dryness at the roots or an over-arid air will tend to make the leaf tips turn brown. This brown tip can either be cut away with scissors or the discolouration can be allowed to travel down the length of the leaf, which eventually dies, retaining a pleasant tan colour. The dead leaves can be used effectively in flower arrangements.

The bird's nest fern gets its name from the mass of interwoven roots from which grow vivid green, tongue-shaped fronds with undulated edges. The botanical name for this fern is *Asplenium nidus* and it comes from such widely differing areas as Australia, India and Japan. Like all ferns it needs a good deal of humidity and cannot stand too dry an atmosphere or bright sunlight. Do not let it get cold during the winter, but maintain a temperature of at least 55°F (12°C). Too much warmth, a dry air or draughts will cause the fronds to curl up and die. The roots should be kept moist at all times and a light spray over the foliage once a week or so is helpful. Only the lightest of feeds should be given.

In the large, useful and decorative family of the begonias, two foliage species stand out. They are *Begonia masoniana* and *B. rex*. The first consists of one type only, with the characteristic crinkled leaf surface bearing a rough facsimile of a Maltese cross. The second has vast numbers of cultivars which provide us with some of the most vivid leaf colourations. *B. rex* leaves can be green, gold, silver, white, red or purple. They can be smooth or crinkled and some appear almost metallic. All have the characteristic lop-sided, heart-shaped outline.

Both species are easy to grow in the average home, requiring warmth (50°–70°F, 10°–21°C) and good light but not direct sun. An occasional feed during the growing period helps the colour and the size of the leaves. These begonias are not always predictable, and where for a period they may like their roots to be constantly moist and cool, at other times they seem to prefer a drier soil, a higher temperature and a brighter light. It is wise to watch specimens closely and when leaves begin to brown at the edges, light and temperature should be reduced and a little more water given to the soil.

Calathea makoyana, *known popularly as the peacock plant, is one of the most striking plants in the Calathea genus and can reach 4ft (122cm) in height. However, few plants grow as big as this indoors for, like all calatheas, they need special care and will not survive long in hot, dry rooms or in cold temperatures.*

Right: Three species of begonia, B. haageana *(top),* B. rex *(left) and* B. masoniana. *Begonias are a large genus of flowering and foliage plants with some 400 species. They can be divided into three main groups: tuberous rooted, rhizomatous and fibrous rooted. Most of the tuberous rooted begonias grow better outside than in but the rhizomatous include* B. rex *and other foliage species with a great variety of colours and patterns, while the fibrous rooted species have both flowering and foliage types.*

Because it has perhaps the most beautiful foliage of any plant ever grown, the caladium has found its way into many homes and indeed into many lists of house plants. Strictly, however, it is not a house plant at all, for the leaves die down each winter and the tubers from which they grow must be stored and then started into growth again in the spring. So attractive is the foliage that considerable work has been done on producing cultivars and caladiums can now be seen with their large, arrow-shaped leaves speckled, striped, streaked and spotted with white and cream and green and pink and red and purple – a marvellous range.

The caladium's soil should never be allowed to dry out and the atmosphere should be kept humid, though not too close or oppressive. Temperatures should be in the 60° to 75°F (15° to 23°C) range. Draughts, either cold or hot, are dangerous and will make the leaves curl, bend and die. Plants should be kept where they will at no time receive the direct rays of the sun, but where there is good, steady illumination. An occasional feed when the plants are growing strongly is recommended

Below: A large-leaved caladium with, behind, white fuschia flowers. Caladiums are tuberous-rooted plants and their beautiful leaves die down each winter. There are several varieties, with green, pink, red or purple foliage. None is easy to grow again another year but they are so attractive that it is worth keeping them while they are in leaf.

but they must not be over encouraged by nourishment. They are not easy plants for all homes and must be treated as expendable.

Calatheas are again frankly difficult plants for most people, but with care they can be kept for many months, if not years. Like caladiums, they have very beautiful leaves. *Calathea ornata* is a small plant and carries its almost egg-shaped leaves on short stems. The leaves are dark in colour, striped purple and pink, delicate and finely etched. *C. zebrina* has much larger leaves, soft and velvety in texture, apple green in colour, streaked with chocolate brown. Calatheas should be kept warm in winter (at least 60°F, 15°C) and just moist. When the warmer days arrive give a little more water and place them in a lighter position, though never in direct sunlight, and new leaves will quickly appear, aided by the application of regular, light feeds. Humidity is an important factor for calatheas and they will react to dry air, hot air or cold temperatures by curling up their leaves. These will then discolour and die.

Chlorophytum comosum variegatum, the spider plant, St.

Bernard's lily or ribbon grass must surely be one of the most popular and easily grown house plants in the world. It is, in fact, rather like a large tuft of grass, with banded cream and green blades, about a foot (30cm) long and half an inch (12mm) wide, arching out from a central point. Longer stems also arch out from the centre, bearing at their tips a few white and rather insignificant flowers. These develop into baby plantlets which gradually produce roots and can quite easily be propagated into new plants by resting them on or pegging them into a pot or other vessel of soil nearby.

Chlorophytums will grow quite well in a temperature range of 50° to 70°F (10° to 21°C) and make no particular demands on regular watering, feeding or high humidity. The variegated leaves keep their colour best in good light but are less difficult in this respect than most similar plants. It is such an easy plant that it is sometimes neglected and begins to look a little brown and bedraggled. Brown leaf tips can be trimmed with scissors but the best way to maintain an attractive plant is to start afresh and constantly to grow a new one.

Cissus antarctica is one of our most dependable climbers and will live for many years. Many-stemmed and thickly-leaved, it can be grown up a cane or a string to make a pillar or its individual stems may be spread out and trained to cover a wall or lattice work. The cissus is an easily grown plant which will exist on a weekly watering but which repays regular feeding and care. It will withstand a wide range of temperatures, having even been known to survive a frost. When the temperature rises above about 75°F (23°C) an occasional light spray will be useful. The dark green leaves do not demand strong light and appear to grow best in light shade. Regular feeding is necessary to sustain the large number of individual leaves and the rapid growth. It is not affected by draughts but if the air around it is allowed to become too dry some of its leaves will turn brown and drop. It may also become infested by the red spider mite (see Chapter 9 for details of this and other pests).

Cissus antarctica grows so easily and so well that it seems too often to stand in one position in the house or office for such long periods that it collects dust. There are too many leaves for individual cleaning, so it is helpful to take the plant out into a warm summer shower occasionally to clean it or, if this is impossible, to cover the floor around it with newspaper and give it a light spray with clean water to remove the dust from the leaves.

Until comparatively recently the vividly coloured and shining leaves of *Codiaeum variegatum pictum*, or croton, were to be seen only in a greenhouse and were brought indoors only for brief periods. The plants simply could not stand the cool yet arid atmosphere of most houses. Now newer cultivars are available which have had new strength and tolerance bred into them. This is a splendid thing, for croton foliage, green, yellow, red, slashed, streaked, marbled, spotted, is among the most magnificent available to us.

Keep plants in a good light, but not in direct sunlight, out of all draughts and in as humid an atmosphere as you conveniently can. They will stand a range of temperatures between about 55° and 70°F (12° and 21°C) but some care should be taken to see that as the temperature increases so does relative humidity and an occasional spray over the leaves during warmer days will be helpful. Light feeds should be given only when plants are growing well, and the soil should be kept moist. If care or conditions are not right, crotons tend, without warning, to drop their leaves one after another until it is obvious that the plant is no longer attractive.

Equally spectacular in the colour of its foliage is the coleus, although the texture is quite different. It is soft and delicate rather than tough and glossy. The leaves are marked in green, red, yellow, purple and white in bands, flecks, or blotches and streaks. A well-lit situation is essential, and regular feeding keeps them growing well. Keep the plants warm (60°–70°F, 15°–21°C) and well watered. If they are allowed to become too dry even for brief periods they will quickly droop but an early application of water to the roots will soon make them turgid again. Browning of leaf edges indicates that the temperature is too high or the humidity too low. Well-grown plants will reach 2ft (60cm) or more in height. Pinch out the little spikes of flowers as they appear to keep the leaves attractive. Coleus are easily grown from seed (see Chapter 9).

Cordylines and dracaenas are both members of the lily family and they appear to differ only in the colour of their roots. For some reason, however, most of the cordylines grown as house plants seem to be known as dracaenas. Thus *Cordyline bruanti*, *C. sanderiana* and *C. terminalis* will usually be found in stores and markets as *Dracaena bruanti* etc. All make good house plants and

all are comparatively easy, although leaves sometimes brown if the atmosphere is too dry. *C. bruanti* has dark green, spear-shaped leaves with a fascinating brown or bronze sheen. *C. sanderiana* is more dainty and is pale green and cream. *C. terminalis* has the common name of flaming dragon tree because of the vivid colours of its green and red leaves.

A good light is helpful to all these plants but if it is too strong, or if direct sunlight lingers on them for too long their leaves are apt to brown at the edges and look unattractive. They prefer a little humidity in the atmosphere and an occasional spray in the warmer months is helpful. Watering should be generous during the summer months and rather less during the winter. Regular light feeds should be given when the plants are growing well and temperatures can range from about 55° to 70°F (12° to 21°C).

The cryptanthus is the lowliest of the large bromeliad or room pine family. It is literally the lowliest, for the plants are small and ground hugging. *C. acaulis* is even known as earth star because of the way it spreads its wavy-edged, green and white leaves on the ground. Probably the most striking of this little group is *C. fosteriana*, low growing but with longer leaves than most, interestingly striped horizontally rather than vertically, in tones of reddish brown and grey.

Like all bromeliads they are comparatively easy plants to grow but because they are prostrate the normal central cup or reservoir is so small that it is of little value to them and they must be watered through the soil. They prefer this to be kept on the dry side, particularly in winter. They need good light to maintain their leaf colour but should be fed only rarely with the smallest possible amounts of fertilizer. Their spreading leaves tend to collect dust and dirt and they look much more attractive if they are kept clean. Over-dryness causes the leaves to turn brown and shrivel, but do not mistake this for normal dirt. Temperatures can range between 50° and 70°F (10° and 21°C).

The dainty little cyperus is a grass-like perrenial herb which is found growing naturally all over the world. Its best known commercial form is *Cyperus alternifolius*

Cryptanthus zonatus is a bromeliad, belonging to the same family as the pineapple. Small and ground hugging, it is easy to grow and tolerant of neglect. It will grow in hot or cool conditions and is a good plant for a bottle garden.

Left: Flaming dragon tree, Dracaena terminalis, grows to 2ft (60cm) with pointed, spear-shaped leaves of dark green and vivid purple-red. Good light is essential to keep the leaf colour and it is helpful also to give the foliage a light spray or an occasional wipe over with a moist cloth.

Right: Crotons or codiaeums have hard, waxy, glossy leaves, streaked and spotted with green, cream, red, purple and intermediate colours. New varieties are tougher than the original plants but some humidity is still necessary.

Right: *Three different plants from the Ficus genus. The familiar rubber plant,* Ficus elastica, *looks much bigger here than* F. benjamina, *the weeping fig (right) though this will also make quite a large tree-like plant.* F. pumila, *in the foreground, is more lowly and is a useful plant for shady corners.*

gracilis, with grass-like leaves springing out like the spokes of an umbrella on top of a slender stem. This is a bog plant and its soil must always be kept moist. If the soil is allowed to become too dry or the atmosphere is insufficiently humid, the radiating leaves tend to turn brown and eventually fall. Keep it out of the sunlight, in light shade, away from draughts and fairly warm at a temperature of about 55°–65°F (12°–18°C).

For obvious reasons few house plants have poisonous berries or fruits, but the dieffenbachias do have exceedingly poisonous sap. It is not virulent enough to do great harm to a healthy adult but it acts on the mouth, causing great pain and a swollen tongue. For this reason it is known as dumb cane and the greatest care should be taken to see that none of the sap ever comes into contact with the mouth. Only when the plant is pruned or damaged (both unlikely events) is the sap normally exposed, but in this event it is urged that you wash carefully and immediately. Dieffenbachias are otherwise lovely plants for the home, the office, the store, the waiting room or any other place that will accept their large leaves with the dramatic stripes and blotches of cream and green. *Dieffenbachia exotica*, *D. picta* and *D. amoena* are the species most frequently seen and some of these have improved cultivars. The plants are not always easy to keep for long periods and often just when you think you have achieved success the leaves will begin to yellow and fall. Warmth and humidity are the secret.

Temperatures should not be allowed to fall below about 60°F (15°C) and can go up to around 75°F (23°C) so long as the air around the plant is kept relatively moist. They should have good light but no direct sunlight. The soil should be kept moist but never wet and may be allowed to become almost dry between waterings. Feeding should be regular while the plants are growing well. Like some other plants they show that their roots are too dry or too wet by yellowing and drooping leaves. Brown and curled leaves indicate a lack of humidity.

Dracaenas have been discussed briefly under the name of cordyline and there is little more to say here except to urge readers to look for more varieties than are normally on sale. *Dracaena goldieana* has magnificent alternate horizontal bands of green and gold, *D. godseffiana* is spotted and speckled all over with green and cream; *D. marginata* is spiky and individual with long, green leaves margined with vivid red.

The euonymus is generally thought to be more useful in the garden than in the home, with a wide range of berried or foliage trees and shrubs and climbers. However, someone tried *Euonymus japonicus medio-pictus* indoors with such success that it now seems to be available almost everywhere. It is not a striking or dramatic plant but it appears to be tolerant of most indoor conditions. It must have a light position to maintain the colouration in its leaves and it likes a little humidity in the air but it tolerates a wide range of temperatures, from about 50° to 70°F (10° to 21°C). A light feed when the plant is growing well will keep it active. Too high a temperature or too low humidity tends to make the leaves brown at the edges.

Bi-generic hybrids are rare but the fatshedera, a cross between a fatsia and a hedera or ivy is a very useful specimen indeed. It retains some of the best characteristics of both parents, having large, attractive, palmate leaves from the fatsia and a quick-growing, wiry, creeping or climbing habit from the ivy. The fatshedera is usually trained to climb upwards and it will quite quickly reach 10 or 12ft (3 or 4 metres), but it can also be allowed to sprawl or trail. It is very tough and will survive most conditions. A specimen of *Fatshedera lizei* (the only species except for a type with cream markings) which we once had was by accident allowed to remain for a week in a bucket of water which became frozen solid – yet the plant recovered and lived for some further years.

More ideally, temperatures should be kept at 50° to 70°F (10° to 21°C). Although the variegated form requires good light, the all-green type will exist very well in darker areas. Water thoroughly during summer months and allow the soil to become much drier during the winter. Too dry an air or soil will result in leaves turning brown, first at the edges and then all over.

As we have seen, *Fatsia japonica* is the correct name for the false castor oil plant, sometimes known as *Aralia japonica* or *A. sieboldii*. It is a good indoor plant with large, glossy green leaves of palmate pattern that give it considerable decorative or even architectural value. It grows easily and quickly. It needs no special treatment and in fact is hardy enough to grow well in the garden in temperate climates. Indoors the temperature should not be more than around 70°F (21°C). Make sure that the soil is never allowed to dry out. Under drought conditions the leaves will either curl and brown or may drop as they turn yellow. It will do equally well in light or shade but because the leaves are large they must be kept clean of dust for them to breathe. Over feeding tends to make the plant grow too quickly for convenience indoors: individual leaves can grow to 9–12in (22–30cm) in diameter and the plant itself, growing in a large tub, will reach 3ft (1m) or more with an equal diameter.

Attractive berries are produced on outdoor growing plants but because of the difference in light they seldom appear on plants indoors.

The ficus or fig genus is one of the aristocrats of the house plant world. One of its members, the *Ficus elastica* or rubber plant, in one or other of its several forms, is possibly the epitome of all house plants, being the best known and most widely grown in all parts of the world. Though the most popular, it is not the only useful ficus species available. *Ficus benjamina*, the weeping fig, makes a pleasant tree-like plant with medium sized, glossy green leaves and a slightly drooping way of growing. It will make quite a large tree if desired. *F. lyrata*, the fiddle leaf fig, is large and sturdy, its slightly waisted leaves giving it its popular name. The rubber plant itself has many forms, which are sometimes difficult to keep up with: *F. elastica* has been improved into *F.e.decora* and also into *F.e.robusta*. There are also variegated forms, one of the best of which is *F. schryveriana*, named after the

Belgian nurseryman who first found it. It is a pleasant and tolerant plant, streaked and blotched with several tints and shades of green and cream. *F. diversifolia* is a small, single stemmed, greyish-green plant which holds its almost round leaves out horizontally in company with its curious little berries. It persisted for some time under the common name of seaside grape, *Coccoloba uvifera*, but has now been more correctly identified. The berries, in fact, are remarkably similar in appearance to tiny, immature figs. It is an easy plant to grow, making no special demands and is unusual enough to make a talking point.

The main thing to remember about caring for the fig genus is that they do not like to be over-watered. Try to keep the soil no more than just moist at all times and you are unlikely to lose a plant. The dark green forms of these plants will tolerate a certain amount of darkness indoors but the variegated forms must have good light to keep their colour. They do not require exceptional humidity and temperatures can range from as low as 50°F (10°C) to as high as 70°F (21°C). Light applications of fertilizer should be given during the summer months. The difficulty with all these plants is that they display the same symptoms if they are over-watered as they do when they are too dry at the roots. Leaves will gradually turn yellow, then brown and droop downwards. It is thus necessary to judge whether you have been over generous or niggardly with your watering before you can decide what corrective action to take.

F. radicans and *F. pumila* are different from the other fig species mentioned above. Both are trailers or creepers and the first is generally seen in its attractive variegated form, green and gold. Both tend to be rather delicate but if they are cared for correctly they will grow well and quickly. They require a relatively high degree of humidity and temperatures between about 60° and 75°F (15° and 23°C). Although they require some light this should never be too strong and their feeding should be light and occasional. If humidity is lacking the leaves of both these plants will dry, turn brittle and fall. Like all other members of the ficus genus the roots should not be over watered and, because humidity is necessary, it is helpful to give the plants an occasional spray with tepid water.

The snakeskin plant, *Fittonia argyroneura* (sometimes known as *F. verschaffeltii*), is particularly noted for the beauty of its foliage, its silver-veined leaves having the texture as well as the colouration of certain snakes. It is not always an easy plant to keep for long periods, needing warmth and humidity beyond that normally available outside a greenhouse. Even if you are able to get it to grow well it will never grow large, merely increasing the number of its beautiful leaves so that they cover and hide the pot completely.

Though it may not be possible to keep the plant for more than a few months, it is still worth growing it for the beauty of its foliage. To try to keep it longer, never allow the soil to dry out, never allow the temperature to drop below about 60°F (15°C) and keep the atmosphere as humid as is normally comfortable. A light feed at intervals will be helpful in the production of new leaves but do not overdo it. If leaves begin to curl and turn brittle this is an indication that humidity is probably too low. In this case it may well be worthwhile cutting off affected leaves, spraying the plant and hoping that this will solve the problem. Never allow this plant in the sunlight. If possible keep it in a north window where its light requirements will be adequately met.

Now we come to the father of them all, the hedera or ivy genus, which appears to have been the first of the modern house plants. It is interesting for many reasons, not least for the fact that although the genus has only seven species, there are so many cultivars that it is difficult to know where they begin and end. There are large leaved ivies and small; they can be green, grey, green and white, green and cream, green and gold, grey and white; they can be almost round, they can be almost palmate, sagittate; they can be smooth or crinkled. Most are derived from the common wild ivy, *Hedera helix*, but another important species is *H. canariensis*, the Canary island ivy, thought by some to be named after the canary bird because of the golden colour of the foliage. *H. hibernica*, Irish ivy, has larger leaves than the others and grows better in the garden than the home. Japanese ivy, *H. japonica*, and one from the Himalayas, *H. nepalensis*, are now being investigated to see what they can offer the house plant hedera enthusiast. All ivies are easy to grow in atmospheres that are warm or cold, dry or humid, still or draughty, which indicates one reason why they are so popular all over the world.

Some humidity is necessary, however, and if plants are grown too dry they tend to be visited by the red spider mite (see Chapter 9). A well-grown and handsome plant is one that is kept only just moist at the roots, is fed regularly, is given some humidity and is pinched out occasionally at the growing tip to encourage a branching habit and the production of glossy new leaves. Variegated forms must have good light.

A curiosity normally grown by more knowledgeable indoor gardeners is *Helxine soleirolii*, also known as

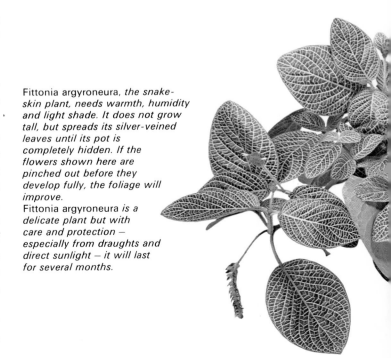

Fittonia argyroneura, *the snakeskin plant, needs warmth, humidity and light shade. It does not grow tall, but spreads its silver-veined leaves until its pot is completely hidden. If the flowers shown here are pinched out before they develop fully, the foliage will improve.*
Fittonia argyroneura *is a delicate plant but with care and protection – especially from draughts and direct sunlight – it will last for several months.*

Left: Fatshedera lizei variegata, *a rare bi-generic hybrid, a cross between a fatsia and a hedera, stands above (left) a variegated* Ficus radicans *and (right)* Pilea cadierei, *an attractive and easy-to-grow member of the nettle family. Fatshederas are very tough and will survive most conditions but like the other variegated plants in this arrangement, they need good light to keep their leaf colouration.*

The young growth of Gynura sarmentosa *is covered with fine, purple hairs so that in some lights the plant appears to be purple and in others merely dark green. A twining plant, it can be trained round a support if it spreads too widely. Its flowers smell very unpleasant.*

The many varieties of Hedera *or ivy are among the easiest of all house plants to grow and do well in warm or cold rooms, in dry or humid atmospheres — even in draughty corners. These variegated plants are examples of a cultivar, Little Diamond.*

babies' tears. This is a tiny, creeping plant bearing masses of small, round, glossy green and white leaves at the ends of thin wiry stems. In no time it will completely cover a pot and creep onto neighbouring territory if this is inviting. Good light is essential but never direct sunlight. Temperatures should range from about 55° to 70°F (12° to 21°C) and a very light feed once a month in the growing period is all that is required. The soil should be kept moist at all times and a light spray over the foliage once or twice a week is also advisable. Too dry conditions will result in dry patches which gradually become bare of foliage.

The hoya is a climber which sends out long, whippy, naked shoots which only later develop their leaves. *Hoya bella* is the species that generally produces the white, waxy flowers (see Chapter 1) but *H. carnosa variegata* is generally the more beautiful. It has thick, fleshy leaves, pale green and gold, which are much more attractive than the occasional flowers. The hoya usually comes from store or market trained around a hoop above the pot and the trail or trails should be removed from this and trained up a wall to help it look its best. It does not need high temperature or humidity but it needs good light to show at its best although it should never be placed in the direct rays of the sun.

Temperatures can be between 50° and 70°F (10° and 21°C) and the soil can be allowed to dry out almost completely between waterings. With normal care the plant should grow well if not luxuriantly. The main indication of over-dryness will be that the whippy growing shoots will turn brown and die, the rest of the plant not being affected.

The kentia is a fairly large palm which, under indoor conditions, may reach 4ft (1·2m) or more, though it will take some years to do this. It has achieved considerable popularity in recent years. It is striking in appearance and very easy to grow but it needs rather more space than most people can give it. The usual species available is *Kentia forsteriana*.

It does not need a specially light situation but it must be watered lavishly and then allowed almost to dry out before it is watered in the same way again. It should receive no more than two or three light feeds a year. Temperatures can range between 55° and 75°F (12° and 23°C) and when they are high it is helpful to spray the plant occasionally with tepid water. If the atmosphere is too dry the grass-like leaf tips will turn brown.

Pink, purple, red, white and green are some of the colours to be seen in the foliage of *Maranta tricolor*, known as the peacock plant or red herringbone. The leaves are magnificent but the plants are not easy to keep in good

condition for long, needing more warmth and humidity than most people can provide in their homes. Temperatures should range between 65° and 75°F (18° and 23°C) so long as humidity can keep in step. Regular light feeding during the growing months will be reflected in the richness of the leaves, and good light without direct sun is also essential. If the plant is too dry or too cold the leaves will curl, become brittle and drop. The foliage of this plant is so beautiful that it is often worth growing plants for the few weeks that they will be at their best and then discarding them when they are no longer decorative.

Monstera deliciosa, the Mexican breadfruit plant or Swiss cheese plant, is one of the curiosities of the house plant world. Its leaves, dramatically holed and slashed, will sometimes grow to 2ft (60cm) across and the plant itself, when trained as a vine, will stretch for 20ft (6m) or more around the walls. Contrary to normal practice, the monstera should be given a pot just a little too large for it if you wish to let the leaves become heavily indented and holed. Never allow the plant soil to stay too wet for too long; keep it on the dry side. When the shoots start growing in warm weather, feed it to get good growth. It is tolerant in its reaction to temperatures and will grow well in anything from 45° to 70°F (7° to 21°C). It is also unusually tough, surviving well in polluted or smoky atmospheres. It will normally grow well in a fairly dark situation but there is a variegated cream and green form which requires greater light. If leaves begin

The cocos palm, Cocos weddeliana, *is related to the coconut but indoors seldom grows to more than 2ft (60cm) high. It needs an even temperature of no more than about 61°F (16°C), plenty of strong light and a well drained soil mixture. Its fern-like leaves all spring on long stems from the central collar of the plant and tend to turn brown with age or if the roots are dry.*

Left: Maranta leuconeura *has two main varieties, kerchoveana and massangeana (here). They are similar in many respects and are both sometimes difficult to grow. A cultivar known as* M. tricolor *still has the greens, creams and reds of the original species, but is rather easier to keep for longer periods indoors. Marantas and calatheas are often confused: the difference is in the number of cells in the ovaries.*

to turn yellow and then brown, this is an indication once again that either too much or too little water is being applied. As the plant grows in size it will send down aerial roots, whippy or thong-like, which can be ignored but which will aid the plant if they are trained into the parent pot of soil or into another pot suspended at a convenient point.

Another palm, similar in some respects to the kentia but somewhat smaller and daintier, is *Neanthe bella*, which grows well and easily in the home and is even prodigal in its production of somewhat undistinguished flowers. Normal living temperatures of 55° to 70°F (12° to 21°C) will suit this palm and it should be kept in light shade. It should be watered by giving the soil a thorough soaking and then allowing it to dry out almost completely before repeating the process. Keep it almost dry in the colder months. Fertilizer should be applied seldom and sparingly, probably not more than two or three times a year. Although it does not require high humidity, if the air is too dry the leaves will tend to brown at the tips.

A tropical fern which is hardy enough to grow indoors in the northern hemisphere is a useful novelty and the nephrolepis has been known and grown for many years, originally in conservatories and hot houses. The two species usually seen are *Nephrolepis cordifolia* and *N. exaltata*, the first, known as ladder fern, possibly a little more coarse than the second. No sun, subdued light and plenty of water and humidity are the invariable rules for all ferns, which should be kept where possible in a temperature of between 55° and 65°F (12° and 18°C). Ferns need very little feeding but when they are growing vigorously in the summer a light feed once a month will be helpful. If humidity is lacking, the growing tips will turn brown as will older leaves, which can be cut away when they begin to look unattractive.

The nidularium is one of those convenient bromeliads which form a central cup or vase in their rosette of spreading leaves. This cup needs only to be kept filled with water to supply the plant's needs. There are several nidulariums, all fairly similar, some of which are *N. innocentii*, *N. rutilans*, *N. striatum* and *N. tricolor*. All have light green leaves, most of them striped and all have the habit of turning a fiery scarlet around the edges of their central cup when the low and insignificant flowers are produced.

Like all bromeliads the nidulariums will tolerate considerable variations in light and temperatures between about 50° and 70°F (10° and 21°C). They normally require little or no food but it is helpful at the beginning of the growing season to water the soil with a light fertilizer solution. Only when plants are old are they likely to lose their attractiveness as leaves begin to turn brown at the edges.

Peperomias are a group which provides a large number of house plants, all of which are neat, compact, easy, interesting and distinctive. *Peperomia argyreia*, for example, is a small, bushy plant with green and silver leaves; *P. caperata* has leaves only slightly smaller, but green only and heavily ribbed; *P. glabella* has fat, green or green and white shiny foliage; *P. hederifolia* is similar to *caperata* but less ribbed, smoother and more metallic; *P. magnoliaefolia* and *P.m.variegata* have larger leaves, fleshy and respectively green and cream and green; *P. obtusifolia* is unusual among peperomias in having thick, chunky leaves so green as to be almost black. All have characteristic 'rat-tail' flower spikes and all except the last must have good light to keep their attractive variegation. Soil should be kept just moist at all times but too much water will sometimes lead to the weakening and dropping of some stems. All are fairly tolerant so far as temperature is concerned and will live happily in a range between 55° and 70°F (12° and 21°C) and all enjoy a fairly rich diet which can be provided by an application of fertilizer roughly twice a month during the growing season. The drooping of the flower spikes is generally the first indication that a plant is being treated incorrectly and brown patches may appear on the leaves if plants have been over-watered or if they object to too dry an atmosphere.

The philodendron is the last (alphabetically) of the great groups of house plants. The genus provides a number of excellent plants that have proved their worth, that are decorative or even spectacular, that make no special demands and that fit happily and comfortably into the home. Probably the most familiar of the genus is *Philodendron scandens*, known as the sweetheart plant because of the heart-shaped leaf it bears in its twining, climbing or trailing growth. It is an old and tried favourite, said to be the inhabitant of more bathrooms than a steamy mirror. It is, however, by no means the only philodendron. The following are all easily obtainable. *P. andreanum* has arrow-shaped, velvety-purple leaves with silver-grey veins. *P. bipennifolium* has large leaves with rounded indentations and *P. bipinnatifidum* is much the same but with more evident indentations and larger leaves. *P. elegans* has indentations so deep that they almost touch the central rib. *P. ilsemanni* has no indentations and its heart-shaped leaf is very much larger with a creamy, spotted finish. *P. imbe* has a deep, almost wine-red colour to the leaves, which open gradually and hang onto the plant almost in-

Pilea repens *'Moon valley' will not grow large, but has attractive, crinkled foliage. It is not always easy to grow. For better leaves, remove the small flowers.*

Peperomia magnoliaefolia *is one of the easiest of the peperomias to grow indoors. They can live in a wide range of temperatures, but need good light and some food.*

definitely. *P. verrucosum* is hairy rather than smooth, with green leaves turning almost pink.

All of these philodendrons will grow successfully in the rather deeper shade away from windows, all like to be watered lavishly and then left until the soil is almost dry and all require regular feeding. They thrive in temperatures of between 50° and 70°F (10° and 21°C) and require regular cleaning of their foliage. The two most frequent faults are over-watering or under-watering, the first indicated by the foliage turning limp and pale in colour and the second by dry, brown edges to the leaves.

The date palm, *Phoenix dactylifera*, makes a small, graceful house plant, which can actually be grown from

Phoenix dactylifera *is a miniature form of the date palm. It will normally grow only to 2ft (60cm) or so but it will live for a long time if it is given good light and plenty of water during the hot months and kept warm, drier and draught-free in the winter.*

a fresh stone. It must be kept warm and sheltered, allowed to be almost dry in winter but given plenty of water in summer and an occasional overhead spray with clean, tepid water to provide the humidity it sometimes needs. Temperatures should be no lower than 65°F (18°C) and humidity should be high at first, though as the plant adapts to indoor conditions the amount of moisture in the air can be gradually reduced. The plant should occupy a well lit position. It should receive a fertilizer dressing only rarely so that it does not grow too large too quickly. As with most plants, the tips of the leaves will tend to go brown if the air is too dry or the temperature too high.

Pilea cadieri nana is a small plant with dark green leaves, regularly marked with silver blotches, which give it the popular name of aluminium plant. It is easy to keep and attractive in a modest way, the leaves being thickly held. It is a relative of *P. muscosa*, a sheer curiosity known as the pistol plant, artillery plant or gunpowder plant because when the leaves are touched the plant gives off a small puff of pollen. It is easily grown, moderately attractive and especially interesting for young children.

Both plants need good light, though not direct sunlight and a temperature of between 60° and 70°F (15° and 21°C). Their soil should be kept moist but not wet and if days are dry or temperatures high, a light spray of moisture over the foliage will be helpful. Leaves will curl, shrivel, brown and fall if there is insufficient humidity or if the roots are allowed to become too dry. Neither plant is a gross feeder and two or three applications of dilute fertilizer through the year should be sufficient.

The stag's horn fern, *Platycerium alcicorne* is one of the most curious and effective decorative house plants. Its name is particularly apt, for the fertile fronds, grey-green and downy, grow out from a central ball, their tips divided into two and then into two again so that they really do look like stag's horns. The sterile fronds, round and shield-like, surround and cover the pot. A particularly effective way of growing this platycerium is to knock it from the pot and tie it with copper wire or nylon string to a board or piece of cork and then suspend this high in a room so that the antlers look at their most effective. It is an easy and tolerant plant and it is possible even to wait for the fronds to droop before giving it water.

The older, fertile fronds will tend to turn brown and they can easily be detached where they join the parent plant so that younger leaves can continue to grow. The sterile fronds in the central ball gradually die and brown in the centre as they are covered with younger, greener growths. Eventually they disintegrate to feed the remainder of the plant but as a rule this happens only in the wild when artificial feeds are not supplied and every possible food source must be exploited.

Platyceriums are comparatively tolerant regarding light and temperature and will grow either directly in a window or further back in a room. Heat can vary between 50° and 70°F (10° and 21°C). The tough outer skin makes high humidity unnecessary. During their main growing period of spring to late summer they benefit from a regular light feed.

The next plant is equally curious but for a different reason. It is *Plectranthus fruticosus* and although we see it

everywhere we have never found it listed in any catalogue nor ever seen it on sale. The reason for this is probably simply that the plant is so easy to propagate that it would not be worthwhile for a nurseryman to stock it. A growing tip pinched out and inserted in any soil or even in plain water will send out roots and begin growing almost immediately. It grows quickly, making long trails of shiny dark green leaves. Plenty of water at most times of the year and an occasional feed are its main requirements.

Normal living temperatures of 50° to 70°F (10° to 21°C) are suitable and a plant will normally grow either in a shaded situation or in strong light, although obviously colouration will be better in the latter case. Over-watering or under-watering tend to cause some of the main stems to rot or shrivel at soil level and may eventually lead to the death of one of the shoots. As there are many of these, this is not a disaster so long as the dead shoot is removed quickly and the treatment changed. Although plants will grow successfully in a fairly dry atmosphere, the size, succulence and colouration of the leaves are greater in humid conditions.

The pteris is a cosmopolitan genus of many species, known popularly as brake fern, ribbon fern and crested ribbon fern, *P. ensiformis victoria*, *P. umbrosa major* and *P. cretica* respectively. All need a moderately shaded position with sufficient humidity to make an occasional spray with tepid water advisable. Temperatures can vary between about 55° and 65°F (12° and 18°C) and they should need feeding no more than two or three times during the growing season. Evidence that the air is too dry will be shown in a browning of the tips of the fronds.

So long as these plants are kept fairly warm, out of direct sun or draughts and given plenty of water they should do well. They are perhaps a little insignificant by themselves so look best either in a group of ferns or planted in a miniature garden. They make excellent bottle garden residents.

An unusual plant which is better known in warm than in temperate regions, yet is not difficult to grow, is the boat lily, *Rhoeo discolor*. It gets its popular name because its flowers appear in small containers, almost boat-shaped, at the base. Its leaves are long and narrow, dark green above and pinkish purple on the underside. It likes a warm (60°–70°F, 15°–21°C) and well-lit position and plenty of water during the warmer months, but when the weather is cold it should be kept almost dry. When it is growing well it can be fed regularly with light applications of dilute fertilizer but this should be stopped during the winter. Humidity is less important than the

quantity of water at its roots, but a spray of tepid water over the plant during the warmer months will not do any harm. An inward folding and browning of the leaves will indicate that the soil or the atmosphere is too dry.

Rhoicissus rhomboidea or grape ivy is another plant that will grow almost anywhere under almost any conditions and always look good. It is a natural vine and can be trained upwards as a pillar or spread out to cover a wall. The leaves are a dark and shining green above and a soft and almost furry brown underneath. It will grow almost anywhere in the house except in strong and direct sun and it will stand draughts. Although it does not need a high degree of humidity, if the air is too dry the plant may be attacked by the red spider mite; so under dry summer conditions it is useful to give the plant an occasional spray with tepid water. Temperatures can range from as low as 50°F (10°C) to as high as 75°F (23°C). Water well during summer months but reduce amounts slightly when the weather is colder. Because the vine is so rampant, it will require regular feeding to keep it at its best. Older leaves will fall and a yellowing and crinkling of some of the foliage may suggest that an attack of the red spider mite is beginning.

The familiar and unkindly named mother-in-law's tongue, sharp and sword-like, is deservedly popular because it provides a much needed contrast in shape and texture and will grow in almost any conditions, even in direct sunlight or in draughts. The only thing it will not tolerate is too much water. Grown well, *Sansevieria trifasciata* reaches 3–4ft (1–1·2m) and constantly produce new shoots so that after a while it will be necessary to divide the creeping rhizome into a number of new plants. It will also produce a few tiny and insignificant shoots bearing flowers which are so heavily and sweetly perfumed that their scent will fill an entire house.

As a semi-succulent it requires plenty of good light and will even grow in a south window where it may get two or three hours of direct sunlight a day. It does not require humidity although a certain amount will help to produce the flowers. Normally a sansevieria suffers only if it is overwatered or too cold. The soil should be kept only just moist enough to keep the leaves plump and the temperature should be between the extremes of 55° to 75°F (12° to 23°C). If the plant is not being cared for correctly, stem tissue may soften at or near the soil level and the individual spears may bend and fall. Because a sansevieria requires watering only comparatively rarely, it should receive at the same time the light feed that will enable its shoots to appear at frequent intervals.

Mother of thousands, Aaron's beard, strawberry geranium are all common names for *Saxifraga stolonifera* and all have validity. This saxifrage sends out large numbers of hair-like stolons which carry at their tips baby plants. The leaves are rather like those of some geraniums. The baby plants need merely to be rested on the soil of another pot for them to root and begin growing. Try to keep the plant in light shade, preferably on a shelf or in a position where the stolons can hang down. Water freely in summer but give much less in winter. Spray to give additional humidity when tem-

peratures are high and feed once a month in summer. Moderate temperatures, from 55° to 70°F (12 to 21°C) are suitable. Only total neglect will kill this plant but when it is old some of the stolons will gradually dry and finally die.

With the not particularly apt popular name of umbrella tree, *Schefflera actinophylla* makes a useful tree- or shrub-like house plant with glossy, green leaves. Be careful with the water here, keeping the soil no more than just moist during summer and almost dry in winter. A fairly light position without direct sunlight will keep the plant growing and in summer a degree of humidity will be necessary to counteract the comparative dryness of the soil. If the soil is too dry and the plant is not sprayed, leaves may dry and fall. Temperatures should be no more than average, about 60°–70°F (15°–21°C). Feed lightly during the summer months.

The scindapsus, with its vine-like growth habit and its heart-shaped leaves, is remarkably like a golden variegated *Philodendron scandens* but is, perhaps, a little more delicate. *Scindapsus aureus*, its botanical name, tells us that it is golden in colour and each of the several forms available varies mainly in the size of the leaves and the depth of their colour. To keep its colour, a scindapsus must have good light but direct sunlight may brown the leaves. Plenty of water in summer and much less in winter should be the rule. Temperatures should be between 60°–75°F (15°–23°C), although in the higher range, humidity should be increased. If the air is too dry, brown patches will appear on the leaves, gradually spreading until the entire surface is coloured and the leaf eventually falls. Although not a gross feeder, scindapsus appears to need a little more food than many house plants and a regular fortnightly feed in the growing season will help to keep the leaves large, shapely and well coloured.

Senecio macroglossa variegata, from South Africa, is very similar to a variegated ivy in its leaf shape and texture and only something different in its habit of growth shows that it comes from another family entirely. It should be kept warm (60°–70°F, 15°–21°C) at all times and given plenty of water during summer. Because it is still active in winter the rate of watering should not be cut too drastically at that season. The foliage is somewhat more sparse than that of ivy, so a careful arrangement of the trails is called for to produce the required impact.

As a variegated plant it requires strong light but only brief exposure each day to direct sunlight. Humidity is provided to some extent by the comparatively high water requirement but when days are long it may be helpful to give a light spray with tepid water. Leaves browning at the edges or drooping and falling show that there is insufficient water at the roots or that humidity is too low. Food requirements are modest; a light feed no more than once every three weeks should be adequate.

The goose foot plant, *Syngonium vellozianum*, is so-called because of the characteristic shape of the leaf. The leaves are dark green and grow from the main stem. It is not a particularly significant or lovely plant, but a cultivar known as emerald gem is rather more interesting because its main veins are picked out in white. The syngonium will tolerate rough handling and poor conditions, but simply because it is rather undistinguished it is worth looking after it well to make it look its best. Warm conditions (60°–70°F, 15°–21°C), freedom from all draughts, light shade, gentle regular feeding, moisture at the roots in summer and much drier conditions in winter are the things that will make it thrive.

If the main points of the leaves droop and curl it suggests that the plant is too cool, too hot or too dry at root or leaf level. To correct the situation, examine recent handling methods. During the warmer months a protective humidity is advisable and a weekly gentle spray of tepid water will help in this.

The tetrastigma is not a plant for anyone in a small home, nor is it a plant for those people who are terrified

This well planted bowl contains (l to r, back row) Asplenium nidus, *the birds nest fern,* Ficus elastica, *the rubber plant and* Dieffenbachia exotica, *dumb cane. In front is* Neoregelia marechati *with the scarlet central cup that is characteristic of bromeliads.*

that their plants will take over and strangle them to death! We once estimated that in our home a *Tetrastigma voinierianum*, also called the chestnut vine because of the shape of the leaves, grew more than 100ft (30m) in two years! The tetrastigma has a thick, downy stem which is exceedingly brittle when young, so some care is required with the growing shoots. Leaves are large and glossy green with tan undersides. This is really a plant for the store, the hotel, the showroom or perhaps even the office rather than the home, although those who have the space to indulge it will have an exciting time.

It should receive strong light even to the extent of moderate direct sunlight. Obviously if it is to be as well lit as this it will use quantities of water and when the leaves are many and far ranging it may require heavy watering two or three times a week. Temperatures should vary between 60° and 70°F (15° and 21°C) throughout the year. Humidity is of less importance than a fairly accurate estimation of the requirements of water at the roots. If this is too sparse a certain drooping of the leaves may be observed although it will frequently be found that this is due to a fracture of the brittle stem. To grow to such an extent and so swiftly a tetrastigma obviously needs regular feeding but too much at one time may result in uneven growth and the appearance

of unbalanced leaves, one quite small and one large.

Tradescantias are normally so familiar that they are disregarded and untended and are too frequently seen only as browned and stringy lengths hanging dispiritedly from a dry pot. This is a great pity for, like so many other plants, tradescantias look good only when they are treated well. There are actually many species of tradescantia, although few ever seem to be labelled. *T. albiflora* has small, shiny, dark green leaves with red undersides and *T.a. tricolor* has leaves striped with cream and pink. The leaves of *T. blossfeldiana* have purple undersides. *T. fluminensis aurea* is the type most frequently seen, with white and cream stripes on a pale green leaf. The more vividly coloured form, with silvery green leaves, the central vein dark green and the undersides purple is *T. reginae*. Temperatures should be those we enjoy ourselves, between 60° and 70°F (15° and 21°C). A light feed at intervals as short as a week will keep the young plants plump, growing swiftly and in good colour. There is really no excuse for brown and shrivelled trails. They should be cut off as soon as they are noticed. Even healthy trails should not be allowed to become too long. Nip off the growing tips and root them (they strike very easily) in the same pot to begin another plant. Tradescantias have the popular names wandering

jew and wandering sailor because they grow so easily.

The vriesia is another invaluable bromeliad. The species most generally seen is *Vriesia splendens*, which has strap-like leaves horizontally banded in chocolate and green, arching out from the central rosette, cup or vase, which should always be kept filled with water. The leaves alone are attractive, but the flower is most striking (see Chapter 1). *V. fenestralis* has leaves of a paler green and those of *V. tesselata* are spotted with brown. Like all bromeliads, the vriesias are easy to care for. They need light to grow really well and will even tolerate direct and hot sunlight for brief periods.

They are tolerant in their temperature requirements, which can be between 55° and 75°F (12° and 23°C) and they have no particular need of high humidity. Feeding is not normally necessary but a single dose of fertilizer can be given directly into the soil early in the growing season before the flower spike is mature.

Only after they have flowered do they begin to look old and worn, showing their age by browning and brittleness of the arching leaves. At this stage it is generally more profitable to propagate new plants from the offsets produced and to discard the old.

So similar to the tradescantias that it is often confused with them is *Zebrina pendula*. It is recognizable because it is slightly larger and fleshier and has more vividly coloured leaves, shining with an almost metallic silver, striped with green and mauve and with a solid purple underside. It needs good light to keep its colour but is better out of direct sun except for brief periods. The soil should be kept no more than lightly moistened at all times, and a regular light feed will keep the plant growing well. Overgrown shoots should be nipped out and used as cuttings and any that turn brown should be ruthlessly pruned away. Temperatures can be anywhere between 55° and 75°F (12° and 23°C) and it is seldom necessary to provide any extra humidity for this plant.

Cacti and Succulents

In every country and in every continent the constant cry of the beginner house plant enthusiast is, 'How often do I water it?' For those who have this problem cacti and succulents are the perfect plants on which to begin, for not only are they extremely tolerant of most poor indoor conditions such as dry air, but they have their own in-built water supply in their thick and fleshy stems. So long as this fact is understood and they are consequently watered comparatively rarely, they will grow and flourish.

All cacti are succulents but not all succulents are cacti. They are grouped together here mainly because they have roughly the same habit of growth and because they require much the same treatment. They like plenty of sun almost without exception but they do not necessarily need high temperatures, for some are found growing in the wild on mountain sides where the winds can be fierce and the temperatures low and most grow under desert conditions where daylight brings burning sun but night time temperatures approach freezing point. At night time, too, many enjoy very heavy dews which help to keep the plants plump and healthy. But their nature, their physiological operation, is such that they can live for long periods on the water they have stored in their fat stems. Although they may survive under hot, dry sunlight for many days, even months, at a time, there is usually a period each year when heavy rains drench the land and at this time the plants soak up all the moisture they can get and store it in their stems.

Cacti only occur naturally in the American sub-continents – both north and south. Other succulents come from many parts of the world. Some cacti, for example some of the opuntias, have so taken to other soils in other continents that not only do they appear indigenous but they have become weeds which must be ruthlessly controlled if they are not to take over certain portions of land completely.

The main thing to remember about growing cacti under artificial circumstances is that they require as much sunshine as they can obtain, especially in the temperate conditions of North America and Northern Europe, and significantly smaller quantities of water than most house plants. To qualify the latter statement it should be said that during cold and comparatively dark winter months cacti need the minimum of moisture necessary to keep their swollen stems plump and turgid. Yet in summer they can absorb as much moisture as most other house plants, and indeed require this if they are to grow and to produce their frequently extra-ordinary flowers. As a rough average in temperate areas of the world most cacti will require watering no more than once a month in winter, rising to perhaps once a week in summer. As a rule they have a small and shallow root system and require little or no feeding. They have no need for the special humidity required by many other indoor plants. Because they grow in nature in locations where there are extremes of temperature, cacti have no particular need of special temperatures in the home. They will not, however, accept frosty conditions.

Cacti can live for long periods indoors, some of them hardly appearing to grow at all in twenty years and others reaching such heights that they need tying to cane supports. Some will flower and once they have produced their blooms they are likely to do so regularly. Flowers can be small and almost insignificant or huge, magnificent and flamboyant. Most flowers are fairly short lived. Some appear at night and are gone by morning.

All cacti have areoles, little buttons or cushions from

As plants of the arid regions of North and South America, cacti can survive dry periods without losing too much weight. When the heavy rains drench the land they soak up the moisture and produce their flowers. The taller growing cacti will seldom attain flowering size in a pot, but most spherical or short columnar species will readily grow to mature size and will flower.
Watering indoor cacti plants during their winter resting period can sometimes inhibit flowering during the following spring or summer.

Opuntia macrorhiza

Rebutia grandiflora

Cactus flowers are usually short lived. Where many are produced on one plant they tend to be small but where there are fewer flowers, they are usually flamboyant. This is one of the many hundreds of Mammilaria species.

which spines project or which produce fine hairs, barbed at their ends, called glochids. Handle cacti with the greatest care, for these spines can be most painful and if stuck in the skin they are sometimes very difficult to remove. Always use heavy gloves, a cloth or a folded band of newspaper to handle cacti.

So long as you can give your plants plenty of sun there is a tremendous range of cacti and succulents from which you can choose. Many are of more interest to the connoisseur than the amateur enthusiast and the following alphabetical list mentions only a few plants, those that are known to do well under normal home conditions and those which are normally comparatively easy and inexpensive to obtain.

The agave is a succulent grown mainly in the garden. Of the three hundred or so species, all American, several make good house plants. One of the best is *Agave*

Astrophytum myriostigma
shown below is
about 5–6in (13–15cm) high.
The rest are drawn to the same scale.

ephalocereus senilis

Echinopsis
multiplex

Lemaireocereus chichipe

Astrophytum myriostigma

Rhipsalidopsis gaertneri

victoriae reginae, about 6in (15cm) tall, with a mass of fleshy finger-like leaves curving upwards from a central point at soil level.

From South Africa and Arabian regions come some two hundred species of aloe, many too large again for the home. *Aloe variegata*, sometimes known as the partridge-breasted aloe because of the spots and stripes on the meticulously arranged stems, grows well indoors

Echeveria harmsii, *often marketed as* Oliveranthus splendens. *The flowers are shown here at approximately life size.*

Echeverias are succulents, growing naturally from northern parts of South America to southern North America. Echeveria secunda is the hardiest of the many species. It has the characteristic rosette of waxy leaves and produces its flowers freely in the spring.

and produces fine red flowers. It grows to between 3in and 9in (7·5 and 23cm) in height.

A small genus of cactus containing only four species, the astrophytum is globular, ribbed and appears to be covered in small grey scales. *Astrophytum myriostigma* has a number of varieties, grey and stone-like, with flowers either yellow or yellow with a red splash in the centre.

The bryophyllum, a succulent, has the curious habit of producing tiny plantlets like a fringe between the teeth of its leaves. These fall to the soil and most root easily and quickly. The yellow or pinkish flowers grow on a stem which can reach 3ft (1m) or more. *Bryophyllum diagremontianum* has glaucous-green, tooth-edged leaves patterned with red-purple markings.

Another oddity is the old man cactus, *Cephalocereus senilis*, so called because of the many long, white, fine hairs that grow from the areoles and cover the entire plant. It likes the full sun.

The tallest and largest of the cactaceae belong to the cereus genus. Though in their natural habitat some species grow to more than 50ft (15m) in height, there are some two hundred smaller species which can be grown indoors. Some have magnificent, funnel-shaped flowers but these tend to open only at night. *Cereus azureus* grows erect with prominent ribs. It is a quick grower. *C. jamacaru* is perhaps easier to grow, columnar, blue-green and bearing yellow spines.

The crassulas are a large family of succulents which give us numbers of easily-grown and easily-flowered plants. They are usually quick growing and hence need some pruning or cutting back from time to time. They all come from South Africa and most have small, fleshy, grey-green leaves, sometimes covered with a bloom. Flowers can be red, white or a pale cream.

Echeverias come from the southern United States to Argentina but most commercial varieties are from California, Texas and Mexico. They are easy plants, producing pretty flowers freely year after year but enjoyable for the beautiful rosettes of clustered leaves. They grow and spread easily.

The flowers of the cactus echinocereus are always large, always beautiful and usually last for up to a week, making the genus particularly popular among cacti lovers. Yet some species are more noted for the variation in the colours of their spines. *Echinocereus rigidissimus*, for example, is called rainbow cactus because its different coloured spines are arranged in rows or layers around the stem. There are many species and a collection is always worthwhile.

Equally worth collecting are several of the 36 species of echinopsis, a genus of cacti which come from South

America but only on the eastern side of the Andes. They are all easy to grow and to propagate and although all are sun lovers some need a little light shade in the hottest part of the hottest days. These are perhaps some of the easiest and most rewarding of cacti and so are suited to cultivation by children, in schools, or by beginners who wish to make a collection and gain experience.

Most epiphyllums are epiphytes, and grow on tree trunks in their wild state. They have achieved enormous popularity because of the splendour and number of their flowers and because they are comparatively easy to grow. Much work has gone into hybridising various species and the large trumpet-shaped flowers are now of several colours. After they have flowered the plants should be given a rest period for a month or two, with just enough water to keep them plump. At other times they should be watered more freely, for they are quick growers. Some epiphyllums drop their buds instead of flowering and this may well be due to a change of conditions – a change of light or perhaps draughts through a window. If possible, always keep them in one position.

The small white and pink blooms of haworthias stand out from slender stalks above dark green rosette-like plants with studded tubercles. They are easy plants to grow, not spectacular perhaps, but interesting and with a tolerance that makes them suitable for the beginner.

Haworthia fasciata, stemless and speckled with white tubercles, is one of the easiest and best.

The kalanchoes belong to the same family as bryophyllums (Crassulaceae) and in some respects are similar to them though they do not have small plants growing in the teeth of their leaves. They like to be warm and to have plenty of light. One or two of them tend to become drab and leafless after they have flowered, but on the whole they grow easily and quickly so that new plants can always be brought along. *Kalanchoe tomentosa* seldom flowers indoors, but its thick, chunky, oval leaves, glaucous green and red-spotted by the rim, provide a good reason for growing it.

Though they belong to a different family, the kleinias are similar in many respects to the kalanchoes. *Kleinia tomentosa* is a lovely white, felted plant, but requires rather careful attention in winter. It should be kept rather dry, warm (60° to 70°F, 15° to 21°C) and given as much light as possible. *K. articulata*, the popular candle plant, is more suited to average taste and skill.

The lithops look rather like living stones, small, ground hugging, roughly conical and divided into two. The two divisions of the plant are, in fact, two leaves. The yellow and white flowers grow up between them from a very much shortened stem hidden at their bases, making the leaves themselves look almost insignificant.

Flowers from Bulbs

Plants grown indoors from bulbs, corms and tubers are not strictly house plants according to our definition, because they do not continue to grow throughout the entire year. Instead they grow, develop, come into flower and then die down again. With the correct treatment some can once again be brought into bloom for the following year.

However, there are many bulb flowers which are so spectacular and at the same time so easy to grow indoors, that they fill a definite niche in the house plant world. Many people, in fact, who normally grow only a few house plants as background decoration, never fail to pot up a few bulbs of hyacinths or hippeastrums simply because of the pleasure brought by the flowers at a time when normally outdoor blooms are scarce. Interestingly, where there are long, cold winters, spring-flowering bulbs are grown more freely than in places where the weather improves early, giving people the opportunity to enjoy natural outdoor growth.

Bulbs, it has been said, are nature's prepacks. Each bulb comes complete with its flower neatly tucked into its centre and its food and its protection folded around it. Given normal care no bulb flower can fail to develop and appear, although it may possibly be dwarfed, twisted or otherwise misshapen if it has been damaged by bad handling or unsuitable treatment.

SOILS AND CONTAINERS

With one general exception all bulb flowers to be grown indoors need some medium to hold and sustain them. The normal material is called bulb fibre and is sold as such. It is made up of six parts of granulated peat by bulk, two parts of crushed oyster shell and one part of crushed charcoal. This must be moist and the way to tell whether it is at the correct rate of dampness is to take up a handful and squeeze it. When the fingers are released the ball of bulb fibre should hold together, yet it should disintegrate easily when touched. No moisture should be exuded when the ball of fibre is squeezed.

Some bulbs will grow perfectly well in water alone and a special type of container known as a hyacinth glass has been developed and marketed for this purpose. Here the bulb rests in the top of the container, its base fractionally above the water level to start. Roots grow from this base down into the water. It is possible to use any convenient container of the right size and a pur-pose-made hyacinth glass is not necessary. So long as the jar or other container will accept the bulb in its top, even with some propping, and can accommodate the considerable volume of roots that will later develop, it will suit. But it is always best to hide the bulb away from

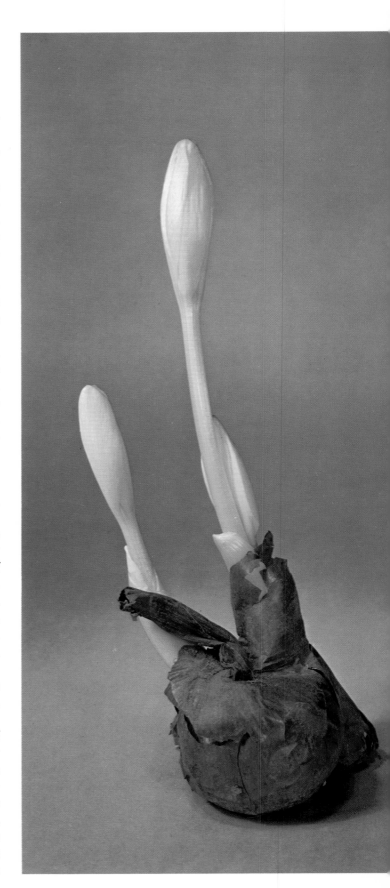

crocus

Corms are thickened underground stems. They shrivel away each year, producing a new corm above or to the side of the old.

Bulbs are underground buds which each year produce a single plant. They vary greatly in size and shape. Some, such as onions, are better known for their food value than their flowers.
Inside the bulb, protective layers of food surround the flower, which lies ready to develop when conditions are suitable (above, right). In the ground, roots develop to absorb moisture and minerals while the shoot, nourished by the stored food from the previous year, is drawn upwards towards the light. After flowering, the foliage should be allowed to die down naturally, so that the leaves can manufacture food for next year's growth.

Left: Colchicum autumnale *is popularly known both as autumn crocus and meadow saffron, although it is neither a crocus nor a saffron. The flower stem appears before the leaves, and it can be grown without soil or even water. However, it grows better if it is planted in the normal way.*

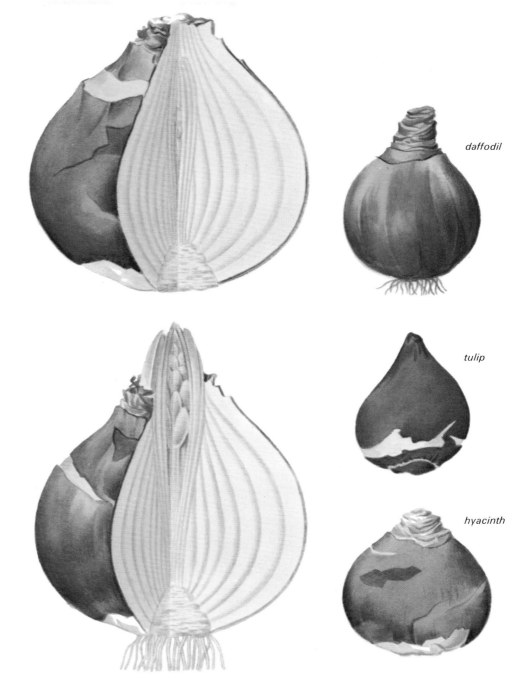

daffodil

tulip

hyacinth

all light, particularly at the early stages. The simplest way to do this is just to slip over the entire unit a cone or dunce's cap of dark, heavy paper. This can be removed easily enough to see if the water needs topping up or if the bulb has developed enough to warrant its removal.

Not all bulbs will grow well in water alone, nor will some accept the next medium, pebbles and water. In effect, of course, the bulbs are still growing in water alone, for the pebbles are there merely to hold them in position.

The one exception mentioned earlier is the colchicum. Bulbs of this are normally available in early autumn and they need merely to be exposed to the air, to light and to moderate warmth such as you would expect to find in most homes, and the flower stem will grow and develop into a pale violet flower which will last for some days. This is really a curiosity only, one for the children. It will not repeat the process in the following year, but will need to be planted in the soil so that it can gather the necessary nourishment into itself again.

Although bulbs can be grown in water alone or, like the exceptional colchicum, in no medium at all, it is still best to grow them in bulb fibre, in peat or in a specially-prepared compost or soil. In each of these cases it is not necessary to use flower pots with drainage holes so long as there is a layer of some drainage material at the base of the container and so long as a certain care is exercised in watering. Special bulb bowls can be bought and although there is actually nothing special about these except the name they do give an idea of the size and depth that is most generally useful. About 3in (7·5cm) is the minimum depth you should use. Shallower bowls will not leave room for a useful layer of drainage material such as broken crocks or charcoal nuggets. Deeper bowls will sometimes allow a double layer of bulbs to be planted.

As a general rule large bulbs such as hyacinths should be planted with their tips just above the level of the bulb fibre. Small bulbs, such as snowdrops, should go deeper and a useful guide is to plant each one 1½ times as deep as the height of the bulb. If you want a bowl filled to overflowing with flower colour, you can plant, for example, a layer of daffodil bulbs, just an inch (2·5cm) or so above the drainage layer, cover them with bulb fibre and then plant another layer above and between the first. All the bulbs will somehow agree among themselves to appear above the soil at the same time and eventually to flower simultaneously.

FORCING SPRING-FLOWERING BULBS

Nearly all bulbs which flower in the spring expect to go through a cold period before they begin to grow and eventually to flower. This being so, it should be possible to produce early flowers by cooling the bulbs artificially and thus persuading them that they have been through a winter and that spring has arrived. Indeed this is now being done so successfully with certain varieties that 'precooled' or 'prepared' bulbs can be bought for a modest price and will flower several weeks ahead of the more normal type. This special conditioning is, however, a once-only treatment and in succeeding years these bulbs will flower only at the normal time. Bulbs for forcing must be obtained from the specialist merchant and will not be available before the correct period of planting nor kept on sale after the latest possible date. Bulbs from the garden are not suitable.

In addition to the cold conditions which prepare the bulbs to begin to grow and eventually to flower when the warmer, longer days arrive, a period of darkness is also necessary. It may be possible to grow and flower certain bulbs without keeping them dark, but they will not produce flowers as large, as perfect, as well coloured or as long lasting as those from bulbs which have been given a period of cold and a period of darkness.

The old method of cooling was to plant up the bulbs and then take them out into the garden, bury them in ashes and clinker to keep out or discourage slugs, snails – even mice – and leave them there for a number of weeks so that the natural cold of the weather would condition them and they would be hidden even from the weak rays of the wintry sun. There is no reason why this same operation should not be carried out today, but there are easier methods.

One good way is to wrap the planted bowls in black

FORCING SPRING BULBS

1 Plant hyacinth bulbs with their tips just above the bulb fibre.

2 Cover the bowl with black plastic. Put it in a cold place and keep the bulb fibre moist.

3 When the shoots are well out of the bulbs, bring the bowl into a cool, light room.

4 Do not bring it into a warm room until the flowers appear.

5 Give less water when the plants are in flower but add a liquid feed once a fortnight until the leaves turn yellow.

Clivias, popularly known as Kaffir lilies and sometimes called imantophyllums, are not really bulbous plants but grow from a fleshy root which takes about seven years to mature from seed. The foliage is evergreen and the showy flowers can vary from yellow through orange to red.

plastic sheeting or place them in a black plastic bag and then leave them in some cold situation outside, on the balcony or even in a cold room. Always make sure that the bulb fibre is kept moist at all times. It is too easy to put the bowls away and then forget them, only to find later that they have dried out and the bulbs will not flower as they should.

Bulbs should not be brought out into light and warmth until they have formed a good root system. This is visible where the bulbs are grown in water alone, but of course it cannot be seen under bulb fibre. Instead look for top growth and leave them in cold and dark conditions until the shoot is well out of the bulb. In the case of some small bulbs such as snowdrops and scillas it is best to wait until the flower is beginning to show colour before you bring them indoors.

This suggests that in some cases very little time is saved by growing bulbs specially for indoors, and this is in fact the case. It may very well be better with some bulbs to leave them growing in the garden until they are about to come into flower and then to dig them up, pot them and bring them indoors where they will quickly open their flowers. They will unfortunately almost as quickly fade and die, after which the bulbs can be planted outside again for another year.

In every case the foliage helps to feed the bulb for the next year's growth and should be left on the plant after

If you have a deep pot, it is possible to plant more bulbs by placing them at different levels in the fibre. They will flower at the same time and their blooms will be at the same level.

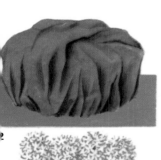

3

Forced spring bulbs are almost foolproof, for the flower already exists inside the bulb. Tiny bulbs such as snowdrops should not be brought indoors until the flowers show. If larger flowers have yellow leaf tips they have been over-watered. If they flop they have been given too much heat. A rotting bud means that water has collected in it.

the flower has died until it has so yellowed or browned and withered that it can be plucked away from the bulb at the lightest touch.

There are summer-flowering bulbs as well as spring and not all require the cold treatment. Unlike spring-flowering bulbs, most summer-flowering bulbs can be kept in their pots, or repotted and grown indoors again the following year.

BULB FLOWERS FOR THE HOME

So long as they are treated as temporary decorations in the home, almost all bulbs can be grown in temperate climates, although where temperatures are high there can be problems with certain species. In the following notes, local conditions will, of course, have to be borne in mind.

Acidanthera are related to gladioli, but the flowers are, perhaps, more starry and have a dark central blotch. Plant the corms five to a 6in (15cm) pot in spring and keep them warm (60°–70°F, 15°–21°C), and moist while they are growing. They will flower in late summer and after this give them no more water until the foliage has died down. Then remove the bulbs from the bowl or pot, clean them and store them in a frost-free place through the winter.

The bletia or blettilla is a pseudo-bulb and is really a small garden orchid carrying spikes of magenta blooms. It is easy to grow and highly rewarding. Merely press the bulbs into a fibre or peat-based mixture in early spring, water lavishly and in about six weeks or so the dainty flowers will appear. They need great quantities of water compared with most other indoor plants, so to prevent any unpleasant smells it is well worth while incorporating a few nuggets of charcoal in the base of the compost. After the flowers have finished (they last up to 3 weeks) the bowl should be placed outside in a cool place or indoors in a north-facing window and the watering should be cut down until the autumn, after which it should cease entirely so that the bulbs become dry and ripened through the winter. In early spring repot and begin again.

From South Africa come the lovely clivias, kafir lilies or imantophyllums, with yellow, through orange to red flowers, and strap-like, evergreen leaves. Pot the bulbs in late winter and keep the compost moist, even adding a balanced fertilizer during the summer. When the shoots appear, keep the plants in good light but not direct sun and top-dress the soil each year. After flowering, allow the soil to dry out in the pot and repeat the process next year, adding a little fresh soil to the top, and making sure that both old and new soil are moist.

Freesias, among the most sweetly scented of all flowers, cannot really be classified as house plants for it is impossible to grow them indoors in many parts of the world. However, if they are grown in the garden or the greenhouse, a few pots can be brought into the house when they are ready to flower.

Right: There are two forms of haemanthus – the blood flower, Haemanthus multiflorus, shown here, which flowers in spring on thick 1ft (30cm) stems; and H. albiflos which has white, cup-like flowers and blooms rather later in the year.

We have already mentioned *Colchicum autumnale*, which will grow and bloom without the stimulus of water or soil. This, the meadow saffron, can of course be planted up in soil and will flower in summer through almost to winter depending on the variety. Some give huge blooms and colours go from white and pink to lilac, carmine and purple. The leaves, curiously enough, follow in spring, so to some the flowers are known as 'naked ladies'.

Convallaria or lily-of-the-valley do not really come from bulbs but from what are called crowns. They are highly versatile and can be bought natural for the garden, pre-cooled for forcing, even in succession through the year. In some areas they can also be obtained ready planted in little containers which are guaranteed to come into flower in exactly three weeks, so you can order them for a special occasion such as a birthday.

When ordering, specify that you wish them for pot culture rather than the garden and plant them with the tips just above the surface of the soil. Keep them dark and *warm* (at least 60°F, 15°C). In about ten days or so they will have grown to 4 or 5in (10 or 12cm) and can be brought out of the dark and moved gradually, day-by-day towards the light. Forced crowns will not force again. Plant them in the garden and after a year or so they will grow naturally.

Crocuses, particularly the large-flowered Dutch hybrids, can be potted up in winter to flower in the spring, but they are an example of the bulb flowers already discussed, those that cannot be forced into early bloom. It is thus easier in some ways to dig up plants from the garden, pot them and bring them indoors when they are about to come into bloom. In this way you can also get good yellow flowers, which are some-

times difficult to obtain from corms which are grown indoors from the beginning. Replace the corms in the garden after they have finished blooming.

The pineapple flower, *Eucomis bicolor*, gets its name from the way its flowers are arranged at the end of the thick stem, surmounted by a tuft of leaves. Bulbs should be potted in autumn or spring and in the first case water should be given only sparingly until spring. When the flower spike appears it is wise to begin feeding also. After the flowers have finished, allow the pot to dry out gradually, remove the bulb and clean it, repot it and begin again.

There are several varieties of galanthus or snowdrops, some large and some small. They should not be brought indoors into the warmth until their flower spikes are showing colour. The flowers will not last indoors nearly as long as they will outside, but they are a real promise of spring and as the bulbs can be planted back in the garden after they have finished flowering indoors there is no loss.

It is not always easy to obtain bulbs of the haemanthus or blood lily, but it is worth trying, for the red flowers are very striking. Bulbs of the early flowering species should be potted in autumn, the others in spring, making sure in each case that the bulb is half in and half out of the soil, several bulbs to a bowl or pot. Do not begin watering significantly until you see growth appearing, then increase the amount and begin adding a liquid feed. A haemanthus likes plenty of sun. When the flower fades decrease the watering rate until the soil is almost dry, but keep the plant still in full sun. This ripening period is important to get good flowers the next year and is well worth observing carefully in view of the difficulty of obtaining bulbs. Plants are at their best in about their fourth year. Propagation is from offsets removed at planting time.

The hippeastrum, amaryllis or belladonna lily must be one of the most spectacular of all bulbous plants, with its huge, vivid yet most delicately-coloured flower. The large bulbs can be bought specially prepared for forcing (in which case follow carefully the directions given) or natural. They should be planted with a third of the bulb above soil level. Water carefully at first and more freely when growth begins. When the flower spike shows, begin a feeding programme, but reduce both this and water when the flower begins to fade. Allow the soil to dry out and the bulb to ripen and then repot in winter in fresh soil.

The familiar large-bulbed, large-flowered hyacinth is not the only type available. Much daintier are the Roman or multiflora types with more than one stem carrying fewer flowers. These tend to flower earlier than the larger ones, quite early in the winter in fact and with care it is possible to plant a succession, once every two weeks or so, to ensure that you have flowers right through the dark days of winter. But never mix pre-cooled and normal bulbs together and never mix kinds in one bowl. Bulbs which are past their best are not attractive and will not compliment those that are just beginning to open.

From southern parts of the United States and warm South America comes the too little known hymenocallis, white-flowered and striking in appearance. Pot up the bulbs in early spring and water them freely right through to the end of the summer, gradually reducing the amounts after that until the soil is almost dry. A weekly feed during the summer will help to produce large blooms of hymenocallis for the next year.

Hyacinths are probably the most sweetly scented of all true indoor bulb flowers. They come in many different colours, red, pink, blue and white, each individual bell being a complete flower in itself.

Flower bulbs are extremely delicate and should be handled gently. If they are bruised this often shows in malformed or uneven flowers later in the year.

Hippeastrums, frequently called amaryllis, are spectacular bulb flowers, growing 2 to 3ft (60–90cm) tall, with white, pink, red or striped blooms. The large bulbs should be potted one to a container, half out of the soil, and kept in a light, warm place. It is possible to choose types that will flower at almost any time of year.

More and more lilies are proving suitable for growing indoors and some are being produced ready planted in pots so that they require nothing but the addition of water to start them into growth. The best lilies for indoors are the Asiatic hybrids, *auratum*, *bulbiferum croceum*, *formosanum pricei*, *hansonii*, Honeydew, Jamboree strain, *longiflorum*, *martagon album*, the Potomac hybrids, *speciosum*, *testaceum* and Verona. Allow space when planting for a top-dressing of fresh soil. Pot the bulbs at any time during the winter or early spring and keep the soil only just moist until the new shoots are visible. When the flowers appear water freely and give a weekly feed. Keep the plants in a cool and airy place. Re-pot in late autumn.

Many narcissi or daffodils will grow indoors and the best thing to do is to consult a bulb catalogue or a bulb merchant to discover which types are most to your liking. Some, such as the fragrant Paper White and the yellow Soleil d'Or, will flower very early in the winter. Cragford is a variety which grows well in water alone and is often grown in water with pebbles to hold the bulbs in position. The large-flowered King Alfred, the double Texas and the white Mount Hood all do well indoors and there is a particular charm in growing forms of the smaller and miniature types in pots where they can be admired and examined closely, rather than in the broader areas of the garden.

Narcissi can be grown in succession so that you are never without growing flowers. Keep them cool and dark until the shoots begin to show, then give them good, but not too bright, light. Keep them cool until the buds appear. Do not overwater, or the leaves will turn yellow at the tips. Feed about once a fortnight until the flowers die down. When the plant has finished flowering, allow the pot to dry out completely. Like other spring-flowering bulbs it will not be possible to force narcissi or daffodil bulbs a second time, but they will grow well in the garden.

Gorgeous pink colours and beautiful shapes are provided by nerines. Pot them half in and half out of the soil in autumn, three to five to a 6in (15cm) pot which has plenty of drainage material at its base. When the shoots appear, place them where they get really good light and feed and water them thoroughly when they are in flower. Let the pots really dry out when the flowers are finished. It is essential with the nerines to ripen the bulb well, so lay the pot on its side in a good warm place, 70°F (21°C) or more. Then in the autumn merely scrape away the top inch (2·5cm) or so of old soil, replace it with fresh and begin again. Repot after about four years.

Snowdrops, crocuses and daisies were dug from the garden and planted together in this bowl. A few stems of winter flowering heather and a tall piece of jasmine complete the arrangement.

There are spring-, autumn- and winter-flowering oxalis, which should be planted respectively in early spring, early autumn and early winter. Plant the bulbs half an inch (12mm) deep and half an inch (12mm) apart in pots or bowls. Put them straight into a south or west window and begin watering, lightly at first until the leaves begin to grow, then more regularly and with a feed as the flowers form. When they begin to die, cut down on the water and let the bulbs rest in a cool place until they are ready for re-potting at the correct time.

Pleione formosanum is a pseudo-bulb, commonly called the window sill orchid. It has pink petals surrounding a tube of creamy white dotted with gold and brown. It is an easy bulb to grow, needing only to be pressed about one third into the fibre in late spring and given moderate warmth and water. It will flower in early summer. Other species are *P. humilis*, white with a brown speckled tube, and *P. limprichtii*, pink with a scarlet speckled tube.

Although scillas are more familiar in a woodland clearing or a rock garden than in the home, they will grow well indoors. Pot the bulbs in autumn about an inch (2·5cm) apart and an inch (2·5cm) or so deep.

Left: Much work has been done with lilies recently and it is now possible to buy bulbs of plants such as Harmony, shown here, already planted in a dry container. Only water is needed to start it growing.

Above: When narcissi are grown indoors they sometimes get too tall and tend to flop. An inconspicuous stake in the centre of the bowl will serve as a support for them all.

Give them a light feed when they begin to come into flower and withhold water when the flowers begin to fade and die.

Known as the jacobean lily, *Sprekelia formosissima* makes an attractive plant for the home. Bulbs should be planted towards the end of winter, the top third of the bulb showing above the soil. Water lightly at first and then more freely as growth begins and give regular liquid feeds when the flower spike appears. As autumn approaches and the flowers fade let the soil dry out and the bulb ripen. Next winter remove the bulb from the pot, clean off its soil and re-pot it in fresh soil.

Tulips are perhaps a little more difficult to grow well indoors than most other bulb flowers, but if the right varieties are chosen and some care given they can be very rewarding. The early dwarf varieties can be grown successfully in bulb fibre but most of the others prefer to be potted in soil. It will take about ten to twelve weeks of cool darkness before they are ready to bring into light and warmth and even this process should be gradual rather than sudden. It is a good idea, for example, to put them into a dark cupboard at first, or some similar dark place with a temperature of about 60°F (15°C) for

a week or so to get good stem length before the bowls are brought out. Keep the bowls out of bright sun.

The vallota, from South Africa, is known there as the George lily and in Britain as the Scarborough lily, apparently because some bulbs were washed up there after a shipwreck many years ago. It makes a splendid pot plant, a foot (30cm) or so tall and bearing numerous beautiful scarlet flowers in late summer. Pot the bulbs in early summer with the tip only just below the soil surface. Water lightly to begin the growth and increase the amount as development takes place. Instead of re-potting the bulb feed it well with liquid fertilizer so that it will last up to five years before needing re-potting. Dry it out when the flowers fade.

Less vivid and with a rather faded, old-fashioned air, the veltheimia nevertheless makes a good pot plant. From the top of the bulb eight or ten strap-like leaves with wavy edges arch outwards and from the centre a long scape or flower stem rises bearing the many flowers. These, an inch (2·5cm) or so long, are tubular, pink with a green tip and yellow interior. Treat it in almost exactly the same way as the vallota, but plant the bulbs a month or two later in the year.

67

Containers for House Plants

The traditional clay or terracotta flower pot is almost as old as horticulture itself. It has a convenient shape, it stacks well, it is porous, it absorbs moisture, it is cool and, perhaps most important of all, it has an affinity with the soil it contains. But it is heavy, breakable and outdated.

The modern flower pot is made of plastic. It is roughly the same shape and the same colour as the old traditional pot. It is not porous, it does not absorb moisture, it is not cool. It is light in weight, smooth and easily cleaned. It stacks well, occupying much less space than is required for clay pots. The plastic is breakable but less so than clay.

Many house plant enthusiasts greatly regret the gradual disappearance of the traditional clay pot. There are two main reasons for this. The first is a simple matter of weight and stability. The old pot was heavy and the plant it held was therefore relatively steady and safe. More important was the fact that the old clay pot would absorb and release moisture and would allow, to some degree, the passage of air through its walls.

The porous nature of the clay not only helped to keep the root ball of the plant in a pleasantly cool condition, but it also helped to keep the soil moist. As the soil dried out between waterings it could absorb a little extra moisture from the walls of the pot. When the soil or the potting compost dried out completely, it tended to remain in close contact with the pot walls, for both dried out at the same rate. Unfortunately this is not the case with the modern plastic pot. When the soil or compost dries it tends to crack away from the smooth pot sides, leaving a dangerous gap. The water that is added then tends to slip down this crack at the sides and the soil itself does not benefit.

No house plant of any type should ever be grown in the home, office, showroom, hotel foyer or anywhere else without some barrier between the pot and the horizontal surface on which it stands. The most obvious reason for this is to save marks or stains being made on furniture, shelving or even floors. Even a simple mat or a saucer will prevent this damage.

THE COVER POT

All plants should have their pots protected, hidden inside another, larger pot, called a cover pot or a plunge pot. The space between the two pots should be filled with some absorbent material such as peat, sawdust, crumbled Florapak or Oasis (see Chapter 11), even sand. This means that when the plant is watered any excess moisture which may trickle through the drainage holes at the base of the pot will be absorbed by this packing

All plant pots should stand on or in another container. The *Hedera helix Chicago* here has its pot completely hidden inside a copper wine cooler. The chlorophytum just has a saucer.

Right: Citrus nitis, *the miniature calamondin orange, in a traditional clay pot. Pots like this are becoming scarce though many people still prefer them to the plastic variety.*

material. It remains to some extent as a reserve of moisture. With the old clay pots, this kept the pot wall moist and cool and even with plastic pots it can still feed moisture through the drainage holes to the dry soil inside the pot.

More plants are killed by over-watering than from any other cause. Unless such over-watering is reckless and ignorant in the extreme, a cover pot with a good layer of absorbent material will save the plant.

There is another function for the cover pot and its absorbent layer. The atmosphere in our homes and offices is too dry for most plants. It does not produce the natural humidity required to some extent by all plants. The layer of moist material between the pot plant and the cover pot helps to remedy this by continually releasing its moisture into the air. This means that a minute cloud of moist air is continually moving up around the leaves of the plant.

The packing material, however, must never be more

than just moist. It must certainly never be so wet that the plant pot swims in a soggy sea of liquid peat, for if this is the case the plant will drown. It is easy enough to add a little water to the soil of a pot if the plant it contains appears to be thirsty, but it is almost impossible to dry out a soil that is waterlogged, certainly impossible to dry it out quickly enough to save the plant.

COVER POTS AS DECORATION

Cover pots are valuable for house plants not only as a means of looking after their health. They also have a decorative role to play, for they can be selected to tone with the surroundings in which they stand. They can be chosen for their colour, for their shape, for their texture, even for their sentimental value. They need not, in fact, be flower pots or containers at all. They can be a saucepan or a soup tureen, they can be a large shell or a drinking mug. One of our most satisfactory and satisfying containers is a large piece of bracket fungus which contains a mixture of little ferns. It is satisfactory because it is light in weight and completely waterproof and it is satisfying because it is a natural material which goes well with the plants it supports.

Cover pots should be large enough to conceal the plant pot entirely so that at a glance the plant appears to be growing from the larger, exterior container. A large cover pot also allows space for a good layer of absorbent material. Yet it is obviously absurd to place a tiny plant in a large container merely for this purpose and as aesthetics as well as practicality are involved here it is sometimes necessary to search around for an attractive and satisfactory answer. For example, a small and delicate pteris fern looks ridiculous with its diminutive pot concealed in a much larger urn, so look for a slim goblet of china into which the flower pot just fits. There is no space for peat to go between the sides of the fern pot and the goblet, but there is plenty of space for it underneath the plant pot. Even if the fern is potted in a plastic pot which can absorb and release moisture only from its base, this is now correctly protected by the peat.

It pays to be adventurous with cover pots. Look at your plants and you will see that some grow upright like trees, some can be trained like vines, some sprawl and some droop or flop. Choose your containers to suit. Sprawling plants can have long or wide, low containers to hold them. Where some plants hang downwards, lift the pots in a tall container or stand them on a pedestal so that the plant can behave according to its nature and show to best advantage.

It may be that some cover pots are too precious to be used as plant pots. They might become scratched or stained. In this case put a little peat into a waterproof plastic bag, insert the plant pot in this so that the actual plastic will not show and then place the bundle in the container, which will thus be protected from contact and from water.

Some containers might be excellent but for the fact that they are cracked or leak for some other reason. Again, place the plant pot inside a polythene sleeve and the disadvantage will be overcome.

In some parts of the world house plants spend a great deal of their time outside rather than indoors and here cover pots can be a distinct disadvantage, becoming filled with water at the first heavy shower. To remove the plant pots from their cover will leave them so top heavy that they blow over in the slightest breeze. Try using cover pots with a good central drainage hole. When the plants are indoors plug the drainage hole with an ordinary wine cork and remove this when the plants go out into the open again.

Some plastic cover pots, flower pots, troughs, tubs and the like are available without drainage holes but with special weak spots in the base which can easily and quickly be punched out if required. Others (and this applies to many pottery examples) come with a good drainage hole and a special matching saucer; the pot can be lifted out of its saucer and replaced in a minute.

Containers should be chosen with some care if they are to serve their decorative purpose. The container is secondary to the plant and while it should be chosen to harmonize, to flatter the plant as well as to fit attractively and comfortably into its surroundings, it should not be so striking, so unusual or so dramatic that attention is drawn to it rather than to the plant it contains. For this reason patterned containers are sometimes difficult to use unless the pattern is discreet and the colour harmonizes with the flower or foliage colour. Green, as would be expected, is effective and shades of grey and brown are also generally suitable in almost all surroundings. White is usually suitable.

Sophisticated materials such as silver and cut glass tend to grate on the eye. Softer metals such as pewter or copper and brass seem more suitable. Plain moulded or blown glass is less oppressive than the sparkle of cut glass. Shapes appear to matter less than materials and plain colours are more generally effective than patterns, particularly where these are naturalistic and recognizable.

Containers can always be painted easily enough if they are of the right materials and if you will not damage them by so doing. Poster paints will last for comparatively brief periods but normal emulsion paints will

Below: Philodendron scandens *has rightly gained a reputation for being both easy and attractive. It is normally marketed clipped to a central cane and will grow well in a small pot for many months. It can also be transferred to a larger container and trained to climb more freely.*

A cover pot packed with a good layer of absorbent material such as peat, sawdust, even sand, not only conceals the pot inside, but provides a constant supply of moisture to the plant.

Hanging in a window like this, plants enjoy maximum light, though south windows will be too bright. The containers look decorative and also catch any drops of moisture from the pots inside. Left, tradescantia and right, chlorophytum.

alter the appearance of a container more or less for ever so long as reasonable care is given to it.

But there is no real reason why you should have to resort to painting an existing container when so many other possibilities exist. Apart from what is available from the shops, mainly modern and mass-produced designs, there are the contents of the antique stores and junk shops, many of which are ideal for house plants of all kinds and all sizes. As has been mentioned, it does not matter if these containers are cracked and might leak. A chip or other disfigurement is more serious but often faults can be hidden by exposing only one side or altering the height at which the arrangement stands. Saucepans, bowls, teapots, sugar basins, soup tureens, storage jars – almost the whole contents of your kitchen may be potential containers for plants.

NATURAL CONTAINERS

There are also a number of house plants which were originally epiphytes. In their wild state these grew high on the trunks of jungle trees and they still maintain a root system which fits them for this kind of growth. They include many of the bromeliads, as well as some of the ferns such as the dramatic *Platycerium alcicorne*, the stag's horn fern. These plants look at their best when growing on a piece of bark or on a well-shaped branch from a tree.

They will not, however, grow there without some concealed assistance. There are two problems to be overcome: how to get the roots to cling to the wood of the branch and how to water the plant once it is 'planted' on the wood. To anyone who has grown plants of this type it will be obvious that nearly all have a root system which is small, compact and closely knit. These roots normally cling in the wild to a niche, a hollow, a joint or even a wound in a tree, to some place where there is a natural collection of dead leaves and other debris from the tree and its neighbours and where moisture tends also to collect. The roots of the plant anchor themselves into this moist debris (which is rich in humus), and the plant grows and flourishes. The roots do not actually grow into the tree wood and they extract no benefit from, nor do any damage to the tree itself. The plants are not parasites, merely epiphytes.

Most people buy plants of this kind growing in pots. In some parts of the world it is possible to buy plants already growing onto pieces of wood or onto bark. Although this may be helpful it deprives the enthusiast of the chance to do something creative and out of the ordinary. On the whole it is worthwhile trying to do it yourself and obtaining the extra satisfaction.

First, choose your piece of bark or bough, driftwood

When a bowl of plants is placed inside a container of beauty or value, it is a simple matter to enclose the pot in a plastic bag.

Right: In its natural state Platycerium alcicorne *grows clinging to a forest tree. Indoors it can easily be attached to a piece of wood or bark and hung on a wall.*

or other anchoring point. The size and shape of this will depend entirely on your own taste and inclination and where you intend to place it in your home. Preferably it should look natural, which means that it should not be an obviously cut and planed piece of timber. If there is a special niche, such as the junction of one branch with a main trunk, so much the better, but this is not essential. It is possible in many places to buy a piece of rough bark which may be anything up to 3ft (1m) or so in length and this can be an excellent and aesthetically satisfying location for an epiphyte; the roots will settle happily into the rough surface provided. It is also possible to pick up in the woods a piece of half-rotted tree trunk, strangely shaped and interesting, which will look absolutely natural with a plant growing onto or into it. Like the piece of bracket fungus mentioned earlier this also has an ecological affinity with any growing plant.

Take the bromeliad, aechmea, cryptanthus, vriesia or whatever you have and knock it from its pot. If you have watered it previously the root ball will be moist

1 *You will need bark or wood, a bromeliad (e.g. cryptanthus), sphagnum moss, copper wire.*

2 *Knock the plant from its pot, taking care not to damage the root ball. If the soil is moist it will cling to the roots and will not spill.*

3 *Hold the root ball firmly in position on the bark, working it into the surface. Add the ball of moss.*

4 *Tie the plant with its mossy cushion to the bark.*

and pliable and it can be worked with the fingers into and onto the surface of the bark or timber. Then, holding it in position, add a ball of sphagnum moss, bun moss or any similar material which is moisture retentive yet has a firm texture. Even a piece of material such as coarse sacking will be helpful. Finally, bind the whole ball into place using string or, if possible, copper wire. This is flexible, strong, non-corroding and non-staining. Then take a critical look at the plant arrangement you have made. You will probably find that by moving the plant a little, bending it within the confines of its flexible copper wire, you can get a more pleasing effect. Sometimes the entire root ball of an epiphyte can be nailed to a piece of wood, preferably with a copper nail, and it will grow well for years.

The piece of wood or bark can be hung on a wall or stood against one, depending on its size and its shape. There remains the problem of watering. Bromeliads need only to have their central cup or vase filled with water to maintain their health and their growing capacity. However, a little moisture at their roots from

time to time does no great harm, especially when the roots are liable to become extremely dry, as they will in situations such as this.

Certain other plants, such as the stag's horn fern, definitely require moist roots (see Chapter 2). In this case try if possible to arrange the piece of bark or timber so that it can be removed, taken to a bucket or bath and immersed completely in water for half an hour or so. If it is then allowed to dry before being replaced it will last under normal circumstances for two or three weeks at least before another soaking becomes necessary. It may also be possible to dribble a little water onto the root ball once a week or even to direct the jet of a spray over the plant without harming the surroundings.

Unless the plant is growing high in a hot room it will not normally be harmed by occasional dryness at its roots. In their natural state most of these epiphytes sometimes go for long periods with very little water at all and are then flooded by tropical storms which soak the roots completely. This is, in fact, exactly the kind of condition to which you will inevitably subject them.

House Plants as Decoration

There is no more effective or less expensive way of furnishing a room than with house plants. Put one or two pieces of furniture, such as a table and a couple of chairs, in an otherwise empty room and the room still looks bleak and cold. Add a plant or two and immediately the atmosphere changes; it becomes softer, more intimate, more comfortable.

This is important. If most people were asked why they like to grow house plants in their home, why they like to have them in their offices or work places, they would find it difficult to give a satisfactory reply. In general terms homes contain what can only be called 'soft' plants: flowering plants, those with plenty of colour, those of indeterminate shape, those which develop and change. In commercial premises, such as beauty parlours, hairdressers' establishments and the like, again it will be gentle plants which are soft and colourful that are used.

On the other hand, 'establishment plants' are used in open plan offices. Rubber plants, philodendrons, sansevieria, all present an image of respectability. The foyer of a large and modern hotel may well add to these something a little more exotic, perhaps a large and spreading *Ficus lyrata*, or a *Monstera deliciosa*, with its slashed leaves. Meanwhile the smallest city office is made more friendly by an impatiens or a cineraria.

The use of plants in our places of residence, work and congregation, such as hotels, restaurants and show-rooms, is both a matter of personal choice and an almost impersonal, almost unconscious seeking for comfort and reassurance. We can, and perhaps we should, see in what way we can make use of these instincts.

For instance, it is both a compliment and a re-assurance when we greet the visitor to our homes with a plant or two in the porch or entrance hall. Immediately he feels that he is entering a warm and friendly place. This is an important fact that should be understood by those who have to rely on waiting rooms – doctors, dentists and lawyers, for example. If light permits, these plants should be flowering and in bright and welcoming colours, even if the plants have to be renewed at intervals.

In living rooms the situation is different. The atmosphere here should be quiet and restful. Plants which are too strident in colour should be avoided and indeed in some rooms there can be too many plants. The aim should be to provide or create one major plant arrangement which will act as the decorative focal point of the room. This may consist of a single plant or a group but it must blend easily with the major decorative colours of the room or echo some important decorative theme. There may, of course, be other plants or plant arrange-

Colour is a vital part of the decorator's skill. The plants in the bowl are azalea, scindapsus, tradescantia and rhoicissus. Their soft greens and whites go well with the more permanent colours of the room.

Below, right: Large plants, such as Fatsia japonica (left) and monstera help to furnish a room.

ments in the room but they should be of a minor nature and subservient to the main scheme.

However important the major plant and however subservient the minor plants, none must be in a position to cause spacial difficulty. No plant in any living room or any place where numbers of people are likely to gather should ever impede progress or even risk being brushed in passing. Nothing is more embarrassing to a visitor than accidentally knocking over a plant or even brushing against it and removing a flower or a leaf. And it does no good to the plants to be constantly swished this way and that by passing bodies. Always ensure that your plants decorate rather than dominate, that people are acknowledged to be more important than plants.

This is even more important in dining rooms, which are places with a specific purpose. No scented plant or heavily perfumed flowers should be allowed too close to the dining table and even the most delicate plant arrangement should not detract from the primary decorative theme, which is culinary or gastronomic.

Climbing rhoicissus and pendant epiphyllum are unscented and are ideal for dining room decoration.

Left: The colours of the flowering begonia and the matching carpet are made to look more striking because plant and carpet are close together. If they were separated the effect would be weakened. An unobtrusive base prevents water or soil from escaping.

The health of the plant should always be considered carefully when arranging a decorative scheme. Available light is the first matter to be examined, before such problems as space, warmth, draughts or humidity. If a plant is one that flowers or if it has variegated foliage, then it must have good light at all times if it is to look at its best for long periods. It must never be placed where the sun will shine on it through the window glass for long, for this can burn or bleach some of the vegetation; but if the situation is too dark the plant will become wan and listless.

Artificial light can compensate plants to a modest extent for being placed in too dark a situation, but this is normally not enough except for brief periods. In artificial light, yellow tends to become white, orange and pink become deeper. Dark red, purple and blue become almost black. Perhaps in the dining room it may be a practice to switch off the main electric light during a meal and rely on the intimacy of candlelight. This is a charming way of entertaining and light of this nature is flattering to humans and to food and wine but,

work of art. Some plants can go on the floor, some can be lifted to other levels, some can be recessed and others projected forward, some can trail from above and others reach upwards from below. They should always look immaculate, with clean foliage and never a faded flower or a browned leaf.

The normal fireplace accessories can be brought into the picture, perhaps to gleam with polished brass or glow with gunmetal. Green and humidifying moss can be wedged between the pots to hold them in place and fill gaps. Some plants can be wired onto a gnarled and twisted piece of polished driftwood.

PLANTS BY THE WINDOW

It is more likely that a fireplace will be decorated in the summer months than in winter, when there is always the possibility that it will be employed for its proper purpose. The reverse is the case with the huge picture windows and the wide sliding doors of so many modern homes, which look out onto the garden or the front of the house and which give such wonderful light to the interior that plants thrive there. Often in winter it is too cold to open the windows or to slide the wide doors aside. This area immediately inside the room is therefore unused by normal traffic and presents a splendid opportunity for a decorative display that can be enjoyed both from within the house and from outside.

The good light found here enables the brightest of flowers to be employed in the scheme, weaving a thread of colour or making a burning bank in the background of normal plant green. If the windows are not opened and the sliding doors not used, you will only have to go near the plants to draw the curtains at night, which means that a considerable space can easily be given to the display.

The floor will be the natural base here and from this it is possible to build a bank of plants, some raised on shelves perhaps or on benches, some standing tall. Although the windows may not reach floor level the doors will, so any low display can be arranged to face both ways, outwards and inwards.

A house with features such as this is almost certain to be modern and well heated, so with the good light also available there is scarcely any limit to the plants that can be used. If humidity is a problem it might be wise to spread a plastic sheet on the floor under the plants. This can easily enough be concealed from view and will make possible a daily spraying or misting of many of the plants.

Once again the decoration will probably be in place for some weeks if not months, so it can be given a certain

The plants in this winter window would be changed in summer when the window is in constant use and when direct sunlight might brown the leaves.

Right: All these plants need good light to grow well. The tall, climbing pelargonium is obviously a permanent fixture, but the other pelargonium, the cyclamens and the sansevieria, can be replaced with other plants when the flowers fade or if a different arrangement is required.

If plants are placed opposite a window, they will turn their leaves towards the light and so face into the room.

permanence. It will be worthwhile installing special portable shelving or benching, perhaps erecting stands and fixing pieces of driftwood or hanging a piece of bark from the wall to hold a stag's horn fern or one or two cryptanthus plants. Opportunities are endless for a really effective and long-lived home decoration.

PLANTS FOR WAITING ROOMS

Even the most glamorous establishment for haute couture and even the most expensive and fashionable doctor's waiting room have a certain impersonality about them. Although plants and flowers can be used to good purpose, they can never be given quite the same importance (and hence effectiveness) as they can in the home. Nevertheless it is worth using them both in a grand and a humble manner.

Where the surroundings are lavish it would be stupid and wasteful to employ earthy and over-simple plants or containers. Colours should be delicate and muted rather than strident and vulgar and more emphasis than usual should be placed on architectural shape and on texture. A well-groomed palm can grow from an elegant, white-painted, antique filligree cast iron container, while on a nearby mahogany table a small group of African violets can nestle together, their pretty flowers standing out from a tin-lined nineteenth-century tea caddy.

The doctor and the dentist must usually be more practical, but nevertheless a plant or two in the waiting room can soften the austerity and can bring comfort and reassurance to those who are weak and worried. The accent here should be on colour, on bright and happy colours, whites and yellows and reds and oranges that warm the atmosphere. Many flowering plants will last a month or so in good condition and are a perfectly practical proposition so long as the light is good enough for them and so long as they get the minimum attention they need. If they cannot get this attention, then it is better to do without them entirely.

THE MODERN OFFICE

One of the most machine-like, impersonal, depressing and arid places in which people today find themselves is a large, modern, open-plan office with dozens or scores of desks and a view from the window only of a similar office across the road or of rooftops far below. In desperation many a secretary will produce a busy lizzie plant brought on from a cutting at home. This will stand for a short time on the windowsill or on the top of a nearby filing cabinet and will quickly wither and die in the arid air. Is there any point in trying? Can

anything be done under these special circumstances?

Although the intention is right, the plant is wrong. Instead of the tender impatiens plant, the secretary should bring with her a tough and handsome vriesia, for example, ready to grow from its cup-like centre a sword flower of flaming gold. Or she could bring a gleaming *Philodendron scandens* and allow its sweetheart leaves to cascade down the side of the filing cabinet.

Employers can encourage and improve the morale of their staff by installing little groups of plants at intervals throughout the floor. Tough, long-lived plants can still be beautiful and they can soften the atmosphere. Built-in plant troughs can hold screens of ivies, cissus and rhoicissus and can provide not only an impression of greater privacy but a more genuine degree of peace and quiet. A volunteer can usually be found to care for these plants and it is even probable that many of the employees would help to pay for their upkeep.

Most horizontal surfaces in offices of all kinds are cluttered with the necessities of business, so special provision should be made for the plants. Even if no formal spaces are available, it is perfectly possible for one or two enthusiasts to insist that occasional cabinets should be left clear to hold not just the casual potted plant but a carefully designed, planned and created plant decoration, of sufficient importance to warrant attention and sufficient beauty to collect compliments.

PLANTS FOR OFFICES

There are several problems or difficulties involved in attempting to grow house plants in offices. The light is sometimes poor, the atmosphere is often dry and stuffy and often no one person accepts responsibility for their care. A number of organizations operate a plant hire system: they will fill or supply containers of suitable plants, tend them regularly and replace plants as and when necessary. If a person on the staff of a large organization will accept responsibility for the care of the plants then the decorations can be supplied much less expensively. The following plants are all suitable for growing in office premises so long as these are not so dark that artificial light is constantly required and so long as there is suitable space provided. Flowering plants are not recommended except for brief periods. On the right is a selection of popular plants, their descriptions and diameter size.

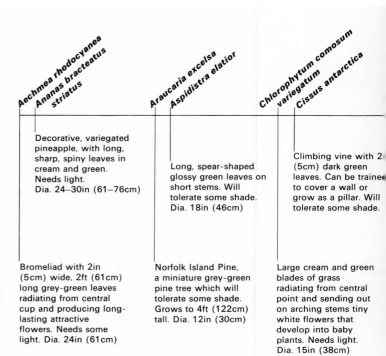

Aechmea rhodocyanea
Ananas bracteatus striatus

Araucaria excelsa
Aspidistra elatior

Chlorophytum comosum variegatum
Cissus antarctica

Decorative, variegated pineapple, with long, sharp, spiny leaves in cream and green. Needs light. Dia. 24–30in (61–76cm)

Long, spear-shaped glossy green leaves on short stems. Will tolerate some shade. Dia. 18in (46cm)

Climbing vine with 2in (5cm) dark green leaves. Can be trained to cover a wall or grow as a pillar. Will tolerate some shade.

Bromeliad with 2in (5cm) wide, 2ft (61cm) long grey-green leaves radiating from central cup and producing long-lasting attractive flowers. Needs some light. Dia. 24in (61cm)

Norfolk Island Pine, a miniature grey-green pine tree which will tolerate some shade. Grows to 4ft (122cm) tall. Dia. 12in (30cm)

Large cream and green blades of grass radiating from central point and sending out on arching stems tiny white flowers that develop into baby plants. Needs light. Dia. 15in (38cm)

xshedera lizei / Fatsia japonica	Ficus species / Hedera species	Monstera deliciosa / Nidularium species	Philodendron species / Platycerium alicorne	Rhoicissus rhomboidea / Sansevieria trifasciata	Vriesia splendens
Similar to *Fatshedera*, with more branching habit and larger leaves. Will grow into a large plant of 4ft (122cm) height. Will tolerate some shade. Dia. 36in (91cm)	The familiar ivy, available in many colours and sizes of leaf. Can be trained to grow up a wall or support or grow as a trailer. Variegated cultivars need light to maintain leaf colour.	Several kinds of bromeliad with strap-like leaves radiating from a central cup. Tolerant, but best in some light. Dia. 15in (38cm)	A large fern with felted grey-green fronds like stag's horns. Good fixed to a wall. Will tolerate some shade. Dia. 10–40in (25–102cm)	Long, sword-like, thick and fleshy leaves rising to 4ft (122cm) or so, green and gold. Needs light to maintain colour. Will take direct sunlight. Dia. 9in (23cm)	
ingle stemmed climber r trailer with large in (10cm) palmate aves. Will tolerate me shade.	All are trees and will grow to 10ft (3m) or so if required. *F. benjamina* has small green leaves, droops elegantly. *F. lyrata* has large, guitar-shaped green leaves and *F. elastica* (or cultivars) is the familiar rubber plant. All will tolerate some shade. Dia. 15–48in (38–122cm)	Climbing vine with large holed and slashed leaves, usually green but variegated form obtainable. Will climb a wall and can then be trained around the ceiling. Green form will accept some shade.	Several species of green plants, some climbing, some with large leaves. *P. scandens* is a climber with 5in (13cm) heart-shaped leaves. *P. bipennifolium*, *P. bipinnatifidum* and *P. elegans* all have large 1ft (30cm) leaves. All will tolerate some shade. Dia. 6–48ins (15–122cm)	Climbing vine with 2in (5cm) green leaves. Can be trained to cover a wall or make a pillar up a central support. Will tolerate some shade.	Bromeliad with central cup from which radiate 1ft (30cm) strap-like leaves banded chocolate and green. Flower is a flat, sword-like, orange-red growth. Needs some light. Dia. 18in (46cm)

Happy Families

All plants and almost all humans are gregarious by nature. They prefer to live together in a community because this way they are safer and more comfortable. This being so, it seems an odd thing that we tend to buy one plant at a time and to stand this one plant alone, divorced from its neighbours, on a table or windowsill as though it were undergoing some form of ostracism or quarantine. We do not buy a single flower at a time but rather a bunch. The growers and sellers of house plants have not yet realized that once their customers have become used to enjoying and handling house plants, they tend to group them together into joint decorations. If this was understood, perhaps it would become possible to buy entire collections of house plants, related not necessarily by family but by their physical requirements.

The reasons why plants seem to do better in communities rather than as individuals are much the same as with humans. One man living alone in a remote part of the country, whether it be in a cave or a modern home, will have no water supply, no sewage, no electricity, no telephone, no roads, no doctor, no stores. Some of these things he will have to do without, some he will have to find for himself. But if someone else comes to live nearby, and another person and another, then gradually a community is formed and between them they either create their own communal conveniences and comforts or they become significant as a group and the larger and wider community provides what they need.

The parallel is remarkably similar with plants. A *Begonia rex* is bought from store or nursery and brought home to be placed on a windowsill. Over the next few weeks it receives light from the window, warmth from the radiator, food and water from the owner plus an occasional clean and trim up. Once in a while, it is forgotten or the owner goes away. It does not get the light it needs, or the heat or the water.

But surely exactly the same calamities can occur if this *Begonia rex* existed not alone but in a community with a number of other plants? Of course they can, but in this case many of the necessities of life can be borrowed from neighbours. The light cannot be provided but plants, like humans, generate a little of their own warmth and they can share this among themselves. As for food and water, one plant always has an excess to share with another.

Perhaps the greatest benefit to be gained by a plant living in a community is the micro-climate each plant generates around itself. It has already been mentioned that the moisture in a plant pot, and more particularly the moisture in the packing medium in a cover pot,

An open, carboy-type arrangement which includes (clockwise from the top) a croton, Begonia rex, *cryptanthus and araucaria. All will tolerate similar conditions and they have been planted together in the same soil.*

Right: A packed and colourful bowl which includes (clockwise from the top) Hedera canariensis, Cyclamen decora, Fittonia verschaffeltii, *tradescantia,* Dracaena terminalis *and, in the centre,* Fatshedera lizei. *Dracaenas, hederas, tradescantias and fatshederas are all quite easy plants, so choose conditions that suit the more delicate cyclamen and fittonia.*

gradually releases a fine film of humidity around the leaves of the plant above it. This being so, two plants next to each other will release twice as much and five will release five times as much moisture. At the same time, every plant, like every human, exudes moisture from the millions of pores in its epidermis or skin, and this moisture also adds to the beneficial micro-climate around the plant or group of plants.

PLANT ARRANGEMENTS

Plants should be grouped together for aesthetic reasons, too. A single flower is a beautiful thing, a natural work of art which, like a picture, can repeatedly be admired. But the flower once examined in detail remains much the same, while the picture is composed of so subtle and delicate a mixture that the more one looks at it the more one sees. So, although it is frequently possible to enjoy and admire a single flower in a vase, most of the time we

prefer to arrange a group of them together to get a wider range of patterns.

Neither should it be forgotten that there is a genuine satisfaction to be obtained by the exercise of taste and talent in creating a plant arrangement. The blending and contrasting of colours, shapes and textures is the work of an artist. At the same time the arranger must appreciate and work within the confines of the physical requirements of the plants. Making a plant arrangement is just as skilled an art as making a flower arrangement, or even as painting a picture.

One reason why the art of plant arrangement should be so satisfying is the sheer freedom of choice open to the practitioner. There is a tremendously wide choice of plants of all sizes, shapes, colours and textures. So far as containers are concerned, there is no limit. It is possible to make a plant arrangement in a shell no more than two inches (5cm) wide and half an inch (12mm) deep and it is also possible to work with the larger area provided by a bathtub-sized trough or tub. It is possible to make dish gardens and bottle gardens. You can make terrariums or you can mix plants or cut flowers in a *pot et fleur* style (see Chapter 10). Some plants will grow in water alone and others need no more than anchoring down with a handful of pebbles.

USING PLANTS IN POTS

The simplest form of plant arrangement is made merely by combining two or more plants together in a single container. Nothing could be easier than to assemble the plants which are to be used, choose a container that will house them and their pots and then arrange them in a style and pattern that pleases you. This will not, however, satisfy the artist or plant enthusiast for long. For example, all the pots appear to be at the same level. The flower pots are too visible and seem almost to be a part of the arrangement. There are gaps between the pots. One or two of the plants flop over the edge of the container, or over each other.

There are, however, advantages in keeping plants in their original pots. They are easy to place in position and equally easy to remove. Where one of the plants in the arrangement is recognized as only a temporary resident, then it is best to keep it in its pot so that it can be removed quickly and replaced by any other suitable plant. Or if the arrangement is not as effective as it was intended to be, again, plants in their original pots can safely be moved.

To avoid all the pots appearing to be at one level it is a simple matter to raise one or two on a little mound of soil or peat. And if you do not wish the flower pots to

Plants do not need to be planted together to make a mixed arrangement. Here a pot of tradescantia is raised by standing it on a block of moist Oasis.

be so visible it is easy to cover them with a blanket of soil or peat or perhaps with pieces of green moss. Pots need not stand upright, they can be leaned one way or another to project the plant at an angle and improve the appearance of the arrangement. Of course, a plant that leans is difficult to water but if there is plenty of soil, peat or moss around the base and the top of the pot this will hold moisture well and release it to the plant in the pot as it is required.

If plants are kept in their pots it is not normally necessary to have a layer of drainage material in the base of the parent container, for each pot can be watered individually, even if the top of the pot is hidden. But where a number of pots are concerned or where the arranger is new to house plants and unsure of his skills, then it may be wise to include an inch or so of coarse sand or gravel.

Most flower pots are round and there must necessarily be gaps between them when they are placed close together in a larger container. Some are square, but if these square pots are placed next to each other the plants they contain appear to be regimented like soldiers on parade rather than grouped in a free and satisfying arrangement. An agreeable compromise can be made by knocking the plants from their round or square pots and slipping the root balls into little pots made from polythene sleeves. These, black in colour and almost invisible, can be obtained very cheaply in a wide range of sizes. They hold the plants securely so that they can be placed into position just like the round pots, but they are malleable. They fit very closely one to another in a plant arrangement, but the roots of each plant are still separated from those of the next. Some pots can be long

Polythene pots are malleable, so this cryptanthus can be squeezed into a corner. The polythene has drainage holes punched in it so that the plant can be watered in the normal way.

This succulent cutting is anchored to moist Oasis by inserting a cocktail stick in the base as a spike. The finished bowl, with mechanical aids well hidden, is shown on p.74.

and thin, others fat; some are tall, some short; yet all will fit in with their neighbours without gaps. This enables a greater number of plants to be fitted into one container. The black polythene is almost invisible, but if any shows it can easily be cut away with a pair of scissors or can be disguised with peat or moss.

These polythene sleeves have drainage holes punched in them so they operate in exactly the same way as a more rigid flower pot and no change in watering tech-

niques will be required. This means to some extent that all the plants in the arrangement must have more or less the same water requirements and this must be taken into account when the arrangement is made.

If an arrangement of some exceptional kind is planned, for example one containing several flowering plants and a very special cactus plant, special arrangements must be made. The flowering plants will require much more water than the cactus, yet all will be in the

Effective plant arrangements can be made without taking plants from their separate pots, so long as they share light, temperature and humidity requirements. Pots can be raised or angled, and awkward corners filled by using polythene sleeves instead of rigid containers. The flowering clivia is a bulb and as it is in its own pot, can easily be removed when its flower fades. Each pot can be individually watered but an inch or so of coarse sand or gravel in the main container will ensure that there is adequate drainage.

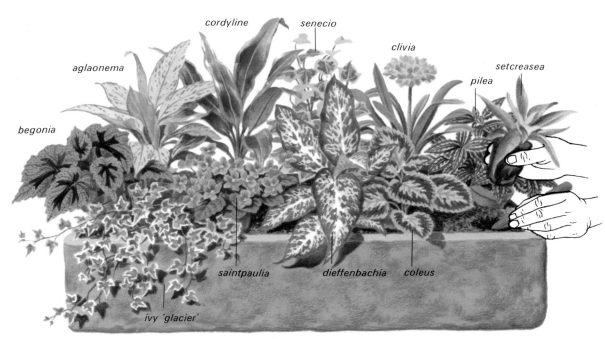

same container and subjected to the same quantities of water. Here all that is needed is to place the root ball of the cactus plant in a plastic bag, one without drainage holes, so that it is separated from the other plants and the water they receive does not get to its own roots.

PERMANENT ARRANGEMENTS

Where a more permanent arrangement is required, it is usually better and more satisfactory to knock the plants from their pots and to plant them all in their new communal home, with their roots all in the same soil. This demands a little more skill and a greater knowledge of the plants and their requirements. It also demands a certain dexterity.

Here the container should certainly have a layer of drainage material in the base, at least an inch (2·5cm) of gravel or something similar and preferably up to two inches (5cm) if the container is deep enough. This should be put in place first and the soil in which the roots of the plants are to be placed should go on top. In order to prevent the soil from being washed down into the drainage layer it is helpful to spread over the gravel a piece of rough hessian or some similar material. Because there may be occasions when rather more water than was intended lies in this drainage layer, it is wise to mix with the gravel a few nuggets of charcoal, or even to make the entire drainage layer from charcoal. This absorbs any foul smell that might arise from the stale water. The charcoal is the type used for barbecue fires, broken up where necessary into smaller pieces. It is normally easy to obtain, light in weight and comparatively inexpensive.

The soil in which the plants are to be placed should be landscaped to some extent before the actual planting. It should be sloped or have miniature hills and valleys made in it according to the position the plants will take. The plants should then be knocked from their pots and put in the soil in the required position. The soil should be well firmed around the roots.

Most plants can be knocked from their pots very easily using the following method. Take up the plant pot from the top so that the palm of the hand covers the soil at the top and the plant itself extends between the first and second fingers. Turn the plant upside down and give the edge of the pot a sharp tap on some firm surface. The root ball will slip out of the pot into the hand and, so long as it is correctly moist, little or no soil will be spilt.

Do not disturb the root ball before or during planting. Keep it intact, for in this way the fine root hairs will not be damaged. If the root ball is too large for its required

position prise away a little of the soil very carefully with your fingers or a pointed stick.

After the arrangement has been completed and all the plants are in place, water it gently and stand it in a cool and shady place for the first few days to allow the plants to settle in to their new home.

Some people, particularly in families where there are children, like to add ornaments to their dish gardens and plant arrangements. It is possible to buy little Chinese figures, bridges, pagodas and the like and a little piece of mirror can be used as a lake or stream. If this sort of thing is to be added, do this after all the planting has been completed.

THE BOTTLE GARDEN

Another type of plant arrangement that has achieved considerable popularity is the bottle garden. Bottle gardens are usually made inside a large glass carboy but they can be created in a wide variety of glass containers, both with wide and with narrow necks. Whatever the container, the basic method of planting is the same, but where the neck is narrow it is obvious that certain different techniques must be employed and certain exceptional tools used.

In the first place the plants to be used must be chosen with care, for they must not only be smaller in size than normal but they should also be those that are slow growing and will not drop their debris on the soil surface. This means, for example, that flowering plants cannot be used, for no flowers live as long as foliage, and fallen petals are apt to rot and lead to trouble. The following plants are all suitable for a fairly large bottle garden and most can be easily enough obtained in an immature and miniature size: *Begonia rex, Carex japonica, Codiaeum variegatum pictum, Cryptanthus acaulis, Dryopteris erythrosora, Fittonia argyroneura, Maranta makoyana, Pellionia pulchra, Peperomia caperata variegata* and *P. magnoliaefolia variegata, Pteris biaurita argyraea.*

There are other plants which will also suit and much will depend on what is available. The two main things to guard against are falling flowers or dropping leaves and over-swift growth so that the interior of the bottle is too quickly filled with foliage.

You will almost certainly have to devise and make your own specialized tools. The following should be all you need. First, a normal table or soup spoon securely tied to a long, thin cane. This, in effect, is the spade. Second, a cotton reel wedged firmly onto the end of another cane to firm the soil over the roots as the plants are slipped into place. Finally, a series of heavy pins tied tightly to the base of a long cane, their points down-

Add moist, sterilized soil to the basic drainage layer of pebbles.

Before adding a plant, knock it from its pot and tease the soil from the roots.

Position each plant carefully so that it will grow well and look attractive.

Add more soil to make quite sure that the roots are adequately covered.

Use a wooden spoon to firm the soil around the roots as you add each plant.

Most plants can easily be knocked from their pots without disturbing the root ball. Hold the pot at the top so that the palm of the hand covers the soil.

Turn the pot upside down and knock it against a firm surface. The root ball will slip out into your hand. If the soil is moist, it will hold together and will not spill.

Slightly moist soil will provide plants with their needs for months so long as the lid is on, but remove it briefly if condensation is too severe. If possible place the jar in a north window, never in a south one.

Left: Only plants with the same water needs are suitable for permanent arrangements in the same soil. Here a chlorophytum is added to cryptanthus, fittonia, peperomia and ivy.

peperomia
cryptanthus
fittonia
chlorophytum
ivy

A garden in a carboy needs more special tools. Soil can be placed with a movable paper chute. Pea gravel and a few pellets of charcoal are good for drainage.

A wooden kitchen spoon, securely tied to a cane, is a good trowel for making planting holes. Make these separately, one at a time, before adding each plant.

Knock plants from pots and reduce the size of the root ball very gently so that it can be dropped through the opening into the planting hole.

ward in a circle. This tool serves to pick up any fallen leaves or other soft debris that will rot and set up mildew inside the bottle.

It is essential that the bottle is absolutely clean inside before planting begins and it is helpful to make every effort to keep the interior clean as work progresses. Normal interior cleanliness can be obtained by putting a handful of shingle inside together with a pint of water and swishing this around until interior dust and grime has disappeared. Several rinsings may be necessary and if these are made successively hotter the bottle will soon dry out when it is completely clean.

There must be a drainage layer in the base, but if pebbles or shingle are to be used instead of the lighter charcoal nuggets, do not merely drop them in from the top as this could break or crack the glass. Instead make the lightest of carpets of peat and slip in the shingle on top of this. It is best to make a chute so that you can distribute the material where you want it.

After the drainage layer, which should be an inch (2·5cm) or so thick, start adding the soil. It is helpful to make this soil slightly moist before it is slipped into the bottle or carboy as it will save having to moisten it later. Spread this soil about in a layer up to three inches (7·5cm) deep, either sloped or with hills and valleys so that the plants can be arranged in interesting positions.

Set out the plants on the table beside the container and arrange them in the positions they are to take inside. It will be difficult to change their positions later.

Then take up your first plant, knock it from its pot and, if the root ball is still too large to enter the neck of the bottle, gently tease some of the soil away from the roots. Hold the plant at its tip and lower the roots into the neck of the bottle. Try to drop the roots directly into the hole you have in the required place. You may have to lean the carboy a little or you may have to swing the plant to and fro and let it drop when it reaches the peak of its arc. With your spoon, then shovel soil over the roots, firming this in position with the cotton reel. Follow the same procedure with the other plants. It will become progressively more difficult as the other plants occupy the interior space, so do not use too many plants.

You can insert a rock or two, or perhaps a piece of driftwood, to give added interest. If the soil used was slightly moist do not add any more water. Keep the planted bottle in a cool place in subdued light for the first few days to allow the plants to settle down. You may find that moisture condenses on the sides in the early mornings. Do not worry about this and do not try to clear the glass. Leave it and it should disappear as the day goes on.

It is not advisable for any but experts to seal the opening, for this generally leads to mildew in the interior unless the balance between the number and type of plants and the moisture in the soil is exactly right. Turn the bottle occasionally so that all the plants get the best light at some time. Water only very occasionally and always very lightly and never give a feed of any kind.

A cotton reel on a piece of cane will firm the soil around the roots. Unless this is done, pockets of air may be left and the roots will die.

When planting is completed leaves are sure to be dusty. A soft, clean paintbrush tied to a cane will clean and groom them to improve their appearance.

Keep your bottle garden in a position where it gets good light but never direct sun. Water open bottle gardens only occasionally.

Tiny ferns and succulents, with a chunk of soft tufa stone, make an attractive ensemble in this outsize brandy glass.

Remember that the slower your plants grow the longer the bottle garden will look attractive. Use your spiker to remove any leaves that fall.

The principle behind the bottle garden is that of the Wardian case, devised 150 or so years ago by a Dr Nathaniel Ward, initially for the safe transport of strange plants discovered in unexplored areas of the world to scientific centres and botanical gardens in the western world. He found that they would travel safely if they were planted securely in large boxes with a timber base and glass sides and top. The boxes were hermetically sealed once they were planted. In this way the plants received plenty of light and needed no watering because the soil in which they were planted was already moist. Neither could the plants be splashed with sea water as they made their journeys across the world lashed to the deck of a sailing vessel.

Wardian cases soon became popular when it was found that they also had decorative uses. They were made in cast iron and displayed in Victorian conservatories, mainly containing filmy ferns. They are collector's pieces today.

THE PUDDLE POT

There is still another kind of plant arrangement, devised by the authors some years ago and called a puddle pot. It consists of taking cuttings of those house plants that will root in water and making an arrangement with them in some attractive and suitable container with

pebbles to hold the cuttings in place. The cuttings grow once their roots develop and the entire arrangement becomes more and more effective until one or more of the plants grows too large for its home. In this case it is removed and potted up in soil in the normal way – a new plant gained.

Complete and mature plants can be mixed with the cuttings. These plants should be knocked from their pots and all the soil washed from their roots before they are inserted. This sometimes results in a more interesting and effective arrangement.

Any type of container will suit a puddle pot so long as it is deep enough to hold water and at least a couple of layers of pebbles. Lay a few nuggets of charcoal on the base of the container in case the water becomes smelly and then fill up with pebbles, adding the water last. In the case of mature plants the roots will have to be put into the container and the pebbles placed on and around them so that the plant is anchored securely. Cuttings need only be slipped into place and held by a pebble or two. Arrange all the plants pleasantly so that the finished effect is pretty and not merely utilitarian. Give a light liquid feed once a week or so and make sure that the level of the water never drops below the new roots that are being formed.

However carefully you feed them, you will find that your cuttings never make large plants until you remove them from the puddle pot and plant them in soil. This is all to the good, for the essence of this type of arrangement is that it should be small and intimate. Mix kinds of plants and if possible colours. One or two flowering plants such as impatiens will grow, flower and make roots very well in a puddle pot.

When all cuttings are in place, add the water. Water is used up quickly by plants which grow in it alone. It also evaporates faster than it does when it is in soil, so examine the pot regularly and top it up if necessary. A weak fertilizer solution added at each watering will keep the plants healthy and encourage them to grow quickly.

Right: The final arrangement contains two species of tradescantia, Begonia rex, scindapsus, Plectranthus fruiticosus, Peperomia glabella variegata, chlorophytum, Rhoicissus rhomboidea and Cissus antarctica. Because the plants will stay in position for many weeks it is important to inspect them daily, removing and replacing any cutting that has not responded well to this method of growing.

Add the first cutting and its anchor stone. These larger stones hold the plants in place. The roots do not become attached to them and they can easily be changed or moved if you feel that the general appearance will be improved by moving the cutting to a different part of the arrangement.

As the different cuttings are inserted and the puddle pot begins to take shape, never lose sight of the fact that this is very much an arrangement of plant materials. Choose pieces that will blend or contrast and will maintain interest over a long period. Anchor each cutting securely with a stone. Leave space for each plant to grow.

Care and Protection

The main requirements of a healthy and decorative house plant are as follows. It is impossible to decide on an order of importance that will apply to all plants, for requirements differ, but this order is right for many of the most popular species.

1	Light	6	Food
2	Humidity	7	Air
3	Water	8	Protection from draughts
4	Warmth	9	Grooming
5	Cleanliness	10	Support

The greatest problem faced by those who are comparatively new to the world of house plants appears to be concerned with watering their plants. They ask anxiously how often they should water them and are genuinely puzzled and distressed when they get no concrete answer. Yet it would seem obvious that watering must depend on such variables as season, temperature, light, weather, size of plant, and size of pot.

To be on the safe side these people give their plants a little dribble of water each day. At some times of the year this is insufficient to moisten more than the top inch or two (2–5cm) of the soil and at other times these little dribbles mount up so that the plant stands in water.

The necessary air cavities in the soil are filled with moisture and the roots drown. More plants are killed by over-watering than by any other fault in handling and this is due to several misunderstandings.

People are apt to equate their house plants with their pets, and in many ways this is quite right, for plants like pets need water, food, warmth, shelter, air, cleanliness and regular grooming. But there is one vital difference. A pet such as a dog, cat or even a canary, can *choose* whether or not to eat and drink. It can take in some of the water in its bowl and leave the remainder for another time. But a plant cannot choose. If it is watered it must accept that water. The most it can do is allow excess moisture to trickle out through the drainage holes in the base of its pot. But too often this pot is standing in a saucer or some other container so as not to damage the furniture and the excess fluid does not, in fact, drain away. So the plant drowns.

It is a simple enough matter to give a plant water when it is obvious that it needs it. The leaves begin to droop and the soil surface is dry. Add some water and in a matter of hours the plant stands upright again, its stems and foliage turgid with the moisture that it has received.

What can be done when you find one of your plants sickening, its leaves drooping and yellowing, and then

Fuchsias are generally thought of as garden or greenhouse plants and are best if they are not kept indoors for too long. Good, bright light is necessary and also a moist soil; regular feeding, spraying and sponging of the leaves are good.

Some house plants have a reputation for being difficult to grow, yet with proper care and conditions most will do well. Hibiscus rosa-sinensis needs a light, airy atmosphere, good light and moist soil. High temperatures and humidity are not necessary.

Marantas have magnificent leaves but need warmth, humidity and good light to keep them in good condition. Temperatures should range from 65°–75°F (18°–20°C) so long as humidity keeps in step. Regular light feeding in the growing period will improve the leaves.

discover that it is standing in water, that its soil is damp and sodden? Obviously you pour away all excess moisture. But what then? You cannot place the plant in front of a fire or a radiator to dry out. You cannot mop up, strain off, rub down and dry out the soil.

There are, in fact, only two possibilities, neither very satisfactory. Which possibility you choose will depend mainly on your knowledge of the plant concerned but partly also on your faith in your own ability. The first possibility is to leave the plant as it is and hope that the soil will dry out and become porous again quickly enough to save its life. Resist the desire to coddle the plant, to move it to a warmer room or to stand it in a stronger light. The plant is dangerously ill. It must be kept in a cool, shaded position and left alone to recover if it can.

The other possibility is to knock the plant from its pot and very carefully scrape and tease away some of the sodden soil from around its root surface. Do not remove all the wet soil, but leave a good nucleus of a root ball. Then plant this in the same pot with dry soil around the wet root ball. Pack the dry soil down quite firmly. Do not give water. Then stand the pot again in a cool and lightly shaded place. Only water again when it is obvious that the plant is recovering.

One reason why too many plants are given too much water is that the true function of watering is misunderstood. When you pour water onto the soil of a house plant it is not merely to provide the plant with the moisture that it requires for life. Correct watering also provides the plant with the air that is necessary for its roots to live an active and healthy life.

The dry soil in a plant pot can be compared to a dry sponge. The sponge is composed of a large number of empty air spaces held together by a mass of vegetable matter or, in the case of a plastic sponge, by a mass of synthetic matter. When you pour a dribble of water onto this dry sponge a portion of its surface becomes moist but the remainder is still dry. When you pour more water onto the surface the moist area spreads until there is an excess of water. At this stage water begins to drip from the base of the sponge. Note that the water has tended to move down through the sponge both by gravity and by capillary action, so that the greatest concentration of moisture is at the base of the sponge. At the top, although the sponge is moist, air holes have once again appeared. If you stop adding water at the top, the water will shortly stop dripping from the base. The sponge will be rather wetter at the base than at the top but all portions will have the air spaces exposed again.

The water has acted very like the piston in a pump. As it was added at the top it coursed through all the air

Codiaeum variegatum pictum *needs good light, but not direct sunlight, no draughts, and as humid an atmosphere as possible. Its soil should be kept moist, and it should only be given a light feed when it is growing well. Spraying the leaves on hot days will help.*

Saintpaulias *need temperatures between 55° and 75°F (12° and 23°C), plenty of light, protection from draughts and regular feeding and watering. Clean air is essential, and for this reason they are not always easy to grow in cities.*

Rhoeo discolor *needs warmth and some humidity to maintain its leaves in good condition. Good light and a moist, rich soil are necessary and shallow pots will allow the plant to spread. In cold weather keep the soil almost dry.*

holes and pushed this air downwards before it. At the same time it sucked air down behind it.

This should be your aim when you water a plant. You should wait until the soil is almost dry and then provide the plant with sufficient water so that the stale air can be pushed out of contact with the roots, so that the whole of the soil in the pot is thoroughly moistened and clean fresh air is sucked down to replace the stale and used air.

For those uncertain about their plants, then, it is wise to wait until the soil surface appears to be dry or is dry to the touch before adding water. Sufficient water should then be given so that it begins to trickle out from the drainage holes at the base of the pot. When this trickle has ceased, the excess water should be thrown away and the pot stood on a dry surface again.

One way to water a pot thoroughly and at the same time to change the air in the pot is to plunge the pot completely in a bucket of water. Bubbles will rise to the surface and when they have finished rising this will mean that all the air cavities in the soil are filled with water. The pot should then be removed and left to drain. Water will rush through the drainage holes in the base and air will be sucked into the soil from above.

This watering by submersion is a rather more complex operation than is really necessary, but it is worth carrying out occasionally to make absolutely sure that the soil in the pot is uniformly moist. It is sometimes quite astonishing how long it takes for bubbles to cease rising through the water from the top of the pot. This indicates that somewhere in the soil there exists a dry spot, an air bubble surrounded, perhaps, by a particularly tough portion of soil into which the water permeates only with difficulty.

All plants need less water in winter than in summer, even though they may live in a warm atmosphere, for nearly all plants rest or grow more slowly in winter. Take note of weather conditions when watering. Dull, dark, cold or wet days reduce the need for so much water for your plants. A plant standing in a south or a west window will need more water than one in a north or an east window. A plant that has been standing in too bright a light can wilt and droop even though it needs no water. Move it to a shadier spot rather than risk drowning it. If a plant droops or the leaves begin to turn yellow yet you can see that the soil surface is moist, then check first for over-watering and secondly for gas in the atmosphere or some other form of polluted air.

Never allow a plant to droop for want of water, always water it immediately the lack becomes evident. Never allow cacti or succulents to droop or to shrivel, give them just enough to keep them plump and turgid.

Some plants (cyclamen and saintpaulias are examples) will begin to rot at soil level if water collects in the top of the plant. In this case either water very carefully, or better still water from the base. This involves pouring water into the saucer or other container and letting the soil absorb this. Do it two or three times if all the water is taken up quickly, but never allow the plant to stand for more than an hour or two in a puddle of water.

If possible always use rain water for your plants. It does not normally contain the chemicals that are necessary in commercial, piped water, nor will it contain so much lime as is suspended in many tap waters. Rain water in large industrial centres is sometimes slightly contaminated by atmospheric pollution, but is still preferable to tap water. When plant foliage is being sprayed or cleaned, rain water should be used in preference to tap water, for the latter sometimes tends to leave a deposit, white and unsightly, on the leaves.

PLANT FEEDING

It is possible to be quite definite and quite scientific about watering, but feeding is less exact a matter and as a result house plants are usually either starved or stuffed. There is, however, one golden rule to be observed with feeding house plants: always under-feed rather than over-feed.

There are two reasons for this. In the first place, too much fertiliser can actually burn the roots of a plant and kill it and, at the least, will certainly give the plant indigestion. As with water, a plant cannot reject the food it is given.

The second reason brings up a matter of vital importance to all house plant enthusiasts. It is very pleasant to see a young house plant bursting with growth. But how long will that plant live if it grows too fast? It may take a while for it to kill itself through over-activity, but it will not be long before it has occupied all the space allotted to it and begun to prove an embarrassment in the home.

House plants should not be pushed along and encouraged to grow large, fat and blowsy, both for their sake and your own. They should, instead, be encouraged to grow slowly and deliberately, keeping their looks and their good health and remaining roughly in proportion with their surroundings. This is another reason why they should be fed only in small quantities.

All the normal proprietory house-plant foods are balanced to provide roughly the same quantities of the essential chemicals for health and growth, but some come in liquid form, some as a powder and some in tablets. Use whichever you find most convenient, re-

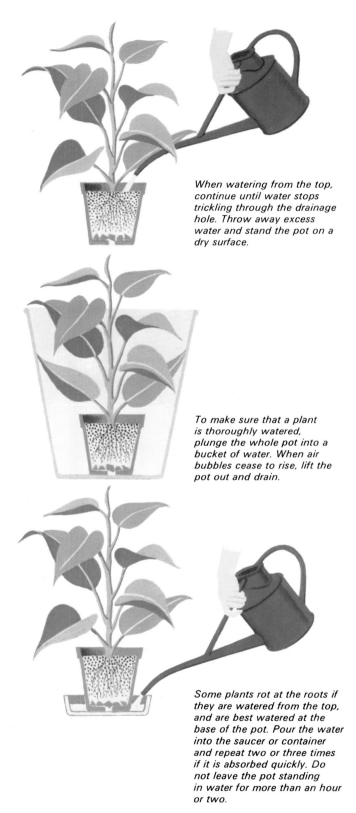

When watering from the top, continue until water stops trickling through the drainage hole. Throw away excess water and stand the pot on a dry surface.

To make sure that a plant is thoroughly watered, plunge the whole pot into a bucket of water. When air bubbles cease to rise, lift the pot out and drain.

Some plants rot at the roots if they are watered from the top, and are best watered at the base of the pot. Pour the water into the saucer or container and repeat two or three times if it is absorbed quickly. Do not leave the pot standing in water for more than an hour or two.

membering that plant roots can only absorb liquids and that powders and tablets must be broken down by the addition of water. Never, never, use more than the stated quantities. Never feed a plant that has just been re-potted nor one that is ailing for any reason at all.

It is normal for all house plants sent out from a specialist nursery to be potted up in a soil sufficiently rich to provide food for the plant for the first few months and it is unwise to feed any newly purchased plant for this reason. Begin to feed a new plant only if the season is right and if it appears to be making new growth.

Because house plants normally rest during the cooler and darker months of winter, sometimes putting on no growth at all and sometimes greatly reducing their normal rate of growth, then their rate of feeding should be proportionate to their rate of growth. Where they are fed in spring and early summer once a week, in winter they should be fed once a month and it will do them no harm if they are fed only once or twice during the whole winter season. If they are to be fed rarely, give them a gentle feed rather than a banquet.

ATTENDING TO THE SOIL

Both watering and feeding are influenced to some degree by the soil in a pot. Take a plant which has been growing in a pot for some months or even years and knock it from the pot so that you can examine the roots. You will probably find that the roots go round and round the inside wall of the pot and that there is very little soil at all. It has all been used up in feeding the plant over this long period of time.

The experienced house plant keeper will almost certainly know that the soil in a particular pot has been used up because he will notice that when the plant is watered the water tends to rush straight through instead of being checked and absorbed.

It will obviously be necessary to re-pot such a plant in fresh soil. But it is not only when a plant has used up all the soil in its pot that it may require to be re-potted. Some plants (some cacti are an example) grow so slowly that they do not use up the soil, but the soil in which they are planted may be so old that it becomes compacted, hard, almost impervious to water and to air. This is another case where re-potting will do much to benefit the plant.

It is possible to be very fussy and insist on special soil mixtures for each different kind of plant, and there is no reason why this should not be a very good thing, but with one or two exceptions it really is not necessary: a single basic mixture of soil can be bought or made which will suit all plants. This can be changed slightly when necessary by adding a little more coarse sand to increase the drainage, a little more peat to increase the moisture-holding properties, or a little more lime if this is what the plant really needs to be healthy.

In some places special standard soil mixtures may be bought in small quantities and it is also possible to buy bags of clean and convenient no-soil mixtures. The benefit of both of these is that as a rule they are sterile, which is to say that all weed seeds have been killed by steaming, baking or by chemical treatment. This means that weeds will not appear in the pot, competing with the plant for the limited quantity of soil, food and water. It also means that if this soil mixture is used for seed sowing you will not have to wonder whether the tiny new plant which appears is the one you have sown or a mere weed.

An easy-to-mix general purpose soil mixture can be made from one-third sharp sand, the grain particles being up to one-eighth of an inch (3mm) in diameter, one third good loam, well-rotted leafmould or rich home-made compost and one-third granulated peat. The loam, leafmould or compost is the only part of this mixture that is likely to contain weed seeds and so it might be worth your while to sterilize this. You can do small quantities without much trouble, either by steaming the soil in a normal kitchen steaming pan or by putting it in a slow oven for an hour. This is not essential and if only one or two plants are involved it will hardly be worthwhile.

RE-POTTING

If a plant has obviously outgrown its pot and needs to go into a larger one, remember always to move it only to a pot one size larger. Pot plants like to have their roots in a pot almost too small rather than too large. The only time a rather larger pot can be used is for a *Monstera deliciosa*, the Swiss cheese plant with its slashed and holed leaves. You will find that these leaves display this characteristic better when the roots have plenty of room to roam.

Remember, too, that when a plant is re-potted this should be done in such a manner that the plant itself hardly knows the difference. The old soil will be caked and hard, so try to ram in the new soil in the new pot with the handle of the trowel or with the handle of a

The striking Monstera deliciosa *should be allowed to dry out almost completely between waterings. Its large leaves (right) grow stronger and more perforated if the plant is kept in a pot that would seem too large for other plants of a similar size.*

RE-POTTING

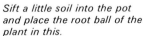

A good soil mixture is $\frac{1}{3}$ sharp sand, $\frac{1}{3}$ good loam or compost, $\frac{1}{3}$ granulated peat.

Remove plant from old pot, holding palm over the soil to prevent it from spilling.

Sift a little soil into the pot and place the root ball of the plant in this.

Drop soil in all round the root ball, firming it with your hands as it goes in.

Right: Though house plants can survive in remarkably small pots, they will not grow well if their roots are too cramped or if they have used up the goodness in the soil. When re-potting, choose a pot that is only one size larger than the old one.

wooden spoon so that the roots are held firmly and no possibility of an air pocket can exist.

For those who have not carried out the actual process of re-potting, here are the detailed operations. Knock the plant from its existing pot and gently prise out as much as possible of the remaining, stale soil from between the roots, being careful to damage the roots as little as possible. Have ready the new pot, just one size larger, and if necessary place an inch (2·5cm) or so of drainage material in the base. This is normally necessary only if the plant likes to have a somewhat dry and well-drained soil. Sift a little soil into the base of the pot and stand the root ball on this. Then drop soil in around the sides, firming it with the fingers as it goes in. Then finally sprinkle some soil on top of the old root ball, but make sure if possible that there is at least half an inch (12mm) between the soil surface and the rim of the pot, for this makes for easy watering.

When the operation has been completed, water the plant in its new pot until soil trickles out of the drainage holes. Stand it to drain for half an hour and then put the plant in a cool and lightly-shaded place for two or three days to recover before replacing it in its normal decorative position in the home.

CORRECT LIGHTING

Although watering and feeding are the problems which appear to give greatest trouble and cause for worry among beginners in the house plant world, they are by no means the only matters to be considered when plants are brought into homes. One vital subject which is given far too little attention is the matter of light.

All house plants have originated and developed from plants that once grew out of doors. Some grew under a hot and blazing sun, others in a shaded forest with its filtered sunlight and still others came from damp and darkened spots beside a stream or in an overgrown corner of a wood. The difference in light between all these places and the quality of light that is normally found in houses is much greater than is generally appreciated. Because of the importance of light for house plants it is helpful and instructive to conduct a little investigation into the light that is provided under differing circumstances and in different places. Use a normal light meter as used in photographic work.

It will be found that the light available in the centre of a well lit room will be roughly one-hundredth of the light available out of doors and roughly one-tenth of the light available immediately inside a window. Actual readings taken on a bright winter day in rural south west England were: outside, 150; immediately inside

Prise as much stale soil as possible from the roots, being careful not to damage them.

Line the new pot, one size larger than the old, with a little drainage material.

Sprinkle some soil on top of the root ball, firming it well down around the roots.

Water the plant well and stand it in a cool, shady place for a few days.

the window of a room, white painted and with windows on three sides, 13; and in the centre of the same room the reading was 1.6.

Eyes are such sensitive instruments that they adapt immediately to these tremendous differences in available light. Plants cannot adapt themselves in the same way, although it is true that practically all the plants we grow in our homes have reached us only after they have developed in commerce for many years and have been hybridized and bred to tolerate the relatively poor conditions we provide. It is interesting to note, however, that the commercial house plant nurseries spend considerable sums of money to develop greenhouses or other structures that will allow the maximum possible light to enter. Even in countries which enjoy greater quantities and higher qualities of light than are available in temperate zones the light available for commercial plant raising is usually filtered and softened rather than excluded.

In fact light is as important as water to the life of a plant, and although a plant may not die if it does not get the light it needs, it will almost certainly not develop the way it should. An experiment was conducted with a young *Hedera canariensis* to confirm this point. It was making normal growth standing near a west window. It was then moved nearer to the wall so that it was in effect around the corner from the window and getting considerably less light. It stayed here for a year and although apparently in good health it made not one inch (2·5cm) of growth. It was then moved again so that the light from the window was directed immediately onto the plant and it put on about three feet (1m) in about three months. Finally it was moved back into the shadows and once again all growth ceased.

It is obvious that the greatest possible advantage should be taken of the light from our windows so as to improve the quality of our plants. The greatest light, of course, enters through south-facing windows and, where on some days this light can be gratefully absorbed by most house plants, there are days when the light is so strong, the sun so powerful, that only cacti and some other succulents can live in it for long. It is possible, however, to stand plants near a south window, at right angles to it, so that the greatest benefit is obtained and the least harm done. It is sometimes possible to place plants in a south window at the beginning and the end of the day, so that the direct sun does not strike them.

In general terms the plants that need the most light, apart from cacti and succulents, are those with variegated foliage and those bearing flowers. This being so it is helpful to reserve for these plants the best positions in the house, those places near south or west windows, so long as this suits the general decorative scheme. At the same time, the light from a north window, relatively steady and unchanging all day, is excellent for large numbers of plants. What matters is not only the quantity of light, the number of hours per day, but also the quality, the intensity of that light.

The nearer the glass you can place your plants the greater the quality of the light they receive and the more active their reaction to the photo-synthetic processes set in motion by this light. Do not, however, allow their foliage to touch the glass. Reflected light is also important. A room decorated throughout in white will reflect much more light than one in more sombre colours.

If a room is really dark it is possible to supplement the natural daylight by using artificial light and sometimes this can be helpful, particularly in cities where the quality of light is bound to be poor both because of the proximity of other buildings and because of the natural darkening pollution in the air. It is not necessary to set up elaborate plant benches with their own special lighting equipment, although this can be done and some plants can be grown successfully using artificial light alone. Most people will be content merely to add to existing light sources in order to keep plants in better health than they would be otherwise. This is a comparatively simple matter.

A normal 75 watt incandescent bulb about 3ft (1m) above a plant will significantly aid its growth processes if the light is maintained for 12 hours or so each day. Place the bulb further away and the quality of the light will decline; bring it nearer and there will be risk of the heat it generates damaging the plant tissue. Cooler light is provided by fluorescent tubes, so these can be used rather nearer to the plant. But the spectrum of the light produced is a little lower and the ideal light is really provided by a mixture of incandescent and fluorescent lighting.

In general terms the best way you can provide your plants with the light they need is as follows. Use very light curtaining material, a fine nylon net for example, on your south windows to filter but not significantly to subtract from this extra high quality light. Use no curtains at all in west, north and east windows, or keep them always opened during daytime to allow the entry of maximum light. If necessary use artificial means to supplement the light necessary for certain special plants. Place plants as near to your windows as you can conveniently manage and if certain plants have to be removed from a light source for some special occasion

When growing plants in a greenhouse or a conservatory, it is necessary to strike a balance between encouraging as much light as possible and providing some shade to avoid over-heating and scorching in sunny weather. With maximum light and more humidity than it is possible to provide in a house, a great variety of flowering and foliage plants can be successfully grown.

such as a party, replace them in good light as soon as you can. Remember that all flowering plants and all those with variegated or colourful foliage need high light intensity. The darker the green of the leaves and the heavier their texture the less light a plant will need, although this must not, of course, be carried to extremes – all plants need some light.

CLEANING THE PLANTS

It is possible to have a plant in the best possible light position which still does not thrive. The leaves are dusty and the light cannot penetrate this dust in order to get down into the chlorophyl beneath. This is particularly noticeable on plants with large leaves. The dark green oval leaves of a rubber plant soon show if they are dusty and are easily enough wiped clean. Use a soft tissue or a soft sponge, moistened with rain water. Never use oil and never use milk. There are certain proprietary leaf-shining materials on the market which appear to do no harm, but they do not so much clean the leaves as give them a high gloss.

Plants with smaller leaves and in particular those with hairy leaves, like some of the saintpaulias, are a greater problem. It is impossible to wipe down each and every leaf of a large and columnar ivy or cissus, for example. It is possible, however, to use a vacuum cleaner with brush attachment to remove some of the dust, so long as this is done very carefully and so long as the suction on the machine is not too fierce. A feather duster or something similar will also dislodge some of the dust but tends simply to move the dust from one place to another.

Where possible the best way to clean plants is to put them out of doors in a soft summer rain so that their leaves can be washed thoroughly and gently. Every possible opportunity should be taken to place plants out of doors when weather and temperature allow. Obviously, tender plants should not be put out into snow or frost and, equally, heavy rain and strong wind should be avoided. But the benefit to the plants of natural rain, high humidity and top quality light is visible both immediately and in the long term.

Many plants have grown too large to be taken outside, or perhaps they are more or less permanently anchored in position by training canes or threads. In this case it is often possible to spray them where they are, using a very fine and gentle spray and first spreading on the floor and surrounding furniture several sheets of newspaper to catch drips and any concentration of moisture. As a general rule it will be found that a plant can be given sufficient moisture for all the leaves to be

Euphorbia *Hoya*

All plants need some light, but generally the darker green their leaves, the less they require. Succulents, flowering plants and plants with coloured and variegated leaves all need good light.

wet and dripping without a great deal of moisture drifting onto the floor and making a mess.

HUMIDITY

The spraying of almost all plants indoors is an excellent activity and one to be most highly commended, for it is the best possible way of providing them with some of the humidity they so badly need. All forms of indoor heating tend to dry the air. We all tend to live in an atmosphere so arid that we notice the dryness of our skin. Much of our furniture suffers from cracks and gaping joints simply because the air is too dry.

It is possible to provide a more humid atmosphere by a variety of means, from the simple provision of one or two pans of water about the house to the installation of expensive electric humidifiers. Which method is selected is of less significance than the fact that something at least is being done. The degree of humidity required vastly to benefit nearly all house plants is one that we would not ourselves notice. It is possible to buy very inexpensively, small and insignificant hygrometers that will measure and indicate the relative humidity of a room and it is worth while investing in one of these.

The figure to aim for on this hygrometer is about 60, which will provide an atmosphere which is not noticeably humid for humans but which is much better for all house plants than the approximate figure of 40 which is so often found in a hot and dry living room or office.

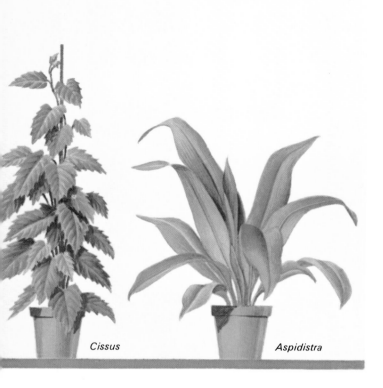

Cissus   Aspidistra

Below: Aspidistras have a reputation for thriving in dark, dusty corners, though all do better with some care and attention. This lovely but seldom seen variegated species, Aspidistra elatior variegata, is just as easy to grow as the plain green plants, but needs good light to preserve the colours of its leaves.

Even the opening of one or two windows for a few minutes will significantly increase the humidity of a centrally heated room.

Individual plants can be given their own personal humidity by sinking their pots inside another container which contains moist peat or some similar substance (see Chapter 5). Another means of doing much the same thing is to stand several plants on a tray covered with moist sand or gravel. This again will send a little moist air upwards around the plant leaves and into the general atmosphere.

When the atmosphere is unusually dry and even the normal means of providing humidity fail to do enough for certain plants, such as the dainty little saintpaulia, it is sometimes helpful to adopt special measures. One way is to take the plant and stand it in some waterproof container, then to place this inside a larger basin. If boiling water is poured into the larger basin the steam given off will swirl around the saintpaulia and do it immense benefit. Leave the plant in position until the water has cooled. When conditions are dry do this once a week or so. Naturally, every care must be taken to see that no boiling water touches the leaves or is absorbed by the roots.

PRUNING AND TRAINING

Many plants, although by no means all, will shed some of their leaves as a normal process of growing. Examples that come immediately to mind are the climbers ivy, cissus and rhoicissus, aspidistras, azaleas and many more. The leaves merely turn brown and either fall off or hang so loosely on the plant that they can be removed at a touch. This is not a sign of disease or pest infection unless it happens to large numbers of leaves either at the same time or over a short period. Sometimes the leaves are actively pushed off the plant to make way for new leaves which are growing.

Although losing leaves is a natural process, this does not mean that it cannot be helped or hastened. All brown leaves should be removed from the plant if they are still hanging there and all that have fallen either on the table surface or into the pot should be collected and taken away. It is possible that to leave them might encourage pest or disease attack. But wait until the entire leaf is brown and dead before attempting to pull it from the plant, otherwise it may cling and you may do damage. If it offends you to see a partly brown leaf on your plant, then cut it away with scissors or a sharp knife rather than tug at it.

It is almost always the older leaves which turn brown and fall and this sometimes means that the lower parts of

Pinching out the growing tip of a plant tends to encourage it to send out new growth lower down the stems and so produce a more rounded, more bushy and more attractive effect.

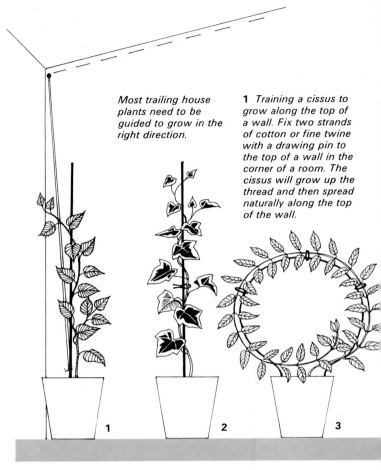

Most trailing house plants need to be guided to grow in the right direction.

1 *Training a cissus to grow along the top of a wall. Fix two strands of cotton or fine twine with a drawing pin to the top of a wall in the corner of a room. The cissus will grow up the thread and then spread naturally along the top of the wall.*

a plant gradually become bare and unattractive. With some plants it is possible to encourage the growth of new leaves by a programme of pinching or pruning. If the growing shoot or tip of the plant is pinched out or cut off, the energies of the plant previously devoted to pushing out or lengthening that growing shoot will be diverted to other parts of the plant and a new twig or branch or new leaves will grow lower down the stem.

Most house plants that are correctly grown will one day outgrow their location. They will block the light from the window, occupy too much space on the bookshelf or fill an occasional table to the exclusion of everything else. Instead of moving the plant, or even throwing it out, it can frequently (though not always) be cut down so that it is smaller in size and equally attractive in appearance. Remember, however, that the result of pruning is frequently to stimulate new growth elsewhere, so be prepared to have to carry out the process more than once.

Again, it sometimes happens that a plant will grow in a lopsided or unattractive shape. A little careful pruning can very well correct this and improve the balance of the plant.

In either of these cases, prune with care. A pair of sharp scissors will probably be found more effective than garden secateurs. Always make clean cuts and, where appropriate, always cut just above a leaf joint so that no bare stem will be left on the plant. Where stems or leaves grow directly from the soil or from a central stem, cut closely to this point so that the amputation is not visible.

Pruning and pinching are not exact sciences – plants have individual characteristics and will not always do what is expected. *Think* what you are about to do. Remember that a limb cut off cannot be replaced. Look ahead at the reaction that is likely to follow your action. For example, when a branch is cut away a greater proportion of light strikes the interior. This is almost certain to stimulate new growth. Is this what you want?

Remember, too, that when pruning a plant you may very well be producing good material for cuttings (see next chapter). So do not thoughtlessly throw away the snippets you have cut off. If you do not want a new plant yourself, someone else will.

PLANTS AND PEOPLE

Some people hold theories that plants are influenced by the provision of stimuli other than the purely physical. They say that talking to plants can help them grow, or perhaps that music will have a beneficial effect. Frequently, advocates of these theories can provide proof of their efficacy by showing plants of quite remarkable size and quality. The soothing voice, they say, has comforted and encouraged the plant, has removed its fears and its phobias, has enabled it to grow contentedly and naturally.

There seems to be no concrete evidence that plants

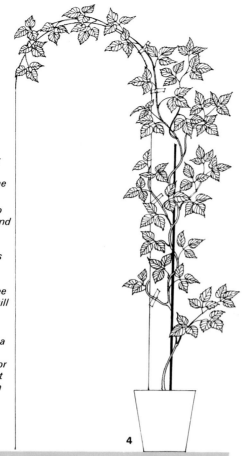

2 *For support or guidance, plants can easily be looped to a cane with a plastic twist. Wire may rust or damage the stem but any soft thread or twine will do.*

3 *Hoyas can grow too long for most homes and are often sold trained round a hoop. To do this, bury the two ends of the wire in either side of the pot. Attach the stem in two or three places and the plant will continue to grow round in a circle.*

4 *A plant growing up a tall cane can easily be trained round an arch or alcove. Use transparent adhesive tape to fasten the stem to the wall.*

can be influenced in any way by voices or by the sounds produced by musical instruments. What would seem more likely is that the person who speaks to his plants, who soothes and comforts them, engenders in himself a mood of tenderness which stimulates him to tend them with greater care and pay more attention to their individual needs than he would otherwise do.

After all, who speaks to the plants which are growing in the wild and which in so many cases are far more beautiful and far more healthy than any which we can grow ourselves?

On the other hand, evidence exists from sources which we must respect, that something, somewhere can quite inexplicably affect the growth of plants. The fact that this agent varies widely and sometimes even produces diametrically opposite results when practised by different people matters less than the fact that our cosy, rational, easily explained world of plant growth and nurture carries with it some metaphysical influence which we cannot see, explain or even understand.

In his fascinating and far reaching *Plant and Planet*, Anthony Huxley discusses this puzzling matter in some detail and he does not dismiss some of the extraordinary claims that have been made. Five minutes concentrated prayer on a plant 814 miles (1,300km) away achieved growth response eight times above normal; giant cabbages, wheat over 23ft (7m) tall; cacti which can add; plants which worry when a dog comes near, that faint

when violence threatens, that sympathise when harm comes to animals and insects close to them. However, he makes suggestions for some possible rational explanation.

Huxley says, for example, that certain vibrations appear to affect certain plants under certain circumstances. Low voltage soil warming wires, which vibrate, appear to give consistently better results than high voltage ones which do not. Trees on the edges of forests are shorter and stockier than those sheltered within, and experiments based on this fact showed that of two identical seedling trees, the one that was shaken violently for 30 sec each morning grew only 1·7in (4·3cm), while the one that was left alone grew 7·8in (20cm). Similar results were obtained merely by the gentle rubbing of the stems of various plants twice a day.

'One concludes that plants do feel in certain ways' says Huxley, 'and that there is much more to be discovered about the ways in which they do so, which may indeed conceivably help the world produce more crops in the future. Their reactions are comparable to those of many animal organisms, especially the simpler ones, from which human beings – who are seldom in such close contact with, say, amoebae or even worms as they are with plants, which they keep around them for pleasure as well as for use – have not found it necessary to invoke emotional responses or telepathic capacities. Plants thrive when conditions are suitable, but there is no other implication of pleasure or enjoyment . . .'

In the authors' possession is a pleasant ivy plant growing from a large pot on the floor beside a west window. Two or three years ago one or two trails from this ivy, trained by string to 'climb' the wall, caught hold of the wall with their roots and clung tightly to the white surface. They then began to climb by themselves, reached the ceiling, and began to cross this. There are now several trails clinging to the wall and the ceiling. This is not particularly remarkable for it is a normal method of behaviour for the ivy out of doors. Why should it not do so inside too?

However, several visitors remarked on this and one went so far as to declare quite unequivocally that the special activity of this ivy was brought on by the fact that immediately beneath it were record players and tape recorders from which poured an almost constant flow of Bach cantatas and masses. This music, he said, stimulated the ivy to behave in this particularly attractive and unusual manner.

Gently, the visitor was led through the house to a little cloakroom by the back door. There was another ivy growing in exactly the same way, climbing and trailing vigorously all over the wall. No music, no voices.

Pests, Diseases & Propagation

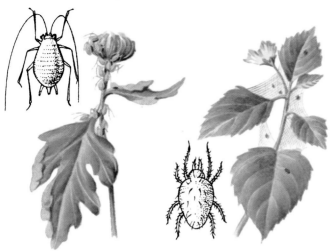

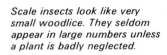

Aphids, usually greenfly, are a common house plant pest. First symptoms are twisted leaves, with some discolouration.

Red spiders collect on the undersides of leaves when the air is too dry. In very bad cases webs may envelop the plant.

White fly larvae excrete honey-dew. After a short time a black, sooty fungus grows on this, gradually covering the leaves.

Scale insects look like very small woodlice. They seldom appear in large numbers unless a plant is badly neglected.

This section of the book is for the enthusiast or the determined, for it deals with any pests and diseases that may strike house plants of all kinds, and describes how to propagate your own plants by the various means available without the special facilities of greenhouse or propagator.

The average house plant owner does not concern himself about these matters. They involve the expenditure of time, energy and indeed money, and unless part of the enjoyment of growing house plants is the challenge that they offer, they are not important. Today most house plants are so easy to obtain and so inexpensive that on the whole it seems cheaper and certainly less time consuming to throw away any plant that is diseased and obtain a new one rather than become involved in curing it and bringing it back to health. Similarly, why go to the trouble of raising your own house plants when the experts in commerce do it so much better and at such little cost? Nonetheless, if you want to try – and it can be very rewarding – this chapter will help you.

PESTS

Fortunately, few pests hit house plants and even fewer diseases. The best way to avoid both is to give each plant its correct care, for a strong plant will either avoid pests and diseases completely or will shrug them off. Any trouble that does arise is usually the plant owner's fault. Diseases spring largely from over-watering and pests achieve serious proportions only if the plants have not been properly examined during their weekly watering.

It is rare for a newly-bought plant to have any pest or disease. Commercial growers cannot afford to allow any trouble in their houses and semi-automatic preventive measures almost always keep plants clean. It is more likely that if a pest is imported it comes from a plant given by a friend or neighbour.

Greenfly and blackfly The most likely pest to be found is one of several varieties of aphid, usually a greenfly or blackfly. Some plants, such as the gay, flowering cineraria, are very prone to attack and should be watched constantly so that any infestation can be stopped at once. The symptoms are first a twisting and writhing of the smallest and youngest leaves of the plants and perhaps a discolouration of some of them. Close inspection will reveal the little insects crawling about and sucking the sap. The sooner these insects are dispatched the better, for they have a rate of reproduction which is alarming and if they are not attacked at once it is probable that other plants will soon be infested.

There are a number of aphid insecticides on the market that can be used to kill the pests and clear the plants, but some of these are poisons and should not be used indoors except under the most carefully controlled conditions. By far the best thing to do is to take the plants outside and spray them there, leaving them until all traces of the spray have dried before bringing them indoors again.

To be on the safe side it is perfectly possible to spray infected plants with plain water or, better still, with soapy water. If the spray is forceful enough the insects will be washed off and the plants cleaned. But this purely mechanical process is not certain. One or two insects may remain on the plant and they breed so quickly that, in a day or two, the growing tips will again be covered.

So long as each plant is carefully examined at fre-

Mealy bug is a small, brown insect covered in a white, woolly coat. It appears in joints or under leaves.

Cyclamen mites attack plants such as saintpaulias, distorting leaves and preventing proper growth of leaves and flowers.

quent intervals no pest should be able to get more than the most precarious toehold on any plant. If an infestation is only light it can usually be dealt with quickly to avoid other plants being affected. But sometimes it is impossible to give plants their normal inspection. By the time they are examined they are already heavily infested. In this case a bath of insecticide might be necessary, for this may be the best and easiest way of ensuring that all parts of the plant are rendered sterile. Fill a bucket or bowl with the insecticide at the correct strength and simply dip the entire plant into this, swishing it about and holding the pot so that the soil does not become soaked also. This is preferable in some ways to spraying, for there is less chance that any of the poison will be inhaled, or get onto the skin.

Always remember that insecticides are poisons. They must be treated with the utmost respect and never used indoors except when the room can be closed for some hours. Use them only according to the printed instructions and after using them always wash carefully all parts of the body unprotected by clothing.

Red spider Another pest which can cause trouble and is rather more difficult to find and identify is known as spider mite or red spider. It is, in fact, not a spider nor is it red, but is a brownish mite almost invisible to the naked eye which collects in colonies usually on the underside of leaves, building a little web for the protection of its young. Red spider must be suspected when the leaves of a plant tend to become speckled, browned or greyish and somewhat distorted.

This is one pest for which the house plant owner must take full responsibility, for it appears only when the atmosphere is too dry and arid. Keep a correct humidity and you will never be troubled with red spider mite. Prevention is easier than cure, however. If for some reason an attack has reached serious proportions the wisest move might be to get rid of the plant entirely rather than risk a spread to neighbouring plants.

If the attack is light, the leaves can be washed down with a moist sponge or the plant can be taken outside and subjected to a forcible spraying. The usual garden insecticides are effective if applied as directed.

Mealy bug Another pest which easily enough escapes notice for a week or two and which can spread quickly to many other plants in the house is known as mealy bug. It is a small, brown insect which surrounds itself with a white, waxy material like cotton wool. It appears as a tiny, fluffy white speck, usually on the underside of leaves and at the junction of leaf and stem. It sometimes attaches itself to cacti. It is difficult to remove and sprays are not normally effective unless applied forcefully and thoroughly three or four times at weekly intervals. If a plant has a bad infestation there is little alternative to this means of clearing it.

If a careful examination of the plant betrays only a few of the little tufts of cotton wool, they can be cleared by hand. The best way is to twist a little cotton wool onto the end of a matchstick or a cocktail stick, to dip this in methylated spirits and then to touch the tuft with this. The white cotton appears to dissolve and the little brown insect in the interior dies instantly.

Scale insects Related to mealy bugs but completely unlike them in appearance are scale insects. These are something like a very small wood louse in appearance, usually grey or black, flat, usually unmoving and adhering close to the leaf. Their epidermis appears to be heavily armoured, for it seems to shrug off sprays of water and even some insecticides. They can be pulled off by hand, prised off with a matchstick or knife or if touched with the methylated spirits wad they eventually succumb. They are seldom to be found in great numbers unless plants have been severely neglected.

White fly One pest that seems to trouble some house plant owners is known as white fly, for the obvious reason that this is what it looks like. They can be cleared by spraying with an insecticide. Another method may seem surprising but is vouched for by a respected authority. It is to place the entire plant inside a plastic bag and seal the opening tightly. The pests should all be dead in some twenty-four hours.

DISEASES

There are only two or three diseases likely to attack plants grown indoors and these occur only when growing conditions are poor. They are various forms of mildew, root rot and wilt, and the most likely cause of their occurrence is over-watering.

Mildew, as the name suggests, appears as a white mildew or powder on the surface of some of the leaves. It spreads quickly and the affected leaves turn mouldy and die. It is a fungus and it can be controlled by a light dusting with flowers of sulphur applied with a puffer pack or by spraying with a fungicide such as Karathane.

Avoid conditions that initiated the disease. Do not over-water. Allow more space and thus air between plants. Keep the soil better ventilated.

Wilt and root rot generally appear at or near soil level. A stem will turn black, will shrivel and fall. Again, do not over-water and try to aerate the soil.

These diseases normally only become serious if plants have been over-watered and then left for several days without attention. If a plant is badly affected it is best not to attempt to cure it but to dispose of it and obtain a replacement. Mildew can be spread to other plants and it is well to avoid this danger.

Most house plant diseases are caused by over-watering. Mildew (above) is a fungus which appears as a white powder on some leaf surfaces. Wilt and root rot (right) generally appear at soil level, causing the stem to turn black, to shrivel and fall. These diseases are difficult to cure and mildew may spread to other plants. It is best to try to avoid the conditions that cause them.

PROPAGATION

The accolade among all house plant enthusiasts must surely go to the man or woman who can say that he or she raised this plant from seed or from a cutting. Yet for many house plants propagation is not difficult and many of the plants seen regularly in homes or places of business conveniently do the job for you and provide you with young plants which you have only to remove and pot up.

Although it is helpful to have special equipment such as a propagating case when you wish to raise your own plants it certainly is not necessary. So long as you are prepared to be philosophical and accept less than 100 per cent success, you will need only the simplest and easiest equipment to obtain results. But you will need patience, a little manual dexterity and a fair amount of time to achieve success.

Root division The easiest method of providing new plants is the division method. One of the simplest of all plants to deal with is the aspidistra. This plant sends up its long, glossy leaves from its creeping and growing rhizome. Eventually this rhizome will fill the pot and the leaves which rise from it will become gradually smaller and smaller. So it will be a simple matter to make from this one over-large plant several smaller plants, the actual number depending on your requirements.

Knock the plant from its pot. Aspidistra roots are tough, so bang the root ball onto a table a few times in order to loosen the soil holding the roots or rhizome. Then with a sharp but heavy knife cut through the rhizome in a number of places so that each piece has several leaves growing at the top and some good roots below. Pot up each of these pieces in a pot only just large enough to take it and use a good, rich and preferably sterilized soil. Make sure that there are no air pockets left. Ram the soil in tightly. Water thoroughly, leave to drain and then place in a cool and lightly-shaded place for the first few days so that the new plants can recover.

Plants which can be propagated in this way by division include aglaonema, begonias, all bromeliads, echeveria, maranta, nephrolepis fern and sansevieria. Even the dainty saintpaulia can be propagated by division. Obviously you would need to be a little more gentle, and instead of banging the root ball on the table to loosen the soil you should tease it away gently. The individual little plants should not be cut from the mass but gently pulled away.

Many house plants can be propagated by more than one method, so you can experiment to find the one which is most convenient, quickest or easiest.

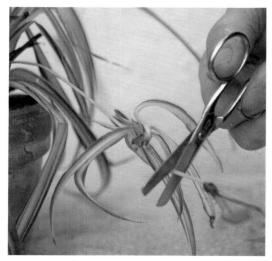

When flowers fade at the end of long stems of chlorophytum, young plants develop. Cut them off when their roots are growing well.

It is even more foolproof to hairpin the young plant to the soil of another pot while it is still growing on the parent plant. Cut the joining stem when the new plant looks well established.

LEAF CUTTINGS (2)

1 Lay the whole leaf flat on moist sand or soil. Peg it down so that it touches the soil closely.

2 Sever the main veins in several places.

3 Roots will grow from cut veins. Pot each rooted section separately.

LEAF CUTTINGS (3)

1 Lay the leaf on a hard surface and cut it into several pieces, each with part of the main vein.

2 Place each piece flat on soil or sand, making sure they are in close contact. Peg if necessary.

3 Each leaf section will grow roots. Pot each one separately when roots are growing well.

ROOT DIVISION

1 Knock plant from pot and loosen soil. Cut through rhizome in several places so that each section has leaves growing at the top and roots underneath.

2 Pot each piece separately.

STEM CUTTINGS

1 Take the cutting just below the point where a leaf grows from the stem. It should be about 6in (15cm) long.

2 Remove the lowest leaves.

3 Plant lowest couple of inches of stem in a small pot. Roots develop after about a month and when the plant is growing well it can be re-potted in fresh soil.

LEAF CUTTINGS (1)

1 Cut leaf from plant, leaving good stem.

2 Fill small test tube with water or use jam jar with paper tied tightly over the top. Punch holes in paper and insert leaf stems.

3 When roots grow, pot plants separately.

Propagation from runners Another easy method of propagation is provided only by very few plants, including the chlorophytum or spider plant and *Saxifraga stolonifera* or Aaron's beard. This method is propagation from runners, as carried out in the garden with strawberry plants. The chlorophytum produces long, arching stems which hang down below the plant, first bearing a few small, white flowers and then developing into tiny individual plants, each with its own ready-formed roots. The saxifrage does exactly the same.

Place the parent pot in some convenient position so that the runners, or some of them, can reach other nearby pots which are filled with soil. Rest the baby plant on one of these pots and if necessary peg it to the soil with a hairpin or something similar. After ten days or so it will be obvious that the little plant has taken root and the stem joining it to the parent plant can then be cut. This method differs only in detail from the previously mentioned process of division.

Leaf and stem cuttings Propagation from stem cuttings and propagation from leaf cuttings are entirely different. The simplest example of taking a stem cutting is to nip off the end of a tradescantia trail and insert this cut end into the soil of the original pot or another pot. It quickly roots and a new plant is made.

With most plants it is helpful to be a little more careful and scientific than this, but the process is an easy one. Take your cutting just below the point where a leaf grows from the stem and about 6in (15cm) long. Take off the lowest leaf or two and then insert the lowest couple of inches (5cm) in the soil of your new pot. Roots should develop in about a month. When it is obvious that the young plant is growing well it is best to re-pot it in fresh soil in a pot only just large enough to take it.

Propagation from leaf cuttings has rather more possibilities, for in most cases it is possible to use plain water as well as soil and in some cases to use not the whole leaf but merely a part of one. African violets can be grown from leaf cuttings. In this case cut the leaf from the parent part keeping a good portion of stem. Insert this stem in a tiny phial or a test tube so that water comes just up to the flat part of the leaf. If you have no small necked vessel like this, tie a piece of paper tightly over the top of a water-filled jar and puncture the paper with a few small holes which will just take the little stems. You will be able to see the roots forming and when they have become prominent and strong you can remove the new plant and pot it up in soil. Alternatively, you can carry out exactly the same process using, instead of water, soil, moist sand, moist vermiculite or even one of the

Propagating a cactus, Mammilaria zeilmanniana. *Cactus plants need a well-drained soil mixture. Make up your own, adding gravel and crushed brick to a normal sandy compost.*

Knock the plant from its pot and cut into sections with a sharp knife. Each section should have some root attached.

Pot up the cut sections in the prepared soil and, because the roots are fibrous and often wiry, make quite sure that they are all in close contact with the soil. Use a potting stick to press the soil down.

Mammilaria zeilmanniana *has soft tubercles and is normally safe to handle. Even sections without roots may grow. Pot them up four to a 2in (5cm) pot.*

The new plants in flower, with 'rootless' cuttings in the pot on the left of the picture. Mammilaria zeilmanniana *is one of the most free-flowering cacti species.*

An aging rubber plant will often lose most of its lower leaves, though the top may remain healthy.

Cut a small nick in the stem a few inches from the top leaves. Remove a portion of the bark.

Moisten a piece of sphagnum moss and tie it round the stem, making sure that it goes all the way round.

Wrap a piece of plastic around the moss to keep it moist. Tie firmly.

After a few weeks the leaves at the top of the plant will look more healthy as new white roots grow from the cut stem (left). Cut the old stem away below the moss ball and plant in fresh soil (right).

foamed plastics that are used in flower arrangement.

With a larger leaf, such as that of a *Begonia rex*, you can get many plants from a single leaf if you want, or you can do exactly the same as you did with the saintpaulia. To get many plants lay the begonia leaf on a table and cut it into a number of pieces, each of which includes a portion of the main vein. Each of these pieces can then be inserted in water, soil, sand or whatever and after a time the new young plants with their new white roots will be seen to be growing. Alternatively, take the entire leaf and spread it flat on a bed of moist sand or soil, pegging it down if necessary so that it maintains close contact. Then with a very sharp knife or a razor blade sever the main veins in a number of places. New plants will grow from these locations.

Plants from which you can propagate using the stem cutting method include aglaonemas, coleus, dieffenbachias, dracaenas, *Euphorbia splendens*, several of the fig or ficus family including the rubber plant, all the ivies, impatiens, both cissus and rhoicissus, peperomia and syngonium. Plants for leaf cuttings include African violets, begonias, gloxinias, kalanchoe, peperomias, some philodendrons, sansevieria, scindapsus and several of the sedums.

Layering and air-layering Two other related forms of propagation are layering and air layering, the second being used when the first is impossible. Layering consists merely of taking a part of the growing plant, splitting or wounding a place in one of its stems and covering this

Far right: Rhoicissus rhomboidea is a climber and a convenient plant from which to layer new plants. The parent plant in the willow pattern jug has grown to 10ft (305cm). Shoots at the base are guided to soil-filled containers and pegged into place. In a few weeks new growth shows and the joining stem is cut.

point with soil so that roots grow from it. It is a process used very frequently in the garden and less often indoors, mainly because of the difficulty of bending a stem into a pot of soil. It can be done easily enough, however, with some of the vines such as the ivies, cissus and rhoicissus and even one or two of the trailing figs.

Obviously it is impossible to layer such a large plant as a rubber plant, although you may often wish to propagate a new one when the lower leaves of the old one have fallen. A tall, naked stem with a top-knot of leaves does not look very pleasant. This is an ideal case for air layering. Wound the main stem a few inches below the top leaves by cutting a little nick in it or by removing a portion of the bark. Tie a ball of sphagnum moss around this wound so that it goes completely around the stem. The moss will be damp and in order to keep it moist cover the ball with a small sheet of plastic and tie this firmly in place again.

After a few weeks the top leaves will begin to look a little fresher. Examination of the moss ball will reveal new white roots growing through it from the main stem of the plant. The moss can then be removed and the new plant (for that is what it is) cut away from the top of the old. The roots can be potted up and a new rubber plant, with foliage now down to its base, is made.

Stem cuttings, layering and air layering are sometimes made more foolproof and the whole process speeded up if you make use of one of the special hormone rooting powders. A pinch sprinkled over the spot where the roots are expected to form is frequently a helpful aid, or the little stem end which is to be inserted in the soil can be dipped in the powder to hasten root formation.

Propagation from seeds The most difficult way of propagating new house plants is to use seeds. It is difficult to obtain seeds of some house plants and others may demand such high temperatures or such high humidity before they will germinate that they are out of the scope of the ordinary house plant grower. You will be advised to check requirements carefully before buying seeds. Cacti, coleus, gloxinia, impatiens and several others are fairly easy.

Fill the pots or boxes with good soil, well drained, fine grained and preferably sterilised. Alternatively use one of the convenient no-soil mixtures. Scatter the seeds finely over the surface and drift just a little more soil over them to anchor them. Cover the top of the box or pot to keep out the light and then put it in a safe, warm spot to await germination. Inspect it occasionally to make sure that the soil or planting medium is still moist and when the tiny green shoots indicate that germina-

Use good, well-drained, preferably sterilized soil for seed growing. Scatter the seeds over the surface, add a little more soil and cover. Keep warm, dark and moist. Remove the dark cover as the seedlings grow and bring them into the light.

When they are large enough to handle, thin out the weaker plants.

When the seedlings are growing well they can be separated and potted up in suitably sized plant pots.

tion is taking place, give the baby plants a little air at first and then, as they grow, remove the dark cover and bring them into the light. When the baby plants are large enough to handle safely they can be thinned out, weaklings being discarded, and transplanted and allowed to grow on until they are large enough to go into their final pots.

In most parts of the world, both where temperatures are high and where they are low, it is helpful to give the young plants greater humidity than is normally available to them in the average home. One easy and inexpensive way of providing this is to slip the pot or the box into a plastic bag and seal the opening tightly. In effect this makes a tiny greenhouse for the young plants. Most newly-propagated plants benefit from treatment such as this for the first week or two of their lives. If the interior of the bag is too humid, so that moisture condenses on the sides too thickly, there is a possibility that the young plants may damp off. In this case open the bag, remove the pot, turn the bag inside out and replace it over the pot.

Plants from stones and pips Lemon and orange pips, date stones, horse chestnut 'conkers', even the large

stone in the centre of an avocado pear are all seeds and all can be grown into plants. This activity is particularly pleasurable to children and it can be instructive too! All can be grown in exactly the same way as other seeds, although as a rule more patience is required. An avocado stone can be grown in a hyacinth glass, its base fractionally above the water until the roots grow down into it.

You can grow your own pineapple plant by slicing off the tuft at the top with just half an inch or so of the flesh and standing this securely in a flower pot filled with a sandy soil mixture. Examine the pineapple carefully first, for in some countries the central growing tuft has been taken out and in this case the plant will not grow. Keep the soil moist at all times and, to give the necessary humidity, stand the pot in a sealed plastic bag.

In much the same way children can grow the top of a carrot, a beet, a parsnip or a turnip. Each of these will grow for several weeks if the sliced top is merely stood in a saucer of water, which should of course be topped up periodically.

A potato vine can grow 3–4ft (1–1·2m) in length in a couple of months. Find a suitable jam or similar jar and choose a potato which will fit it. Do this carefully, making sure that the 'eyes' or growing shoots are at the

top and that the water comes roughly half way up the tuber. Keep it in a cool dark place at first until roots can be seen growing down into the water. When the shoots begin to grow, rub off the weakest, retaining just one or two of the strongest ones and training them along string. If any potatoes appear they will be small, green and unpalatable.

As mentioned at the beginning of this chapter, house plants today are so easily obtained, so good and so relatively inexpensive that they can be considered almost as expendable manufactured products. Why try to cure a plant if it is ill? Better throw it away and buy another. Why try to grow your own plants when this takes time, skill and patience? Better buy some more.

Yet every person in any part of the world who has successfully grown plants in his home or his place of work will always wish to accept some kind of responsibility for the health and long life of his plants. He will wish to create a new plant from one that is old, to make several plants grow where there was only one and to grow plants from tiny and unpromising specks of vegetable matter. These ambitions are good enough reasons to take action yourself rather than discard responsibility and lose a great deal of satisfaction.

Pot et Fleur

In Chapter 7 we discussed the method of growing several plants together in one bowl. One problem with a bowl of mixed plants like this is that after a while the flowering plants will pass their best, while the remaining plants may be doing so well that you are reluctant to move the spoilt bowl. What can be done?

The quick and easy answer is to introduce cut flowers to liven up the bowl. Take out the flowering plant and replace it with a small water container arranged with fresh flowers. Immediately the bowl will be transformed and as the first flowers die you can replace them with

Right: Paeonies and their leaves have been added to a bowl of growing plants, Scindapsus aureus, *Glacier ivy, sansevieria and* Sedum sieboldii. *Pieces of driftwood hide the flower container.*

House plants Begonia rex *and* Dracaena terminalis *arranged with cut tulips, camphor tree buds and driftwood. Black grapes and eucalyptus buds harmonize with the house plant colours.*

others. The next step is purposely to design and assemble groups which might contain plants growing together already, or separate pot plants and many kinds of cut flowers. Then you can begin to use many of the accessories employed in flower arrangement, objects such as pieces of driftwood, cork, dried fungus, bark and rocks, for instance. These play an important role in hiding the 'mechanics' and the containers and flower pot rims. Sometimes they help wedge a plant in a certain position.

When the authors first experimented with this style and realized that it was both very practical and highly decorative, they wrote about it in a national newspaper and invited readers to help name this form of mixed arrangement. There was an enthusiastic response and from the many suggestions the name of *pot et fleur* was chosen.

One reason for its rapid rise to popularity is that it is a form of decoration particularly suited to town dwellers who find it economic, distinctive and yet easy to do. On the other hand, it is ideal for the greenhouse gardener who has the facilities to look after plants which show signs of having been confined or arranged at an unusual angle for too long. Such plants can be nursed until they are fully decorative once again.

CONTAINERS FOR POT ET FLEUR

As in cut flower arrangement, there really is no limit to the variations you can play on this theme. One advantage is that you can use those many containers which are really too large for everyday use in flower arrangements. Flower pots take more room than flower stems. In many homes there are places which would look well filled with a flower decoration yet to make a flower arrangement to fit might take far too long to assemble and be expensive at the same time. *Pot et fleur*, on the other hand, can be quite large and yet use relatively few cut blooms.

Containers can be as varied as a porcelain Georgian foot bath, preserving pans of many types, coal scuttles, tubs, outsize wash basins, baskets, mangers, cradles and other wooden containers, to mention only a few. These would all be for really large *pot et fleur*.

Large flower vases are, perhaps, the most useful containers and arrangements in these can be as elegant as any cut flower arrangement. Once again the shapes and styles of the containers can vary. Pedestal vases and urns with wide tops are great favourites. So many of the house plants are seen best and are often most useful in *pot et fleur* if they cascade or scramble over the rim of the container and the more you lift the part which holds them, the prettier they look.

Besides the cut flowers themselves, you can also use a

flowering pot plant if it will help in the colour harmony. In fact, it is possible in any plant arrangement to make allowances for a flowering plant to be continually renewed when you plant the bowl. At the same time you can leave spaces for the main water vessel for the cut flowers. It all depends upon whether you are going to add flowers to a bowl of growing plants or whether you are going to arrange plants in their pots.

POSITIONING THE FLOWERS

If the plants are to be transplanted, take an empty flower pot of the size you are likely to buy or use when you choose a flowering plant and plant this at the same time. Place any flowering plant used in this, so that when you remove it, you do not disturb the other plants. Try to have its rim just below the rim of the main container. Vessels for the flowers need not be sunk so deeply.

You can use a variety of methods to support and succour the flowers. Cream cartons are a useful size but they tend to be conspicuous even when buried up to the rim. Glass vessels merge surprisingly well and do not need concealing quite so carefully. Metal cones, such as are used for flower arrangements, cigar tubes and some tablet bottles can be used to hold a few flowers or even one stem when this is required. You need not use a stemholder in these. Sometimes you may find it best to arrange two or three blooms and any foliage you wish to put with them and to tie them before pushing them down into these slim vessels. Be warned though, flowers soon drink the small amount of water which is all that these containers can hold. Inspect them daily.

In some cases it is best to use a pinholder as a stemholder rather than wire-netting, especially if the container is tucked away out of sight. You may have to insert the stems without being able to see exactly where they go and in this case a pinholder is best. Never use wire-netting for daffodils and other narcissi unless you can see into the container because it is so easy to pass the stems over the wires. The stems being hollow and soft become split as though they had been purposely sliced and they cannot be anchored properly.

The plastic material called Oasis, cut to the required size, can be stood in any type of container and will suit all but very soft, hollow or fragile stems (see Chapter 11). You can use a cylinder or a small block in a small funnel. Close the end of the funnel to prevent the water from running out. The end of the funnel forms a little stem which goes down well into whatever medium you use to hold the pots and containers in place. Alternatively, the Oasis can simply be wrapped in plastic. (You need to make it waterproof, otherwise the soil will become too

wet for the plants.) If you roll back the top of a small plastic bag and put the Oasis in this you will be able to keep it moist quite safely. Leave some space between the plastic and the sides of the bag so that you can see what you are doing. The rolled edge can easily be concealed at a later stage.

Sometimes it helps the arrangement to have some flowers at higher levels, emerging perhaps from behind a tall stem, such as the support of a climbing plant or a tall piece of driftwood. You can fix holders for these by using adhesive tape or elastic bands, so long as neither of these goes round the actual plant. Or you could use green or very dark party balloons into which a little water has been poured. These are easily fixed in place and just as easily hidden by moving a leaf or re-arranging a stem.

It is usually best to arrange the plant pots and the flower vessels at the same time. In this way you can wedge them together and the objects which conceal the

Left: In this arrangement variegated tulips set the colour, matched by a tall croton in its pot. The yellow croton makes a vivid focal point and a Hedera canariensis *sprawls over the rim of the brass oil lamp holder which forms the base for the container.*

Right: Outdoor hosta leaves complement an early spring arrangement of tulips, cut in bud to last well, sansevieria, variegated ivy and peperomia. As before, small pieces of driftwood are used to hide plant pots and water vessels.

A finished pot et fleur *arrangement of arums, irises and house plants. Below: The plants, including sansevieria, philodendron, ivy and tradescantia are already planted and will be spaced later. The bromeliad (right) is still in its separate pot.*

Cut flowers need containers to hold water and stems. A tablet tube is pushed into the soil for the tallest iris, a metal cone for the arums and the shorter flowers.

More tablet tubes hold the arum lily leaves. As well as adding to the foliage, these large leaves hide the flower containers effectively.

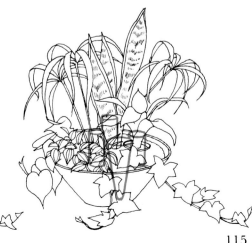

115

Below: An outsize dried bracket fungus, lined with plastic, holds Dracaena terminalis, a tall D. sanderiana, Cryptanthus tricolor and tulips. The driftwood adds height and also masks pots and flower containers.

Right: A shallow container holds pots of Begonia rex and Philodendron scandens. The gladioli are fixed to a pinholder, hidden by stones. The large leaves of the growing plants help to hide the pots.

rim of one can effectively hide the rims of its neighbours as well. While there are several mediums you can use to hold everything in place, soil, sand, bulb fibre, peat and damp moss for example, Oasis is still one of the simplest because it is so easy to arrange all types of holders and accessories into it. You can actually push an entire pot down into it or you can tilt the pot and push just enough for it to hold firm at the angle you want.

A further advantage is that the damp plastic slowly evaporates and so creates a useful degree of humidity beneficial to both plants and flowers. Often, using this as a pot holder you can dispense with separate flower holders. If stems are firm they can be pushed into the plastic in various places among the plants.

CHOOSING THE RIGHT FLOWERS

The kind of flowers you choose to go with the pot plants is bound to depend to a large extent upon your personal taste but there are some kinds which look more at home with exotic plants than others. Fortunately, some of these last well, orchids for instance. A spray of cymbidiums ought, if it is fresh, to last several weeks.

As you might expect, since so many of the house plants used are aroids, their relatives the arums look well with them whether they are pure white, bright yellow or the soft rosy-pink variety which is sometimes on sale. All bulb flowers, such as narcissi, tulips, lilies, amaryllis, nerines and hyacinths, look good but downy or hairy stems and those flowers which have several fussy leaves do not look right. On the whole, flowers from the monocotyledon group are more likely to look attractive than flowers which are dicotyledons. Fortunately, you do not need to have a great knowledge of botany to tell which are which of the most familiar flowers. Apart from the fact that those which grow from bulbs and corms are in the first group, you can pick them out because they have parallel veins in their leaves. Others have a network of veins spreading over the leaf.

Another advantage of using these particular flowers is that most of them do best in shallow water. The only ones to regard with suspicion are tulips which have been forced to bloom early in the season. These must be well conditioned before they are used (see Chapter 11).

However, you can still use many of the familiar and most popular cut flowers in *pot et fleur* and some of the arrangements will be very pleasing.

CHOOSING THE RIGHT COLOURS

When choosing flowers for *pot et fleur*, it is as well to be guided by colour. White and yellow and blue flowers are certain to go well with any kind of green plant mixture

since white provides a clean, pleasant contrast and blue and yellow are themselves components of green. Some greens will be more yellow than deep green and while there are not many glaucous house plants some of them veer a little towards the blue band of the spectrum. Blue flowers arranged with these will make them seem just that little more blue than they really are. As you would expect, if the container is blue or has some blue pattern on it, the colour value will be even greater.

Many people are fascinated by green flowers and for them we would suggest monochromatic arrangements in which such unusual and delightful flowers as green varieties of tulips and gladioli can be used. If you are a gardener, search the bulb merchants' catalogues for these. Hellebores of certain species (these grow wild prolifically in some countries) not only look splendid but last a long time because their 'petals' are really long-lasting sepals. They are also doubly valuable because they flower in winter or early spring, as do also the little olive green iris, *Hermodactylus tuberosus*. Freshly-picked stems of the brilliant green shell flower, *Moluccella leavis*, will bring height to an arrangement.

However, all of this presupposes that plants are

Below: Elegant crown imperials, Fritillaria imperialis, *dracaenas and cryptanthus, arranged together in a wide mouthed urn. As with other* pot et fleur *groups, the cut flowers can be removed when they are past their best and replaced with others.*

wholely green and this is not so. One of the best ways to learn about floral colour harmony, especially if you are also interested in flower arrangement, is to search your own familiar plants for colours other than plain green. There are many more colours and hues than you can see by a casual glance and where you find several you can vary your *pot et fleur* considerably, selecting one colour as the week's theme and another colour to follow. At the same time, naturally, you should bear the colours of your furnishings in mind.

Although you can match simple variegations of white, cream and yellow with green, you can make an attractive complementary harmony by using purple flowers. These need not be pure spectrum purples. You can select from all the pale tints, or colours which have white in them, to the shades which are mixed with grey or black, as well as those hues which are given special descriptive names, such as possibly violet, lavender, amethyst and mauve.

In fact purple, the lovely true spectrum purple, nearer to magenta than to violet, is present in many of our plants. You might find just a trace of it, often unexpectedly, on stems, stipules and bracts or you might

find the underside of a leaf coloured with it. Often this will be a deeper tone or shade, as it is under some cyclamen leaves.

Where you find this colour present, you can find plenty of flowers to go with it. Harmonizing them is fun. Do not be restricted to the full colour. Many pale pink flowers, some tulips, amaryllis, paeonies and even roses have a tint of this purple.

Leaves that are multicoloured, like crotons and coleus and some of the dracaenas, offer you many natural analogous colour harmonies to experiment with. These are neighbouring colours on the spectrum: green, yellow and orange; yellow, orange and red; red, purple and violet, for example.

Flowers also will guide you. Once having decided and chosen a main colour, take a longer look at the flower. If you study a tulip, orchid or dahlia, to take just three examples, you will find that although there appears to be just one main colour, there are in fact many more. The petal tips, the heart of the flower, even perhaps the undersides of the petals will contain other hues. If you copy these you cannot go wrong. Nature offers a wider choice of shades than you might imagine.

Flower Arranging I

Flowers have been picked and arranged, wherever they have been found growing plentifully, by peoples throughout the world and throughout the centuries. The first arrangements were nothing more than bunches of flowers. Later, these were stood in containers. Examples of these early containers can be seen in some museums, old manuscripts and famous paintings. Later arrangements were very different but the earliest examples from both the east and west show that early arrangements of flowers were massed. We see them as decorations in wicker, wood, pottery and, later, in porcelain, metal and also glass.

To make flowers retain their beauty and last as long as possible it was necessary to use vessels in which water or some moist medium could be placed, something like moist sand, peat or clay. These are still used in some countries. It is feasible to use a lump of clay in a bowl even when making a table decoration for a special function. The clay is appropriate, for clay is a form of soil and the flowers have sprung from the soil. The disadvantage of this particular stem holder is that only stiff, nonbendable stems can be easily arranged. If the clay is sloppy enough to take the fine stems then it is unable to hold the thicker ones in just the required position.

Holding the flowers in position is the crux of the matter. Arranged flowers are controlled flowers. The great difference between the flower styles of the west and the orient existed simply because the eastern flower arrangers – or a few of the select among them – thought it important enough to devote great thought and time to the ways and means of anchoring stems so that the arranger had complete control over their placement.

Today, flower arrangement is linked with the home but originally it was part of religion. Flowers were offered up as gifts to the gods in both pagan and Christian religions. In some of the most famous of medieval Italian paintings, for instance, the Madonna is surrounded by angels bearing bowls or baskets filled with blooms. These are usually red and white roses, symbolic of the blood of martyrs. The same flowers would be placed with lilies on the altars of some churches during this period. Today flower arrangements still play an important role in many churches.

THE EASTERN INFLUENCE

Japan borrowed its attitude to flowers from China. At first flowers were the priests' concern but later the professional soldier class was specially designated to be taught the philosophy underlying the strict rules of flower arrangement. Since each stem was the symbol of

Today's flower arrangement is linked with interior decor and the colours chosen reflect those of the furnishings and the surroundings. Designed for a long mantel shelf, this arrangement ranges from almost metallic yellow, to match the ormolu clock, with gladioli, chrysanthemums and carnations, to the white of the heavy lilac.

some higher meaning it was essential that there should be no mistaking its role. This explains why so much thought was given not only to special containers but also to various types of stem holders, all of which had their own names. Originally, only men were allowed to know the secrets of this ancient art.

Until this century, few people in the west practised any style of oriental flower arrangement. Responsibility for the introduction of oriental influences to other countries lies largely with the wives of colonial civil servants and officers serving in the east. Taking advantage of Japanese instruction, they whiled away their time by studying and practising the art of flower arrangement and passed on their knowledge and skill when they returned home.

Meanwhile, in Japan itself, classic style had already given way to less pure forms. Today there are many exponents and schools of the art of flower arrangement. All of them produce different styles of arrangement but all insist that theirs is based on the ancient style and is influenced by its philosophy. Taken abroad and practised in other countries, styles naturally changed even more. Every flower arranger, like every cook, is limited to the materials at hand as well as to local, family or even national likes and dislikes.

In the United States, arrangers took the oriental lines they admired so much and cleverly blended them with the vivid colours and mass effects popular with western arrangers. They created a contemporary style which is now universal but which alters a little as practised in each country.

The Dutch, with their eastern connections and with their logical outlook, adapted oriental styles to suit the bulb flowers for which Holland is so famous; but they also kept and modernized the opulent, truly western arrangements, immortalized in paintings by some of their great artists.

THE FLOWER ARRANGERS

Historically, flower arrangement proper would appear to have been a man's preserve in most countries. Even well into this century it used to be the head gardener's job to see to the flowers within a big house. In between the wars there were more men competing in the 'decorative classes' at the great flower shows than there were women. In Victorian times, nurserymen were known as 'florists' if they grew cut flowers. It is only in recent years that flower arrangement has come to be regarded by some as a purely feminine pursuit. There is no reason why this should be so. Just as there are great chefs, so there are great male flower arrangers in every

Left: In spite of the hours of contemplation practised by the ancient schools of flower arranging, placing the stems need only take a few minutes if simple, basic principles are followed. Give each flower room to display itself. Arrange stems so that all appear to spring from one source and grade the materials, placing the largest at the base or at the heart of the design.

country where there are many people interested in this particular art.

In any international flower show where many countries have a trade exhibit, it is possible to recognize even from a distance which flowers are arranged by, for instance, the Dutch, Belgians or French. Although a recognizable pattern runs through them all, the arrangements themselves differ, stamped miraculously with the arrangers' national personalities. Yet, in the early stages of the show, when the vases are being filled, it is clear that though generally the choice and placement of the containers differ, the same methods of arrangement, the mechanics, the stem holders, the tricks of the trade, are shared. Fundamentally, we all agree to follow the same rules and differ only in the execution of those rules.

More and more flowers are being produced commercially and there is a remarkable degree of uniformity amongst the kind of flowers that are being produced from country to country. Roses, chrysanthemums, gladioli, stocks, lilies, hippeastrum, narcissi, tulips, carnations, anthuriums, arums, asters, marigolds, orchids, dahlias, paeonies and others are usually on sale. Sometimes these are supplemented by a few local flowers and foliage. Many of these flowers can be bought for twelve months of the year because of new methods of growing which enable their seasons to be stretched. In this way, flower arrangers everywhere are assuming an international identity.

The uniformity of commercial flowers does not, however, bind arrangers to a uniform style of arrangement. There are many who arrange only garden flowers and some who also gather wild materials. The diversity of popular tastes in every country will influence flower arrangements. Pottery and all accessories associated with flower arrangement are influenced by local and national preferences. Minor differences in style will depend upon custom, perhaps on superstition, on the materials available and, most of all, on the climate.

Where flowers cannot be expected to live long once they are picked they are often regarded as playthings. In hot countries there are many ingenious ways of using them out of water besides simply strewing them on the dining table. For instance, frangipani blossoms may be threaded on straws or coconut ribs. Other blossoms may be used to tip stripped palm leaf fronds. In some Malayan styles a greater and more imaginative use is made of the longer-lasting foliage. Leaves are cut, folded, looped and set into wonderful and diverse abstract designs as well as being used in the more familiar arrangements with tropical flowers.

Above: Given a variety of materials there is no limit to the designs and harmonies that can be created. The flowers themselves can often serve as a guide for these. Here the light purple tint of the amaryllis matches the variegation in the heart of the 'flower' cabbage, while the glass container is reminiscent of the round and swollen bulb of the flower.

Left: The style of an arrangement is often influenced by the role it has to play in the house. Set table flowers low. Sometimes only one kind of flower is plentiful. Roses, for example, may have to be used again and again in the same container. They can be varied considerably by using different plant material with them. Here they are arranged in a trough and mixed with the bright compound leaves of the robinia, or false acacia tree.

Just as it is possible to tie a country's name to the manner in which its florists and nurserymen display their wares, it is also possible for the experienced flower arranger to tell immediately who is personally responsible for a particular arrangement. The stamp of personality is clearly to be seen for flower arranging is an excellent way to express individuality.

PREPARING THE FLOWERS

Successful flower arrangement begins with the picking of the flower. So many words are devoted to explaining how to keep house plants thriving and happy but there are far too few on how to keep flowers alive and of lasting beauty once they are taken from the plant. This is because cut flowers are not expected to last nearly so long as a growing potted plant. Despite this, most flowers can be helped to give greater value than they do.

The flowers and plant materials to be arranged must be young and fresh if they are to last and the conditions under which they are expected to be displayed must be suitable. Most people, failing to provide either of these conditions, refuse to waste time over careful arrangements which are doomed to wilt only too quickly, and simply stand the flowers in a vessel of water. Few flowers treated so casually will really give true value.

Anyone who loves plants and learns to grow them well will also be able instinctively to select 'good' flowers and other fresh plant materials. For those who are not so confident, there are many practical rules to use as a guide. In this chapter, and in the 'how to do it' section at the end of the book, we show how the experts work, with examples of arrangements which range from simple spring flowers to complicated set pieces.

The variety of materials First of all, what is meant by 'a flower'? Reference has already been made to 'flowers and other fresh plant materials' which indicates at once that there is more to a 'flower' arrangement than meets the eye.

If the reader looks from one picture to another in this book and examines the components of each arrangement, he will see that so far as this particular art form is concerned, it is not necessary to stick too closely to the botanical meaning of 'flower'. The term, as used here, covers not only the bloom but any portion of a plant and indeed any kind of plant material that can be used decoratively.

Everyday flowers, a bunch of flowers, a splendid single specimen bloom from a shop or street stall or from the garden are not the only materials. A great range of other plant parts should be used: branches, for instance,

Not strictly a 'flower' arrangement, this shows the variety of different materials that can be used to make an attractive display. Ornamental gourds with holly, ivy and cupressus are arranged in the lower part of a block of Oasis. The gourds rest dry on a nest of camouflaged wire-netting placed on the plastic.

in bud, leaf, blossom, fruit or simply bare. These can be used fresh or preserved or dried for continued use and are ideal for arid, centrally-heated conditions. Individual leaves of all shapes and colours can also be used – palm, fatsia, croton, aspidistra, hosta; sprays of smaller leaves like ivy or trailing rhoicissus and smilax, fronds of fern, whole rosettes of leaves; sometimes the crown of a whole plant, a saxifrage, mullein, thistle, meconopsis or cryptanthus, nipped or cut from its roots. Entire growing plants can be used either in their pots or removed from them or, in special cases, left on their bulbs.

The fruits of flowers can also be used. These vary from the hard wood-like structures of cones and nuts to the more familiar 'fruits' such as berries. Certain fruits are soft and feathery like those of some clematis; some are encased in showy bracts like the lovely shell-flowers. There are also the everyday fruits we call vegetables – peppers, aubergines, avocados, all with lovely or subtle colours and exciting textures. There are the leafy vegetables, cabbages, beet, ruby chard, even forced rhubarb with its coral-coloured stem and acid-yellow leaf. All of

these are ornamental enough to be used on certain occasions and under certain conditions.

There are many kinds of beautiful fungi, from the edible culinary mushrooms to great bracket fungi which can be dried and which often serve as containers for other flowers. There are true embryo leaves such as palm fronds. There are specially-dried plants and plant parts as well as a whole range of 'everlasting' flowers with petals which are naturally stiff and straw-like and which do not fade or fall.

Skeleton leaves and stems are good material. So is driftwood, rootwood such as the knotted roots of ancient grape vines, also cork and bark. Grasses, reeds and rushes, even seaweeds, all these and many more materials are all 'flowers' to the true arranger. This is a concept borrowed from the ancient Japanese schools of flower arrangement.

Obviously, those who are trying to economize on the use of bought flowers or who have small gardens from which they cannot expect to gather great bunches will be eager to learn how a few blooms supported by other types of 'flowers' can make full-sized decorations. And those who do not paint or sculpt but who feel that they would like to find some creative activity which fits into the general pattern of their lives, may find satisfaction in bringing together the different types of materials just described. If they do, they will be joining thousands of other happy and fulfilled people.

Conditioning cut flowers Those arrangers who prefer to rely solely on true blooms and only fresh plant materials, must be sure that they are always able to select the best.

If the flowers are to continue to look well after they have been arranged then they should be prepared for their new role. Generally speaking, it is not a good thing to cut or to bring home flowers and then proceed to arrange them right away. (As would be expected, there are always exceptions to the rule and you will in time get to know which these are – for example, the narcissi, a group which includes daffodils. All of these take water so freely that they can be arranged straight from out of their wrapper.)

With most fresh flowers it is important to make sure that they are already taking up water through their stem vessels and conducting it to their petals and the tips of their shoots and leaves before any attempt is made to arrange them. Once they are turgid there should be no further problems and in most cases it should then be possible to arrange them in quite shallow containers if that is what is required.

A few tufted stolons from a chlorophytum plant add substance and variety to six daffodils, which were tied together before being placed in the vase. The lemons add colour and form. When the daffodils die, the chlorophytums can be planted separately.

A small bunch of anemones is submerged in a glass of water which forms a pedestal for the main arrangement. On the plate, the flowers are held in Oasis, which is hidden by the fruit.

If stems are not taking water freely, foliage and petals will wilt. Fresh flowers, branches of foliage and blossom, ferns, grasses and all soft materials should be given a long, deep drink. In other words, they should be hardened or conditioned before arrangement. Generally, it is enough to give them from an hour to as long a period as may be convenient. The warmer the room or the hotter the climate, the longer the flowers should be left to drink.

A stem or branch of flowers uses the same pores to give off moisture as it does to breathe. This is why cut flowers can be affected by warm draughts in the same way as a living plant. The longer a stem is kept out of water the more moisture it is likely to lose. It is important to realize that although a cut stem takes up water only through its cut base, it loses that water from its entire surface. This is the reason why a flower pinned to a coat

will soon droop and why so often lovely roses received as a gift away from home will be faded when you return even an hour or two later. Unless first aid can be given in the form of the hot water treatment described later, these will never recover their fresh look; they will bow their heads at the neck and curl their leaves and look a very sorry sight indeed.

There are some flowers which can never be restored to their first beauty. Mimosa, for instance, cannot take up water; it soon loses its fluffiness when introduced to a dry atmosphere. The best way to keep this looking fresh is to push the stem end into some anchorage and place the branches in a glass jar; a tall pasta glass with a top is good for this purpose. Alternatively, anchor the blossom and cover it with a glass dome.

It is important to get to know your flowers because some need more than an hour's stay in a jug of deep

125

water. Unless the vendor has been seen to take the flowers from water it is likely that any bought flowers will already have dried slightly at the stem ends. Sometimes it is sufficient simply to pat the stems against the table surface so that they are level and then cut away a very thin slice from the stem bases using a sharp knife. Usually it is best to split the stem ends upwards for half an inch (12mm), an inch (2·5cm) or more according to the length of the stems. One of the main causes of wilting is an air bubble which forms in the stem at the time the flower is cut. This prevents the flow of water from the stem end to the stem tip, whether bloom or leaf. In most cases, to split the stem will clear this but where the stem is woody, as it is in blossom branches, or tough, as in stocks, the stem should also be stood in hot water.

Hot and cold treatment It might be imagined that flowers which have been cut and immediately stood in cold water would be well provided for, but they will sometimes wilt inexplicably after having been arranged. It is not possible to give a complete list of such flowers, but one remedy is always to use tepid water for conditioning and to follow this up with tepid water when the flowers are arranged. Stems which have been stood in hot water should also be arranged in tepid water.

The depth of the water is important. Where some flowers are concerned – and sometimes, as in the case of chrysanthemums, this might apply to some varieties only – the stems will not begin to conduct the water upwards unless the foliage on the stem, or the greater part of it, is covered by water also. Take care that the water is only tepid. Hot water would damage the foliage.

A way to speed water uptake for these flowers is to split the stem ends and then stand them in just an inch or two (up to 5cm) of water at boiling point. This is a good way of coaxing wilted roses to become turgid again. When this is cool, pour in tepid water deep enough to reach just below the bloom.

Never crowd stems into containers when you are conditioning flowers. Flowers which continue to grow in water faster than others and 'snake' their stems, as for example tulips, are best left in their bunches or else placed heads together and then rolled in paper to keep them straight. They can then be put into deep water reaching almost to the blooms. Once these flowers are turgid they usually behave better when arranged.

If a flower, leaf or branch has wilted after flowers have been arranged, carefully remove it, give it boiling water treatment, let it stay in this inch or two (5cm) of water until it is turgid again and then return it to the arrangement. Some of the daisy family, including gerberas,

pyrethrums and dimorphothecas require this treatment. As a precaution, it is advisable to stand all such flowers in a little boiling water before arrangement.

Those who have to buy their flowers may find that unless these are properly wrapped they may fade on the way home. Usually the treatment already recommended will suffice but should the flowers be of a very frail type, such as annual gypsophila, nigella or saponaria, they are often helped by being totally immersed in water for a few seconds before having stem ends split or trimmed and stood in luke-warm water.

Branches of leaves, particularly young foliage, are also helped by immersion. But it is important to remember that water is heavy and can actually bruise leaves and petals; they should not remain immersed for many minutes. Some blooms, such as sweet peas, may stain or rot if water falls on their petals.

Most flowers and leaves benefit by a light spray of

Left: Scabious, sweet peas, petunias and pansies. Most flowers are best cut in bud or just as they are opening. Sweet peas should have just the lowest bloom on the stem open; petunias and pansies can be cut in bud. Scabious, however, should be more fully expanded. Once most flowers are conditioned they can be stood in shallow vessels.

Right: Pinholders come in several shapes, sizes and weights. Stems can either be placed vertically or will be held equally well at an angle. Where very different weights of stem are used in one arrangement, it is best to use a combination of pinholder and wire-netting. Here the pinholder supports the branch and the delicate snowdrop is carefully placed among the netting.

A candle cup is a small bowl with a stem underneath to fit in a candlestick. It can be used with either a pinholder or with wire-netting. It will fit into the top of a bottle as well as into a candlestick, but make sure that the base is always well weighted.

clean water. Violets like a daily dunking. Some flowers, such as polyanthus, zinnias, wallflowers, cannot be arranged in shallow water even after being conditioned. Others, such as sweet peas and most bulb flowers thrive on this treatment.

If possible, use clean rain water. Some tap water is very limey, though this is not likely to affect flowers grown locally. However, water which is chlorinated can affect both plants and flowers badly enough to kill them.

Choosing flowers The younger the blooms, the longer they will last, because the more freshly gathered they are likely to be. Some are best picked or bought in bud. If you want flower arrangements looking at their best for a certain occasion, allow such flowers two or three days to open out.

If you want to create an immediate effect, it will be necessary to gather or buy mature flowers. A gladiolus spike with several open florets and a full blown rose are both more colourful and decorative than their buds. It is important to condition these flowers well, even if you are in a hurry.

If young flowers are bought you can enjoy watching them develop. More and more flowers are being sold in bud. This is a good thing because, apart from the advantages already mentioned, they travel to market better in bud and become less damaged as they are transported from one place to another. Examples are narcissi, irises, tulips, lilies, freesias, gladioli and many others which are produced on bulbs or corms. All of these continue to develop from the bud stage. Unfortunately, this is not the case with many other flowers. Of those which are sold, roses are perhaps the most bud-like and young blooms are easy to select. They can, however, be cut too young. See that the calyx of sepals which covers the petals is growing outwards and downwards. Try always to pick or buy paeonies and poppies in bud. The buds should be just ready to break. The crumpled petals will gradually expand and become quite smooth as the flower opens.

Sweet peas will last several days if they are cut with at least one of the lowest florets on the stem still unopened. Full-petalled and double flowers, such as chrysanthemums and ranunculus, that have no well-defined centres of stamen clusters should still have a zone of tight, young petals, usually greener and certainly much more immature than the outer petals. Flowers such as anemones and any others in which the stamens are visible should be free of pollen dust. If dust is present then the flowers have already passed their peak.

Blossom such as double cherry should be in bud but forced lilac should not be too immature or it may not take water. Most forced blossom, the double guelder rose included, is inclined to be temperamental and should always be given hot water treatment. Some people recommend smashing rather than splitting the stem ends. While the latter method simply reveals the inner tissues so that the water can quickly reach them, the first is likely to pulverise the tissues so much that they begin to decay in the water. This causes the water to become foul and smelly because bacterial activity is too great; the flowers themselves will suffer.

Clean containers It is often surprising to see how dirty are the insides of some flower containers that people use. No wonder that their flowers do not last as well as they should. Keep all flower containers as clean as all other household vessels. Cleanse them thoroughly after use. Wash any stem holders you use, unless they are simply blocks of foamed plastic. These contain formaldehyde and so, in fact, help inhibit bacterial activity.

Once the flowers are arranged simply keep the water level topped up daily. Make sure that the water has little in it that could decompose and cause trouble. Ensure that the portion of stem which is to go under water is stripped of foliage. Although rose leaves and some evergreens are unlikely to decay before the flowers fade it is as well to get into good habits. A stripped stem end is, in any case, always easier to arrange.

Metal containers tend to keep water sweeter longer than ceramics because the metal slows down the bacterial action. A copper coil placed in the water has a similar though slighter effect. Water fouls quickest in glass, especially when the container stands in sunlight.

Sweeteners and nutrients A few nuggets of charcoal may be helpful in arrangements which are likely to be

The round shapes of pompon dahlias contrast well with sumach leaves, while their colours harmonize.

Right: Primrose lilac and Rosa spinissima *will take water well if they have first been properly conditioned. They will last longer if the lower leaves are removed from the stems.*

A few clippings from the garden will eke out expensive shop flowers like these cypripedium orchids. Here privet, thuja, ivy and cornus have been used but there are many others equally suitable.

in the house for a long time, such as branches of buds and blossom which may be cut at any time after the shortest day and allowed to open slowly indoors. The charcoal helps to keep the water sweet. If a little soluble plant food is used to help sustain the branches – which are often quite large – a 'sweetener' is a precaution against unpleasant smells. Aspirin can be used for the same purpose. There are various nutrients on sale, including rose nutrient which may be used for all flowers; these really do help the flowers last longer. They consist of certain easily assimilated foods. If you have no proprietory brand at hand, a little sugar, glucose and even honey can be added to the water.

Branches of blossom Almost invariably branches of blossom will need grooming, but quite often they need much more time spent on them. Where a branch is loaded with blossom and leaves, it may fail to continue to take up sufficient water to keep all parts turgid. It will be found that the flowers can be kept in good condition by removing much of the foliage. Sometimes, as in lilac and guelder rose, the new leaves grow in separate shoots and are easily removed. To use these apart, simply cut their stem ends and condition them separately. Where the leaves grow closely among the flowers, patience is needed to cut them away but if sprays are wanted that do not wilt this operation is essential and the result is always worth the effort.

With roses, too, a long stem often keeps crisper and the flowers look better if a leaf or two is removed. If there are several stems, remove the leaves from different areas and the flowers will continue to look leafy and yet remain fresh.

MAKING THE ARRANGEMENT

Many modern flower arrangements in which few actual blooms are used depend on beauty of line instead of a mass of colour, yet appreciation of plant line and form

A branch can be made to appear longer by cutting the main stem and leaving the longest lateral to continue the line. Keep prunings for other positions in the arrangement.

Woody stems should be cut at an angle.

Before being impaled on the pinholder, branches should be cut upwards, with the thin blade of the secateurs at the top. This will allow them to take up water freely.

Right: One bloom will make an arrangement if enough accessories are used. Here a single chrysanthemum is impaled on a pinholder with variegated kale leaves. Viburnum berries and driftwood hide the holder.

Left: Guelder rose with driftwood. First impale the branch on a large pinholder, firmly fixed to the floor of the trough. As the laterals are opposite, cut some away to make the branch look less formal. Where suitable these can be arranged lower down.

Far left: Apple blossom with two Artist tulips. On the tree the blossom grew horizontally, but now it stands vertically. It is placed at an angle so that the flowers appear naturally posed.

is not just a modern taste. We may detect modernism and contemporary influences in the way we see the lines designed and interpreted but such arrangements are based on oriental designs and on ancient Japanese in particular.

Where mass arrangements tend mainly to be static, line arrangements, if they are well done, should give a feeling of movement. Fortunately it will be found that this is more effectively achieved with fewer flowers. As a result, line arrangements are also extremely practical and are to be recommended especially to those who have to buy every flower and who are looking for some means to make the most of the few.

Those who have never done more than stand a few flowers in water should begin learning flower arrangement proper by making patterns with the minimum of material. There are several examples illustrated in these pages which should prove helpful and there is further pictorial advice at the end of the book.

A curve of colour Those who have to buy bunched blooms are certain to find that often they tend to be uniform in length of stem and size of flower. Yet even these can easily be made more formal. Narcissi, for example, and particularly the trumpet daffodils, can be arranged in a long curve rising up from a shallow dish – a lovely crescent of colour. This is a pleasant, easy and logical way of displaying a bought bunch or even a handful of first flowers from the garden. Stems are shortened so that each bloom can be seen and admired. It is a style which is easy to do and which has become quite popular.

Not only narcissi, with their fluted leafless stems, can be made into curves this way. Most unbranched flowers can be used and even as few as three can sometimes be both effective and colourful, depending on what kind of blooms are used. A curve or crescent need not stand upright, it can also lean on the rim of its container. Floral crescents can be used as patterns within patterns, perhaps surrounded by a frame of foliage arranged in a triangular or oval shape, perhaps framed by long leaves or branches whose lines follow those of the flowers.

Stemholders It would be difficult to devise this type of arrangement without the use of a special stemholder, one which can anchor the flowers firmly and yet allow the arranger to set them at the required angles. Known generally as pinholders these follow the principles of the ancient Japanese stem holders known as *kenzan*. You can buy them in many sizes and they are circular, crescent-shaped, oblong; some hook or loop into each other; there are also tiny ones, sometimes sold in an

Arums are most effectively arranged if each bloom points to a different direction from the one placed below it.

Right: Although this arrangement looks informal, the yellow ribes blossom has been well groomed before being arranged on a pinholder. The daffodils, too, have been cut to size.

interlocking 'belt', which are excellent for some miniature arrangements or for holding just one flower or stem.

To make flower arranging sessions easy, relaxing and enjoyable and to avoid worry about whether or not the flowers will stay in place, it is advisable gradually to build up a stock of these holders. They are especially good for use in shallow containers but can also be useful in deep containers if you want to have extra tall or heavy flowers or branches rising up.

There is more information about ways of using these holders and anchoring them in the practical section at the end of the book.

Although they may seem to be expensive at the outset, pinholders should last a lifetime. It is possible to devise

other means of holding stems upright in just one area of a shallow dish and the resourceful are certain to find ways of doing so but few methods are as efficient or as time saving as using the heavy metal pinholders. For lightweight stems an upturned nail brush which has plastic quills instead of brushes can be used so long as it is anchored securely. Sea shore stones well pitted with holes, even a potato sliced and anchored, will take woody stems cut on a slant. This makes a good holder for a Christmas table decoration.

Another method is to use a ball of squashed wire-netting pushed into a thick ring of plasticine. This is effective for light-weight flowers so long as they are not tall. It is good also for fine stems. After the first few have been wedged in place by using a leaf or a portion of thick stem, the others interlock and hold well. It is important to arrange a little on one side and then a little on the other, or stems will not interlock properly and the arrangement is likely to topple over.

In recent years various expendable, plastic holders have been introduced. These are blocks of water-retentive foamed urea. Oasis, sold world-wide, is perhaps the best known.

When well soaked with water these blocks are quite heavy and can in most cases be used in place of pin-holders. It is possible to buy an adhesive, Oasisfix, which will anchor the dry block and still hold it firm when it is soaked. Probably the greatest value of these holders is that they can be arranged completely without a con-tainer – that is to say, you can make an arrangement on a plate, or any other surface, so long as you bear in mind that the plastic should never be allowed to become dry. It can of course be used dry in all kinds of dry arrange-ments.

Only a very short portion of the stem need be inserted. This is another advantage and opens up great oppor-tunities to the arranger. It means that so many lovely blooms and other materials, once barred because they had short stems, can now be used.

In building up a complicated arrangement or com-position the plastic again is useful. Dry blocks can raise plants and accessories as shown in Chapter 10. It is also possible when arranging fruits to push part of the surface of, for example, an apple into a dry block so that you can have it facing the way you wish.

Finding the 'line' Often when first using pinholders, there is a tendency to arrange the stems upright, so that the ends are well and truly impaled on one or more points. However, although a vertical stem is sometimes of great importance you are much more likely to make

an arrangement which pleases you if you experiment with arranging stems so that they incline away from the vertical. Stems can be laid on the pinpoints quite easily. If they are very woody, they may have to be given a little extra push with the thumb. If woody stems are cut on a slant these are then easier to push down among the points of the pinholder.

If, for example, you want to make an arrangement in which a branch of leaves or blossom is the main feature, having decided roughly how tall it should be, stand it upright on the pinholder and study it critically. Now push it a little to one side or the other and go on increas-ing the angle until the tip of the tallest stem or longest

A vertical arrangement of lilies, Enchantment, with Iris sibirica seed pods.

Far left, above: First fix a heavy pinholder on the floor of the bowl. Arrange the tall lily stem quite near the back, leaving space for the iris. If the lily cluster seems top heavy, remove some of the buds or blooms to arrange low in the bowl later. Keep the stems well clothed with leaves except where they are in water. Save the short pieces of stem you have cut off.

Far left, below: Continue the line downwards, tilting each stem a little forward from the vertical of the tallest one. If any lily stems are too short to reach the water with the flower in the correct position, slip them into a hollow water-filled stem. Gradually make a frame of iris pods behind the flowers. Save cut stem ends. Use the leafy cut ends of the lily stems to hide the pinholder and to help to cover the stem bases. Arrange short-stemmed blooms and buds arising from the base.

Left: Take the cut ends of iris and cut the tip of each one on a slant. Arrange them in a fan at the base of the lily stems. Space them well and try to make them flow outwards. If they are crowded, they will not give the same sun-ray effect.

What type of stemholder used is really immaterial. If you intend to use many stems of varying thicknesses, such as grasses with thicker-stemmed flowers, cut the piece of wire-netting a little larger than recommended and squash it up well so that there are plenty of narrow apertures for the fine stems. Another way of dealing with this mixture is to fill the lower half of the container with a block of Oasis and to rest wire-netting on this. Alternatively, simply fill the bowl with Oasis, but not too tightly or you may find difficulty in topping up with water. A rectangular block is advisable in a round bowl because this gives four points at which to direct the vase-filler when topping up water daily.

If many really short-stemmed flowers are used the plastic can reach well above the rim of the bowl. If a pedestal bowl is used you will find it helpful to raise the plastic this way because some of the lower stems, particularly those you want to be pendant, can be inserted into the plastic upside down, or nearly so.

The centre stem is the important one, so get this in place first of all and make sure that it stands well. If you have variety in the flowers you use do not place the largest flower at this point, let the large blooms lie in the low levels. This stem also defines the height of the finished arrangement.

The side stems should be arranged next and these not only define the length of the arrangement but dictate its style. If you have placed a short stem in the centre and long stems at the side, by the time you have placed the intermediate stems in place and made sure that nothing else in the arrangement is vertically taller than the centre stem, you will have made a half-ovoid shape. On the other hand, if side stems and central stem are about equal, the result will be a half-globe. If the side stems were very short and the central stem quite tall you would be preparing a conical shape.

The face of a clock Whatever pattern you hope to make, the basic procedure is the same. It may be helpful to imagine that the bowl is a clock face. Place a stem down through the stem holder in the very centre. See that this flower or whatever material it is stands quite vertically. Now, place a stem at three o'clock and another at nine. Push these two stems in *across* the wire-netting, towards the base of the centre stem at roughly right angles to it. You can now see how wide the arrangement is going to be. This is the time to shorten the stems if you think that the finished arrangement will turn out to be too large.

Turn the bowl (never walk round it if you can help it) and place two more stems, one at six o'clock and the

A formal arrangement with stocks, guelder roses and viburnum.

Top right: Fill the bowl with a mixture of foamed plastic and wire-netting to hold the different weights of stem. Arrange the centre stem of single stocks first at 'twelve o'clock'. Although it is curved, its tip should be over the centre of the base of the bowl. Next add the two side stems at 'three' and 'nine', to define the length of the arrangement.

Centre right: Stems pointing roughly at right angles to the centre are arranged next round the rim.

Right: Arrange intermediate stems of stocks and viburnum between these low ones and the centre stem. Note that all the stem ends are stripped.

Below: Short pieces, side stems of guelder roses are recessed among the stock stems to fill out the bowl and hide the stem holder. Finally, arrange the roses. None of these should be taller than the stocks and all should be placed so that they seem to spring from the same source.

other at twelve. These determine the depth of the arrangement. Now fill in the spaces round the rim with one, two, four, five, seven, eight, ten and eleven. You have now made a good start.

From now on no stem other than the first one you arranged – the centre stem – is vertical. Every other component should lean from this important centre to a greater or lesser degree. The next move should be to determine the outline. Adjust the bowl so that you have the centre and the first two side stems you arranged in profile and arrange a stem half-way in between them. This one should lean at roughly 45 degrees from the centre. Arrange another on the other side to match it. Then place intermediate stems between these. Now give the bowl a quarter turn and repeat. Then turn again and so on until the main shape is done. You can now fill in with shorter stems and leaves if necessary.

This is the basic method and has been given in detail because the style is so important. It underlies so many of the kind of arrangements you might wish to make for special occasions. The method just described is for a formal arrangement which, when done, is roughly a half-globe or sphere.

You can play many variations on this theme simply by altering the stem lengths. Often a complete half-globe is too wide for a table centre. Having defined the width, to make the arrangement narrower remember that the twelve and six o'clock stems should be much shorter than three and nine. The intermediate stems should be varied accordingly.

If you want to make a decoration which is really low and close to the table surface, follow the same procedure. If you want to make a really tall, large arrangement to stand in the centre of a room where it will be seen from all angles, exactly the same rules apply.

Practising with straws Drinking straws provide excellent material for practising to assemble this style of arrangement quickly. Keep on practising until you find that you can place the straws unerringly in the right place, first time.

There is a further advantage to be gained by using straws as practice flowers. When a bowl is completed it will not look as attractive as it might if all the blooms are at the same level, looking as though they had been pushed uniformly into the surface of a ball. It is much better to recess some of them, either by cutting their stems much shorter than the rest or by pushing the stems in a little deeper. Straws are so uniform in length that you learn very quickly where it helps to insert only an inch (2·5cm) or so of stem and where a longer portion is best inserted. Straw practice soon helps the novice become proficient in breaking up the formal outline.

Helpful hints There are many ways to make flower arranging easier. For example, to insert flowers with less trouble, hold the flower stems near the base and not right up close to the bloom. If you do the latter you are more likely to bend the stem and you have nothing like the same control over the placement of the stem.

Also, it is always a good idea to make the most of any possible curves. Even the seemingly straight stem can usually be found to have just the hint of a curve in it. In symmetrical arrangements, see that the curve, no matter how slight, always flows away from the vertical centre stem. If the tallest flower does not have a straight stem make sure that the actual bloom or tip is directly over centre. Spend a minute or two on this preliminary and you will have no difficulty later on.

Never complete one side of the bowl first. Keep turning it, unless it is an outsize arrangement, in which case you may walk round it. When flowers face one way, like daffodils for instance, let them look away from the centre stem. This will help to create the effect that all the materials you have used flow from a centre point. Obviously, it is not possible to get all the stem bases in the small area at the base of the central stem, but if you point them towards it, you will achieve the effect. Do not let stems be seen to have been crossed. Let them do this only below rim level. The more they cross there, the more they will interlock and hold each other in place.

Candles If you like to use a candle or two in your table decorations, treat the candles as flowers. When you set one or more, treat these as the axis and let all the other components flow from their bases. One candle offers no problem. If two are used, take a point in between them as the axis. If three are used, use the centre candle and so on. By observing this simple rule you will get an arrangement in which everything clearly belongs together and is planned.

There is no problem about arranging candles. If you put them into wire-netting you may have to hold them upright as you wedge them in place with a leaf or two or a piece of thick stem. They are easily inserted into Oasis. If you want to have them standing well up from the level of the flowers, splice each candle to a false stem. Two pieces of strong twig on each side are usually sufficient. Tie or bind them together.

Bending the rules Once you have learned the rules you can bend them slightly to suit yourself or perhaps

the flowers you use. For example, if you think the usual arrangement is too formal, arrange the centre and side stems in position first and then, instead of 'sketching' the outline as recommended earlier, cut the flowers and group them at varying levels, recessing deep colours to give interesting contours to the general mass. If you are using mixed flowers and shapes you may find that these give greater impact if they are grouped in their kinds or colours rather than simply dotted about. Take care, though, that they are not grouped into zones that are too well defined. Let them merge one with another.

If you have short-stemmed flowers and if these are formal in shape and inclined to look still, such as some dahlias or carnations, try using a raised bowl or a pedestal vase or container of some kind. You can add grace by introducing trails of leaves or blossom, or berried or budded stems, and letting them hang well below rim level. Arrange some among the flowers also or they will look too much like an outer frill.

Faced arrangements Apart from its art and even therapeutic value, flower arrangement should be value for time and money. If flowers are to be stood against a wall where no one will see them from the other side, then there is no point in wasting half of them by putting them out of sight.

'Faced' arrangements are used for arrangements which look out into the room. There are many styles of these. Some have already been discussed, since most line arrangements are designed for this role even though occasionally a line arrangement can be devised for a table centre. Others will be discussed later.

Since the traditional half-globe has just been dealt with so fully, it is logical to turn to the traditional symmetrical design on which so many other decorations are based. This is a delightful and very useful style for it can be used quite simply, with everyday flowers in the home, or it can undergo a glorious transformation and appear as the most splendid arrangement at a wedding or reception of any kind. According to the shape and the evergreen materials, you can even make it symbolize a Christmas tree. With a few complementary materials it is an attractive and easy way to display the wonderful yet very formal and uniform flowers the commercial growers produce. It can also look quite beautiful made entirely of wayside grasses.

As before, the arrangement begins with the centre stem because this still has the most important part to play. Now, instead of standing it vertically in the very centre of the container, its base is pushed down against the rim, keeping the vertical stem as a central point.

A formal arrangement of viburnum, alstromeria, delphiniums and carnations:

Top left: As viburnum branches in all directions, begin by cutting opposite side stems to make a flat branch. Arrange this well back against the rim. See that its tip is over the centre of the container's base.

Centre, left: Cut away more of the upper leaves to prevent wilting and crowding. Arrange some of the cut-away stems at the sides and over the rims. Height and width are now defined.

Left: Fill in the space between the first stems with more viburnum and the tall delphiniums. See that no other tip rises above the centre flower. Arrange short stems over the rim.

Above: As you arrange the stems, hold them firmly towards the base and always push them in towards the centre. Make sure that each stem reaches over the rim and down into the container. Let all stems lean to the left, right or forwards from the centre stem. This should be the only stem that is completely vertical.

From now on the principles are much the same as those of the half-globe styles, except that one side only is to be shown. The half-globe is halved; its rounded quarter is displayed and the cut face kept to the wall.

The centre stem goes in place first and defines the height. The two side stems at right angles to it define the width and the tips of the intermediate stems sketch the outline. Side stems which curve lower than the two width-defining stems accentuate the shape and can be used to bring both informality and grace.

Linking the container Often in low arrangements, especially in those designed for the table, the container is seldom or hardly noticeable but in these taller arrangements it tends to become much more conspicuous, although faced arrangements can be low as well as tall. You might, for instance, want to make a long low decoration for a shelf, or one just a few inches more than a foot high (30cm or so) for a side table. Tall vases do not have to be used, although both tall and pedestal vases will, of course, add a little useful height. It is important that the container should never dominate the flowers – they should appear as a linked unit. This is easily done.

In both tall half-globe arrangements and in any variations on that theme, as well as in the arrangements we are discussing, one way of achieving this linked effect simply is to curve the lower stems so that they carry on the outline of the arrangement and do not stop horizontally at rim level, which would leave the rim exposed. The rim should be hidden in these styles. When selecting materials for arrangement, set aside those with nicely curving stems for this purpose. Gardeners are more likely to be able to do this than those who have to buy their flowers but it is possible even in shops to find some suitable material and there are certain kinds which can be preserved, such as beech and eucalyptus, and which can be used time and time again.

You can help yourself create suitable downward and outward flowing pieces of foliage by cutting them skilfully. When you cut the laterals or side-stems from branches – this includes blossom and berries as well as foliage – never cut them close to the main stem unless you are removing them simply to make one long slender piece. Instead, always cut them with at least an inch (2·5cm) of the main stem attached. If possible cut the stem down to the next lateral. When you come to arrange the pieces you will find that when you insert the piece of main stem in the container, the lateral will naturally flow away, usually at right angles to it. It will flow away naturally over the rim without any coaxing

on your part. If you want it to flow in a downward direction, use wire-netting ends as recommended earlier in this book.

Avoiding a flat plane When you assemble a faced arrangement take care that it does not end up as flat as a plate with all the contents on one plane. This is all too easy to do. For an attractive flower arrangement you need features. As you work, turn the arrangement from time to time so that you can see it in profile. The tall central stem should be upright and those stems placed in front of it should all lean away – very slightly at first and then more and more as they get nearer the rim. Facing the front again, you will find that it helps to recess some of the larger materials, especially those of deeper hues, into the heart of the arrangement. After a little practice it will be found that all these things begin to fall into place quite naturally.

The triangular outline As mentioned earlier this method can be fitted into several outlines; the tips of the flowers can fall inside an imaginary oval or a great circle or into parts of both. You will probably find that when you begin without a premeditated plan you will produce arrangements which fit inside a triangular outline. So much depends upon the materials you use. Specimen blooms, such as large chrysanthemums (especially when you have only about six), seem to fall quite naturally into a series of triangular patterns within a triangular frame.

In fact, a great many flower arrangements could be said to fall within a triangular outline, Japanese styles included. This pattern does not have to be both symmetrical and formal. Nor does the triangle have to be upright. It can lie at an angle.

Asymmetrical styles The lazy 'S' discussed earlier was only one form of asymmetrical style. Such styles do not have to be restricted to that one letter. They can be much less studied. If you dislike the formal traditional styles – often they need the containers, setting or even the occasion to do them justice – there are many delightful ways in which flowers can be arranged asymmetrically yet still, if required, on a grand scale.

Asymmetrical styles are a good way of displaying garden materials, especially when it is possible to gather long stems of blossom to give height and curves and to make attractive, downward-sweeping lines. Flowers which grow naturally can so often give a guide to the flower arranger. Take the flower which appeals to you most, arrange it in the angle it seems most willingly to

Byzantine cones are extremely attractive and can be made from all kinds of materials, including those with short stems. Here box and spray chrysanthemums are used with croton leaves.

go and then build the whole arrangement on this indication.

If you bear in mind the imaginary centre stem you cannot go far wrong but be sure first to determine where the centre should logically be.

In some styles, the space you leave between flowers often speaks louder than a mass of blooms but when you leave space make sure that it has a meaning and that it does not appear simply as a gap in the arrangement.

Flowers can be quickly assembled in a vertical line and make a distinctive arrangement. This is a good style to follow if you have low ceilings and want to give an illusion of height. In fact, the line consists of a cone stretched to its limit.

Quick arrangements Flower arrangement can become a completely absorbing hobby in which you take hours on one arrangement or you can do the flowers in just a few minutes. One quick method is based on a shallow dish with pinholder fixed in place. Five or more daffodils are arranged in the hand in such a way that each flower is above the other. This is easily done. Hold the lowest flower first, trumpet pointing downwards, and place the stem of the next flower on this one with its bloom just a fraction of an inch away from the first one. The third stem lies on the other two and the third flower is just above the second. Continue until enough flowers are arranged, then cut the stems level leaving at least two or three inches (5 to 7·5cm) on the lowest flower. Then stand the bunch on the pinholder.

At this point, you can pull a flower or two out of line to make a shape. Have ready at least three large leaves which can be arranged clover-leaf fashion at the foot of the stems. The arrangement is complete. You can actually do this between the time you see your guests pull up and the time they enter the room where the flowers are – provided that someone else goes to the front door to greet them.

This line can be followed with any uniform flower, dahlias, roses, chrysanthemums, irises. Tulips are not so amenable. Generally speaking, flowers with firm stems are best for this line.

Tied bunches You can save time and still make effective arrangements by first arranging the flowers in the hand or, in some cases, by tying them before they are put into water. This is a good method to use with containers which have narrow apertures; it is also good with glass containers because no obtrusive stemholders are needed. It works with roses just as well, so long as the stem ends are dethorned first. Roses have the advantage of sufficient good foliage to arrange at rim level and hide the tie. The leaves should add to the general attractiveness of the arrangement.

In this method, it is usually quite a simple matter to hold the bunch upright, or at some other angle if preferred, and then to wedge it in place with complementary materials. You can also use some of the cut-away stem ends for packing behind the bunch, where they will not be seen. These tied bunches are easier to keep in place if one or more stems reach the base of the container. You can usually judge this quite accurately from outside but another good way is to select the lowest flower, cut its stem to the right length, and leave room for the tie which should come at or just below rim level.

Foamed plastics Those people who like to have plenty of flowers about them and are always looking for time-saving methods should find foamed plastics very useful. Cones and globes of these make it possible quickly to fashion unusual party decorations or long-lasting dried flower montages. A pair of cones can be used as an effective buffet decoration; instead of the usual containers, fill two matching wine bottles with water to weight them and simply press the cones down on their

Using allium flowers and stems.

Left: Arrange the flowers in the hand and cut stem ends level. Fix a pin-holder to the floor of the dish. Arrange the lowest flower towards the front of this and place its cut stem vertically at the back of the holder.

Left: Take the next shortest flower and arrange it behind the first. Place the stem end to the right of the first stem. Let it lean away from this but keep the stem bases near each other on the holder so that they fan out.

necks. If these are first fitted with little wicks – pieces of string will do – which go down into the water inside the bottle, you can keep the flowers fresh for a day or two longer than merely by spraying them. However, as a rule, buffet decorations are for the day only.

Bottles can also be used as pedestal vases by buying or devising candle cups. These are little bowls, fitted with a stem that should fit into a candlestick; as a rule they fit well into bottles also. To make your own, fit small plastic bowls to corks, using a strong adhesive. These bowls can be filled with any type of stem holder depending on the style you have in mind.

The bowls can also be used in conjunction with all kinds of containers, so long as they sit firmly on the rim. Slim vases give height to an arrangement and you can often find your ideal colour in these kind of 'pedestals'. Glass ornaments, too, can be brought into service this way. The glass looks better if it is filled with water. This also ensures that it is well weighted.

The importance of colour Colour plays an important role in flower arrangements and there are several helpful hints on plant colour in the section on *pot et fleur.*

Ways of adding colour are fairly limited once you go

Continue adding flowers and stems in this way until the tallest flower is placed. The two tallest flowers should fill the spaces between the fanned stem ends. Finally, hide the pinholder with smooth pebbles, and add sufficient water to cover all the stems. Again, water is an important part of the arrangement and should be kept clean and fresh, especially in this light-coloured dish.

Soft Maid of Orleans kniphofia blooms are contrasted with spiky variegated zebra grass. A further contrast of texture is provided by fresh ligularia leaves, their brown undersides matching the bowl's interior, and rippled dried hosta leaves. When making the arrangement the flowers are placed in position first, then the zebra grass and last of all, the leaves.

beyond the flowers and fruits themselves. Candles are useful, especially in table decorations. Seashells introduce pleasant pastels and look well in low-line arrangements. As you would expect, they look their best in those styles in which a good expanse of water has been left free as a setting for them.

For Christmas and for party flowers generally, do not hesitate to bring in non-natural products, such as tree baubles. Paint cycas leaves for a wedding in hues to match either the bridesmaid's dresses or the general decor, then sprinkle them very lightly with silver. This is useful in seasons when colours in the true flowers are very limited.

Monochrome arrangements can be very decorative and bring great enjoyment to the arranger who has to search for the colours, tints, tones, shades and hues. All-white and all-green top the list but you should be guided by interior decoration because flowers should always suit their surroundings.

Contrast of texture In these arrangements a contrast of texture becomes important if the components are not to look dull. If a certain amount of matt material is used then there should also be some which is glossy, certainly

at the focal point. Use leaves which are nicely ribbed, such as hostas, or gleaming, like fatsias newly cleansed of any dust; lichen-covered branches, hairy or woolly leaved materials such as the long spikes of stachys and verbascum, are also good. You will soon get a good eye for contrasting textures of all kinds.

Contrast of shape Contrast of shape as well as contrast of texture helps to make an arrangement both more pleasing and distinctive. If you have to buy flowers look round the shop for contrasting material, not just something to go with the flowers (you will only be persuaded to buy a branch or two of foliage) but something which will contrast with them in shape and yet make an agreeable combination. Do not, for example, buy irises and then choose some round flower, such as anemones, to go with them. Although quite different kinds of flowers, they are too much alike to be arranged together. Both need a spicate or tapering shape for true contrast and this will enhance the flowers themselves.

Leaves of the shape of gladioli foliage look well with many flowers which have round outlines. New Zealand flax is similar but less available to many people and it is inclined to be a little large for the average home.

Gladioli leaves can be pressed and preserved for use time and time again.

Other good contrasts for round flowers are grasses, reeds, long tapering leaves such as aspidistra and sansevieria (aspidistra can be dried and kept like gladioli – save the next brown leaves which appear on your plant), graceful sprays of leaves and fern fronds like those of nephrolepis and some seed heads such as orach and belladonna.

The stem ends of the flowers themselves can be used to contrast with their own outlines. When smooth-stemmed flowers – narcissi, amaryllis, sometimes gladioli and irises – are arranged in curves and crescents, save the stem ends cut from the shortest flowers. Trim these by cutting the portion which was nearest the flower on the slant. Usually the lengths already vary enough. Arrange these stems in a fan at the side of the flowers and make sure that the cut portion points outwards.

When foliage is scarce – town dwellers often have a problem in this respect – make use of foliage from house plants. Many of these can help provide attractive contrast to such stems as gladioli, which are spicate and narcissi, which need wide leaves for contrast. Although it may appear at first that you are robbing the plant, you can actually benefit from such leaves as *Begonia rex*. These usually begin to root in water and so can be used as leaf cuttings once you have finished with the flower arrangement.

For this, try to make a really long-lasting arrangement, beginning with the leaves. If you assemble the stem holders in such a way that the begonia leaves can be held in a block of Oasis, they can stay in it until they begin to grow roots. (Subsequently, when the arrangement is broken up, the young begonia plants can be potted up into the soil still in the Oasis, just as though it was an ordinary root ball.) Arrange the leaves in a clover leaf shape and place something pleasant and natural – such as gourds – at the focal point between them. You can change this from time to time according to the kind of flowers you arrange with the begonia leaves. One basic arrangement may last as long as four months with various modifications.

Winter arrangements Making flower arrangements in winter or at other times when there is either no quantity of flowers at hand or none which will last, is a test of any arranger's resources. In some countries there is always something to be found if you live out of town or if you have a garden. A branch or two of evergreen can make an attractive frame for a few fresh flowers or fresh leaves – pick one of two from several house plants. You can even use fruits or bright vegetables, such as peppers.

Like house plants, cut flowers are influenced by indoor climates and they will not live long in hot, sunny rooms. Fortunately it is possible to dry many true flowers and other plant materials and from these to make beautiful decorations.

DRYING AND PRESERVING FLOWERS

There are certain flowers which produce blooms quite unlike any others. They have tough, straw-like petals which do not shrivel, drop or shatter so that the flowers will only disintegrate if they become mouldy – as they do if kept in damp surroundings – or when they finally become brittle with age. They can last years and are, in fact, known as everlastings. Certain kinds are known as immortelles. Collectively, with any other plant material which is used in a dry state, all are known as perpetuelles.

Most of them belong to the daisy or Compositae family and there are both annual and perennial kinds.

It is possible to grow them in the average garden and it is also possible to buy some of them. Although the number of species and their varieties in cultivation are fairly few, there are more that are worth introducing into cultivation. Most of these types of flowers are to be found in Australasia and Africa.

The daisy family Probably the best known of all are the so-called strawdaisies, *Helichrysum bracteatum*, and their many varieties and strains. If they are well grown and from a good strain the daisies are an inch to two inches (2·5 to 5cm) across.

These particular daisies come in a fine colour range which stretches from a white (not a very pure white) through various yellows (some very pale some deep and gold), orange, pale pink, rosy reds (occasionally quite bright), crimson, light and deep bronze to a dark daisy which is almost black with an off-white centre. The colours last quite well if the flowers are not placed in bright sunshine. They stay bright for a year or two.

Helichrysums deserve their popularity because their straw-like petals gleam more than do most other dried materials. One disadvantage is that the stems become so brittle when dried that the flower heads snap off easily. For this reason, heads only are usually gathered and these have to be mounted on false stems. You can see how this is done with grass stems by referring to the diagram on p. 157.

Possibly as well known as helichrysums are statice, botanically *limonium*, of which there are both annual and perennial kinds. The first come in a fairly good colour range. From the strains and varieties of *L. bonduelli* and

Limonium, Ionas, helichrysum, acroclinium and rhodanthe. Dried flowers need massing. If stems are inserted upwards into the stem holder, a much deeper arrangement can be made.

L. sinuatum we get a bright yellow which, though not as robust as the blues, is a useful colour which shows up well in mixtures. This, the 'sunset' or 'art shade' of the seedsman's catalogues, grows on more delicate stems than the blues whose stems are thicker and flatter. Well grown, all these types of annual statice should be on fairly long stems, 18in to 2ft (45 to 60cm). The stems are often much branched; to make arrangement easy as well as to get the most from the flowers, these are best divided.

Before cutting the stems, examine them for their best points. By judiciously removing the lower stems, even when the flowers on these grow almost to the same level as the main centre stem, you can make good long slender stems to give height to arrangements. These and any others can be further lengthened by mounting them on thick florist wire. Usually this can be simply inserted up the stem ends for an inch or two (2·5 to 5cm) until it holds firm.

The tiny flowers grow in clusters studded along the stem ends. By dividing a stem carefully and then mounting suitable pieces, the arranger can collect many nicely curved pieces to go low in an arrangement. Dried materials all tend to be stiff in appearance and it is wise to seek any means of developing softer lines.

This statice is often on sale while still green and fresh and it can be used first in fresh arrangements and again later. In any case, you should not attempt to dry any

stems on which the flowers are undeveloped. They should be wide open. Statice can be dried, like most of the other everlastings, very simply. Tie the stems tightly (they shrink as they dry) into small bunches and hang them upside down in a cool, airy, shady place.

Candle-wick statice, *L. suworowii*, is more often seen in fresh flower arrangements than in dried, possibly because it is a little temperamental. When bought or cut, it should be mature – immature stems tend to droop the tips of their chenille-like stems – and it should be given hot water treatment. Do not arrange or dry it until the stems are turgid.

If you want to go to as little trouble as possible, you can arrange any of these statice in water and simply let them assimilate this as they dry in *situ*.

When dried, and especially when placed in hot, dry rooms, statice will after a time become brittle and shed part of its flower clusters. When you find this happening you can delay disintegration by spraying the flowers with hair lacquer. This is a good method of keeping intact many fluffy plant materials such as dandelion clocks, thistle heads, willow herb and lichen-covered branches, to name just a few.

The perennial statice or sea-lavender, is different in appearance, the florets being very tiny indeed but massed on much branching stems. Best known as *L. latifolium* and *L. incanum*, these are most useful as fillers in very large arrangements but neither is highly decorative.

Next in popularity to helichrysums in the daisy family are two much daintier flowers, *Helipterum manglesii*, sometimes called *Rhodanthe manglesii* and *H. roseum*, often called *Acroclinium roseum*. These two are quite different in appearance. The first carries several small flowers on its slender, fairly soft stem. The flowers are of soft rose or white, both made pearly in appearance by the silver bracts of the calyces which surround the petals. The others are much more like marguerites in appearance and they may have yellow or black centres with white, very pale pink or deep rose petals. Fresh, they are very fragrant, though the scent is delicate. They look well in fresh arrangements as well as dried.

These and any other everlasting daisy with which you are familiar should not be allowed to become too mature if you want the flowers to keep a good shape and remain bright once they are dried. The guide lies in the eye or centre disc of the flower. This should be young and firm. Once the many tiny florets of which it consists develop, the flower will not dry so well. All the daisies should be gathered just as they open.

Lonas inodora is another daisy, although it might not

appear so. The tiny yellow buttons are borne in small clusters and the flower looks a little like a miniature tansy. It is useful because it provides another shape, colour and a change of texture. It is an annual as are also the immortelles *Xeranthemum annuum, X.a. ligulosum* and *X.a. perligulosum*. These are pink, white and purple daisies with spiky petals, the first named being single flowers the other two double and very double. These are the exception to the general rule and need to be fully expanded before they are gathered, otherwise they remain shut and look like tiny shuttlecocks. They will grow as tall as 2ft (60cm).

Ammobium alatum or sand flower is a tiny daisy, white with a brown centre. The little flowers are produced on thick, statice-like, flat stems. These need to be divided and the flowers set individually in small arrangements, or they will be of little decorative value.

The kinds of flowers described above are most likely to be available everywhere and all are easy to grow. There are, additionally, certain perennials including *Anaphalis margaritacea*, the pearly everlasting, and many helichrysums, some of which have attractive downy 'silver' stems and foliage. These, however, will not grow in cold climates.

Other flowers to dry Apart from these true everlastings, which are flowers that would dry on the plant even if they were not gathered for this purpose, there are a number of flowers of the softer types which can be dried, some more successfully than others. Generally speaking, these need to be dried quickly. Once again, tie them into small bunches (spikes of delphiniums should be tied as single stems) and hang them upside down in a warm, dry but shady place. An airing cupboard is a good place, or some dark corner of a house or apartment near to a radiator or some source of heat. Do not put them near smoke, for this will probably discolour the flowers.

It is impossible to give a list of all of the flowers of this type. Included here are those likely to be well known by most flower arrangers. The reader is urged to experiment. Many discoveries may be chance ones. A flower which dries in an arrangement, when others have simply withered or dropped, is always worth putting to the test. The attractive alchemilla will dry in this way. Some rambler roses, helianthemums, zinnias of certain colours, pompon chrysanthemums and pelargoniums grown indoors will also often dry obligingly on the plant.

Even among these soft-petalled flowers, the daisy family still proves to be of great value. There is a great range of 'thistles' from the blue echinops or globe thistle to the garden eryngium (a different plant from the wild

Eucalyptus and beech leaves, pine cones, protea centres, lupin pods and tree beans, achillea, hydrangea and rushes are just some of the 'flowers' used in this perpetuelle design.

sea-holly, which is very spiny and difficult to arrange) and the wild wayside thistles. Cardoons and artichokes both keep their colours for a long period if you gather them at the right moment; even if you miss this, the fluffy seed heads are beautiful when treated with lacquer.

Yarrows or achillea should also be included here. These have flat umbels of soft or mustard yellow florets and good, tall stems. Some have silvery, fern-like leaves which are worth pressing. Others are perennial gypsophila which, when dried, resembles perennial statice; delphiniums and their annual types the larkspurs; salvias (in particular the delightful heavenly blue *Salvia farinacea*) and the little clary, the decorative value of which really lies in the coloured tips of the stems; stachys, verbascum, hydrangea and catkins of all kinds. These should not be quite mature when they are cut.

Seed heads Once the arranger realizes that in dried arrangements it is possible to use seedheads, the whole world lies ahead. Each country has much to offer and those from some regions, such as lotus seed heads, are so beautiful that they are imported to all parts of the world.

A short list of some of those we have found most useful may be helpful to people who live in areas where wild plants abound. There is no need always to pick these and so detract from the beauty of the countryside for other people. Some of the most decorative, such as cones and many other 'wooden' seed cases, can be found under trees from which they naturally fall. Others are on sale from time to time. These include poppy capsules, yucca, okra, morning glory, camphor tree, magnolia and onion (especially those from the decorative alliums). These are some of the larger types. Beyond, there is a limitless choice of smaller, often spicate, sometime umbelliferous, sometimes branching flower seed stems. You can wait until they are dry before you pick them but do not give weather or animals a chance to spoil them. Most seed stems are best gathered when the seed is ripe but before the stem has changed colour.

Some seed heads are much more decorative than others, and either the whole structure or only part may be used. The shining moons of honesty or lunaria, for instance, are hidden until the outer cases of the seed pod are removed. The vivid orange 'lanterns' of physalis hide a juicy orange berry, which is less important than its cover for arrangements.

Making the most of grasses Grasses, which include cereals, play an important role in dried arrangements. If you want these to look fresh rather than ripe they should be gathered just as the flowering portion of the stem is emerging from its protective grass sheath. Dry grasses in the same way as everlastings. They should keep their colour quite well for a long period although they will gradually bleach once arranged.

Apart from wheat, barley, oats, millet and rice stems, all of which are extremely decorative and look surprisingly well with sophisticated flowers, various kinds of sweet corn or maize can also be employed. Sweet corn husks can be opened and turned back in such a way as to make a flower. If you wish to use the corn, cut it away and on the remaining spot fix some other centre, such as a teasel or a pine cone. Strawberry popcorn, a tiny form with strawberry-like cobs, is well worth growing or seeking out in a street market.

Whatever you gather for drying, try to pick it on a dry day and well before the frosts begin. Should you have to gather wet material, first swing it back and forth to release loose drops of moisture and then hang it up, well spread out, so that the air can circulate among all its parts freely. Once it is much drier you can, should this be more convenient, make the material into smaller bunches for ease of handling and arranging.

Using glycerine Important for perpetuelle and winter decoration is a stock of preserved foliage and certain seed heads. The latter include the fluffy styles of certain clematis including the wild European *Clematis vitalba* or old man's beard, the garden species which leave behind them a stem of feathery whorls such as *C. macropetala* and those of the clematis' near cousin, the lovely pasque flower or pulsatilla. All these can be preserved using glycerine.

By the same process you can also preserve immature seed heads and downy flower spikes such as verbascum and statice. It is always a good thing to experiment. The process is inexpensive, takes little time and will provide you with useful new materials.

The stem ends to be treated must be stood in a solution of one part glycerine and two parts water. Only an inch or two (2·5 to 5cm) is needed. Boil the water, add it to the glycerine and pour the mixture into a deep but narrow vessel so that a little goes a long way. When treating spreading or heavy branches, place the container, which can be a disused food tin or jar, inside a bucket or some larger, deeper container to prevent any tendency for the whole thing to topple over. Treatment may take some time, so put the container in a safe place.

Conditioning is important even for plants that are to be preserved. Unless you are sure that the materials you wish to preserve are taking water, you might be wasting your time by standing them immediately in the solution, even though this is warm. Before treating them, split the stem ends and let them stand in water overnight if possible; in the morning you will be able to tell at a glance which stems, if any, have failed to drink. Discard these and treat the others.

The fluffy seed heads referred to earlier should be gathered almost as soon as the petals have dropped; the seed styles are formed, in fact, while they are still green. Unless they are in this condition they will not be able to take the water or solution. If you fear that it is too late to preserve them by the glycerine method you can prolong their usefulness by spraying them with hair lacquer. Gather them, make sure that they are dry and then spray them.

Preserving colour It is not possible to state a definite length of time in which stems should stay in the solution, because so much depends upon the materials themselves. For branches of leaves it may be three or more weeks. There comes a time when it is possible to see the effect of the solution on the leaves. First the main veins darken or turn colour and then, gradually, the whole leaf surface is affected. Evergreens usually turn a shade of brown.

arranged. Gather only mature fronds, those with dark spores on their undersides.

Skeleton leaves Dyed skeleton leaves are of great value when more colour is needed but those which are left in their natural state are likely to be even more attractive. These shadow leaves give a soft, smudged look to arrangements in which many stiff-stemmed materials have had to be used.

It is possible to buy skeletonized magnolia and large ficus leaves. These are packed flat in bundles, all usually under the name of magnolia. Left as you buy them, they would be much too stiff in arrangements but these and other skeleton leaves can be induced to curl simply by rolling the leaf round a candle, cane, handle of a wooden spoon or whatever is convenient. The immediate curl will probably be much too tight but the leaf can be gently stretched back once or twice until it assumes the amount of curl you want. Begin rolling at the tip and work towards the stem.

If you would like to do your own leaves, the easiest and safest way – safe because it entails no use of acids – is to gather tough textured leaves and let them soak for a few weeks in rain water. This, as you would expect, becomes foul but the bacteria present in the water gradually break down the outer tissues of the leaves. Test these from time to time until you find that you can slip the layers of leaf between the fingers. Take them and wash them well under running water, easing the outer tissues off if necessary. The best way to do this is to insert a thick needle under the outer tissue at the stem end, then pull the whole part away.

Dyeing processes Dried materials can be died commercially but this is less easy for the amateur flower arranger to do. For a start, it is difficult to obtain the right dyes, possibly because these are sold only in large quantities. Domestic dyes, used for dyeing fabrics, work in a limited way. The results are usually unpredictable, although leaves, grasses and immortelles (especially the anaphalis) can emerge quite pleasantly. Their colouring is obviously artificial and the hue is not the one on the packet.

Certain freshly-picked materials can be stood in boiling water to which dye or ink has been added. Results again vary considerably. Skeleton leaves can be steeped in or dabbed over with inks and with Easter egg, and food colourants.

Pressing for preservation Many leaves which cannot be preserved can be pressed. Branches need carefully to

Foliage of deciduous trees such as beech can be induced to keep their autumnal hues if the branches are gathered at the right moment. Not all deciduous foliage can be treated, certainly not soft hairy leaves, although downy or woolly kinds will respond. This should be before leaf fall takes place. We keep watch on the trees and when we see the odd branch or two turning colour we then gather what we need. The earlier in the season you cut and preserve beech, the darker the tone it takes after preservation.

Eucalyptus darkens like most blue-greys but if it is placed in the solution for only a short period – 48 hours or so – it will still keep the characteristically blue-green-grey leaves. This particular foliage will also dry quite well. Eucalyptus does tend to shrivel a little but the brief period in the solution prevents this happening. The same process can be used for green fern fronds, especially those which have been found to curl awkwardly when once be laid flat. The best way to do this is to spread them out on strong paper and pass strips of adhesive tape over the stems to keep the leaves flat against the paper. The branch can then be covered with several thicknesses of newspaper, over which something heavy is put. Under the carpet is a useful place if the leaves are not left there so long that they become damaged by the constant passage of a carpet cleaner. Under the mattress may be a safer place. If you have a spare room which you can use, lay out the covered branch as recommended, cover it with bricks, books, marble slabs or any flat, heavy objects you can find.

Fallen leaves can be pressed with a warm iron. This method often brings a new look to dried leaves which have curled too readily at the edges. It is a good method to use if you wish to preserve fern fronds, such as bracken, found late in the season, when they have already turned colour and have slightly curled. Use a warm – not hot – iron and begin at the base of the stem, working upwards along the main stem and then slowly outwards.

Many leaves can be gathered after they have fallen from the trees. The most useful are those with attractive undersides. They can be found under certain species and varieties of sorbus, maple and rhododendron. Press them between sheets of newsprint or with a warm iron. If you intend to store them, pack them flat, one upon the other. Later they can be mounted on false stems and arranged with their undersides to the front.

Containers for dried flowers The best way to weight the containers for dried flower arrangements is to use sand or small riddle gravel. If nothing else is available use pebbles or plaster. If plaster is used, first line the container with cooking foil; so long as the mouth of the container is wider than the portion in which the plaster has been poured, you will be able later to lift the block of plaster out.

Usually it is sufficient to weight half the container and to arrange the stem holder on this. If you are using wire-netting, the base of this can be pushed into the plaster while it is still moist. If you use sand or gravel, pour in most of what you need, place the netting on it, then pour in a little more to anchor it. Oasis can simply be pushed in place and should hold.

Wire-netting can be fixed in place with adhesive tape. This can be passed over the whole of the mesh as well as its edges. Pinch the tape to reduce its width and wrap it round the thin wire so that no stems are impeded by it. Oasis blocks can be easily fixed to any surface by using Oasisfix. Other adhesives do not work so well. If you tie the plastic in place, use a wide tape so that the surface is

not cut. To remove Oasisfix from a surface, keep wetting your finger as you push it off.

There is no limit to what can be used as a 'container'. Since a dried flower arrangement will probably stand in one place and needs no water, it is sensible to consider whether a favourite ornament might not be used to hold it.

Montage From dried flower arrangement to montage is just a short step, for both use the same materials. It may suit your home or purpose, for instance, to arrange everything on a flat surface and hang this on a wall. Simply fix the netting or plastic and arrange the flower stems through this in the usual way. It is best to hang the base in place before making your arrangement. Gravity can interfere with your designs, especially when long, fairly heavy stems, such as larch cone-studded branches or lichened branches, heavy corn cob flowers and certain 'wooden' fruits are used.

Board covered with a rough weave linen or some other fabric looks well with perpetuelles arranged against it, especially if you can make a colour harmony with these and the fabric. Rush mats suit many dried materials. If these are used, the netting can be stitched to the rush with string taken through in a few places. With netting

156

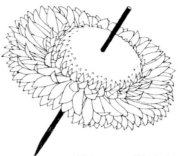

Vivid straw daisies, helichrysums, make bright, cheerful winter decorations if they are generously massed. As they need no water, they can be arranged in a variety of containers, including wicker. With the straw daisies are the orange pods of the gladden iris, achillea, Clematis vitalba *seed heads and some rushes.*

MAKING A FALSE STEM

Helichrysums have stems that become very brittle when they are dry, so it is best to pick the heads only and mount them on false stems.

Make a small hole in the flower head with an awl or an orange stick.

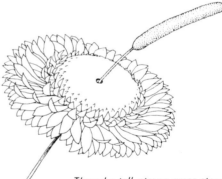

Thread a tall, strong grass stem through the hole, with the grass head at the top.

Cut the grass flush with the flower centre, leaving a long stem below.

you will find that, after the first two or three outer stems are arranged (these may have to be held by cut ends), the other stems will soon interlock and hold fast. Work from the edges to the centre so that each piece of perpetuelle helps to hold the others down. If you want to lengthen stems, splice fine canes or sticks or strong drinking straws, the tough ends of grasses and reeds, or anything which will not easily bend, to the stem of the piece to be arranged.

Picture frames look well filled with perpetuelles. Obviously, the frame should suit the flower as well as its setting. It is even possible to hang an interesting piece of driftwood on a wall and in some crook in the wood to fix a stem holder and to arrange perpetuelles. Many of the woody materials look well displayed like this. Lotus seed heads, cones, 'wooden roses' (morning glory seed heads) and some bracket fungi are perpetuelles you can use in this way, supplemented by large, brown leaves.

CHOOSING CONTAINERS

It is very important that a container should suit the flowers it holds, especially when it supports perpetuelles. It should be of correct proportions, its shape should suit the style of the arrangement, its colour must be harmonious and it should fit in with its surroundings. It should also be heavy, for most dried materials are light.

It is important to remember that there is no water in the container. This is another influential factor in the arrangement. Water not only weights a vessel but influences the arrangement because it bears down upon stem ends and holds them in place once they are anchored in the stem holder.

Perpetuelles can be arranged in the stem holders already described. Most, especially those which are fragile though stiff, are easily and effectively arranged in Oasis. Many perpetuelles have to be mounted on false stems, usually florist wires. These and woody stems cut on the slant will easily penetrate the non-absorbent types of foamed plastic such as Styrofoam, which is moulded into the many shapes – globes, cylinders, circles, blocks, cones and so on which a flower arranger is likely to require. They will also penetrate the type of plastic which is often used for packing. Before you discard any of this determine whether or not it can be used for flower arrangement.

To practise the art of arrangement to its fullest extent, it is useful but not absolutely essential to have a large and varied collection of containers. So long as the few that you have differ considerably from each other you will find that you can play endless variations upon them and the flowers they hold. Meanwhile, if you have the space to store them, you can look out for more.

There is no need to be inhibited by the concept of a 'vase'; if you think in terms of a 'container', always consider the surroundings in which a flower arrangement is to be placed and select containers accordingly, you will do very well. Before spending money on new containers, look round the house. Here most things will already harmonize and the pieces of porcelain, china, pottery, metal, wickerware and wood which you already own, are likely to look well with flowers. If these are not suitable, select things which will go with them – it will not take much practice to arrange and select flowers to suit their styles.

It is also wise to decide where you are most likely to stand a flower arrangement and, when you shop, to search for a container which is right for size as well as colour and style.

Inexperienced flower arrangers tend to go to both extremes when choosing containers. They either buy those which are too small for general use or which are so large that they tend to be uneconomic – unless the arranger practises and becomes skilled in arranging single branches and a handful of flowers.

Whether you are looking through your own things at

If it is to look lovely, water in glass must stay crystal clear. Often subterfuge is necessary. Here, for example, the stems are held in a candle cup fixed to the neck of the jar, and so have no direct contact with the water.

home or searching through shops and market stalls, do remember that the important thing so far as fresh flowers are concerned is that the stem ends should be kept moist once they are arranged.

If you have something which looks right but which you fear is not waterproof, it can usually be lined quite effectively in the ways suggested in the section on *pot et fleur*. Because a stem can sometimes pierce a lining when wire-netting is used, you should, to be safe, line the vessel with plastic and then with a double lining of foil. Quite often a beautiful though porous object can best be used simply by placing a more humble vessel inside it. This can be a pie-dish, gingerbread tin, food tin or any one of the many expendable plastic dishes in which food is packed.

Many people like pitchers and other vessels with handles. Metal tankards, especially pewter, look well with flowers in them and metal containers help flowers to last.

Many of the modern drinking mugs are useful for small arrangements, for a sideboard in a small dining room or for a dresser shelf. Their high glaze and the well designed patterns all contribute to floral colour. They are therefore worth using if flowers are scarce.

With most handled containers it is best to make an asymmetrical arrangement and to place the tallest stem back against the handle. The rest of the materials can

Above: Tansy leaves, dead nettle, hedge parsley and grasses add height to both fresh and dried flower arrangements.

Left: An arrangement like this can be assembled fresh and left to dry. The clematis was first stood in glycerine and hot water to prevent it becoming fluffy when it dried out.

then be arranged to flow away logically from the handle over the rim. This line looks good. If the vessel has an attractive handle, as some tankards do, there is no point in hiding it.

Glass containers If you like glass do not hesitate to buy it but do be prepared to have to spend a little more time on keeping it clean. Flowers in glass containers, especially if they stand in sunlight, tend soon to set up bacterial activity in the water. This becomes cloudy and unattractive. The best way to deal with this is to take the arrangement to the sink and, without disturbing the stems more than possible, let the fresh tap water pour into the glass, thus forcing out the stale.

Cloudy water is not such a problem when coloured glass is used; as you would expect, the darker this is the better. Because plastic contains formaldehyde, you can counteract this bacterial activity by using a piece of Oasis cut so that it fits in the mouth of the glass. As

already described, this can also protrude a little above rim level if by doing so it is easier to make the arrangement and the result is more pleasing.

Cut a piece an inch (2·5cm) or more thick, according to the size of the container and the type of flowers to be arranged. Not all stems enter this plastic easily; hollow daffodil stems, for example, tend to buckle. Make a space at the back of the arrangement, where you can then easily top up the water level, for this must always reach the plastic. When you arrange the flowers keep their stem ends confined to the plastic. Arrange some of them low enough to hide all traces of it.

Wire-netting can be used in much the same manner. In this case you can allow some stem ends to come out below the netting; but if they come out too far below there may be difficulty in masking them later.

Wide glasses of the old champagne type raised on a stem can be used to hold a pinholder and flowers in a vertical line. If you can find pieces of raw glass or glass

Above: One stem of spray chrysanthemums with driftwood. With Oriental styled designs it is possible to make several arrangements from just a few flowers.

Left: An arrangement (shown life size) of a few flowers nipped from a cineraria plant, with hazel catkins and variegated campanula foliage.

Right: You need never be at a loss for a container. These African marigolds are arranged in an oven dish often used in the kitchen.

Far right: Regal lilies and driftwood in a pillow vase designed by the authors. It has a hole below the rim to take the lower-lying stems.

beads to cover the pinholder you can make many attractive arrangements using only very few flowers. An up-turned wine glass can make an unusual pedestal, especially for either another glass of the same shape or size or a bowl in which small and pretty flowers should be arranged.

Cooking-dish containers Many of the dishes and vessels sold for cooking suit flowers remarkably well. Modern oven dishes are so well designed that they seem almost made for the purpose. If you admire a dish but fear that it is so shallow that it will not take enough water to cover the pinholder, you can use a small, deeper supplementary vessel – a little plastic dish or a washed food tin, for instance. This should, like the pinholder, be fixed in place.

To prevent either a pinholder or the small vessel which holds it from moving or tilting, make three or four pea-size pills of plasticine or Oasisfix. Press these, well spaced out, on the *dry* base of the little vessel. Turn the vessel the right way up and press it on to the *dry* dish in the place you want the flowers to stand. Treat the bottom of the dry pinholder the same way. Turn this right side up and press it into the dry dish. Test it by tilting it, or if you are brave enough, by turning it upside down. Both objects should remain firmly in place.

There are many lovely pottery and ceramic pieces made today and although some may not have been designed to hold flowers many do so beautifully. These

sometimes allow a slight amount of moisture to escape from the base and it may be necessary, when they are used on certain surfaces, for the arranger to place a mat below them. In this case, it is suggested that the mat becomes a base – almost in the Japanese sense, a real part of the arrangement.

A base for the arrangement It is possible to buy the various types of bases used in Japanese arrangements from certain shops. Many of them are copies of those which were used in the ancient classical school of this specialized form of flower arrangement. These are of metal and of polished wood and some are of mock jade and other materials. However, these do not suit all kinds of flower arrangements and bases can be 'tailor made' to suit the flowers you intend to arrange.

The simplest bases can be made by covering a cake

board or a table mat with fabric. Cakeboards or similar circular bases are sometimes seen in threes, each one smaller than the other and stepped one on the other, not necessarily placed centrally. This type of base often suits a modern style. If the bases are properly coloured and placed they can do much to bring distinction to an arrangement.

Many flower arrangers like to have a collection of bases, not only of several colours and shapes and sizes but also of different materials, because a base should suit an arrangement in the same way that the flowers and container suit each other. Among those popular in homes as well as in exhibitions are polished slices of wood (some carefully designed, others left with the outer bark still on), pieces of cork, marble, slate and even polished and unpolished rock, thick place mats of all kinds, upturned dishes, plates and ashtrays, tops of lids of tins, flower pot saucers, tiles and shallow wooden boxes. For house plants, *pot et fleur* and flower arrangements, old fashioned trivets of the type once used in the hearth are well worth collecting. These are of iron,

brass and copper and they suit cottage surroundings well.

Sometimes a useful base is marred by a rough surface. Although it would prevent moisture from damaging the surface of furniture, it might scratch the thing which it is meant to protect. Cover the base with an adhesive flocked material. You can also use this on the base of rough containers. It may need changing from time to time but is so easy to use that this presents no problem.

This type of protection is sometimes needed on a pedestal vase, especially in the case of pottery which is not highly glazed.

Decorating waste materials Some of the many expendable objects which are thrown away each day can also make pedestals and attractive containers. Tall, slim tins (those without sharp rims, of course) and plastic bottles and cannisters with their tops neatly and safely cut away can be covered with many different kinds of fabrics, rush matting, foil and even gift wrapping paper if you should find some with an attractive but not dominating design.

Containers of this kind can also be painted – poster paint or shoe white can be used on some surfaces. Or cover them first with an adhesive and then roll them in some material which will give the surface an interesting texture, such as chopped cork, sawdust, seeds or beads, whatever is at hand. For dried materials, you need sometimes not remove the tops of these containers.

161

Cover the surface in whatever way appeals to you, weight the container with sand or plaster and fix a block of Oasis on the top.

Bottle containers You will probably have your own favourite containers, which may be very simple but which ideally suit a particular season. For instance, a flat wide-bellied pottery liqueur bottle – of the kind that once held cherry brandy – is perfect for use in autumn because its gleaming chestnut brown glaze looks so well with a few late flowers, berried branches and brilliant leaves.

Other non-glass bottles are excellent for one-flower styles designed, perhaps, around one long-stemmed rose cluster, one lovely lily, or a tall gladiolus. Where possible or necessary use the flower's own foliage to wedge it into place. If you make sure that the stem reaches the bottom of the bottle, not only does it stand well but you do not have to be concerned about leaving space so that you can top up the water level.

A mass of flowers Sometimes you will want to go to the other extreme and use masses of flowers. It is possible to make a cone of flowers by using a block of Oasis.

You can build up a tower of flowers by using upturned glasses and a series of dishes or bowls. Each glass supports a bowl. Water and flowers surround the glass. In this way you can make two, three or more tiers.

If you want to make a really large flower arrangement you may have to use supplementary containers to give the required height. It is possible to buy cone-shaped metal 'tubes' which are designed to be pushed down among the lower stems. Some can be spliced to canes if the flowers are to stand very high. It is wise to get these into position first and to use plenty of wire-netting in the container which is to hold them. Use it to secure them. Bear in mind that once the cones are themselves filled with water, stemholder and flowers, they will be quite heavy.

With a little ingenuity and improvisation you can make quite short-stemmed flowers fit into a fairly tall arrangement. Choose a pedestal vase in the first place. Raise the back stems in the arrangement by using a slim supplementary container, a tablet tube for instance, well supported by wire-netting. Arrange the stems in this first and arrange the lower ones so that all trace of this holder is hidden. Use enough wire-netting to be able to bring some of the lower stems down low.

In the next section many of the styles of arrangement discussed here are illustrated, with detailed instructions and helpful hints for making a successful display.

Many bottles are attractive enough to hold flowers. They look particularly good when their slim, simple stems hold spreading flowers like these everlasting peas and roses. When they are filled with water, containers like this gleam pleasantly and are well weighted.

Right: If summer flowers like these are to last long, cut them early in the day while they are nicely turgid, and in bud whenever possible. Be sure to strip the stem ends to keep the water clean and sweet. Flowers last longest in metal containers. They tend to clean themselves and so do not encourage the growth of stem-rotting bacteria in the water.

Flower Arranging II

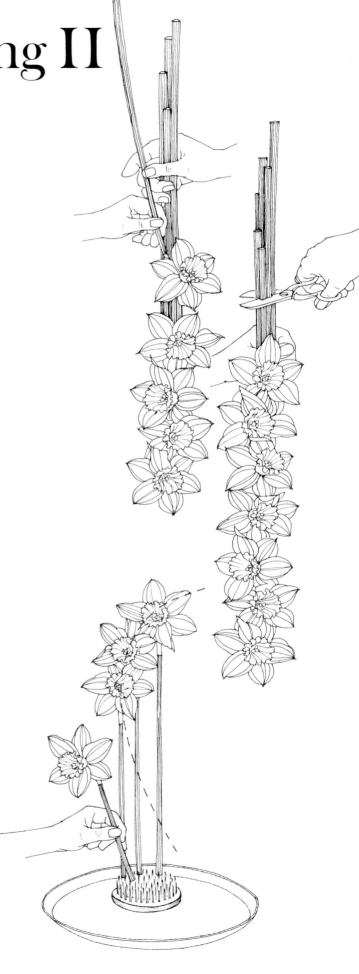

If flower arrangement is to become a pastime then perhaps to some people it is not important for flowers to be arranged quickly. It may not matter if many minutes are spent in coaxing a stem to stay in a certain position. Whether time is important or not, however, the sure placement and positioning of stems is of great importance to the design of an arrangement. If you have a preconceived idea of the manner or pattern in which you would like to see the flowers displayed, then it is essential that this can be done easily and with absolute confidence. If it can also be done quickly, so much the better. And even when time is not important, the less any plant material is handled the better it will look when it is arranged.

Fortunately, there are many sure and effective short cuts to success. Most of these depend on the full use of efficient stem holders. There is really no one holder which works for all types of flowers and every kind of arrangement, although of them all the humble wire-netting is possibly the most versatile for it is so malleable that it can be shaped and squashed into all kinds of containers. In general the varying height, weight, balance, thickness, slenderness, toughness and succulence of stems and flowers means that some holders are much better than others for different materials.

Design, which includes containers, also plays an important part. Stem holders for shallow dishes need to be different from, as well as more securely anchored than those in deep vessels. In some cases, as you will see, actual stem holders can be dispensed with altogether.

Often you can save time and create a more natural effect by letting the materials work for you. It does not take more than a glance to assess their possibilities. For instance, almost every stem has a curve to it no matter how straight it may seem at first and however slight this is it can be exploited and emphasized. Often, especially in the case of foliage and blossom branches, stems can be cut in such a way as to save you both time and temper.

Some flowers take little arranging and will fall naturally into a pleasant pattern but others, especially those which have to be bought and are generally uniform, may seem to call for a little more skill as well as ingenuity. Yet there are many simple basic designs which are easy to do and which provide themes on which many variations can be played.

The illustrations which follow demonstrate these points and many others. By studying, adopting and adapting them you should be able to meet any floral contingency.

Making a curve of flowers

Time is saved when you arrange a line or curve of flowers if you first bunch the flowers in the hand.

1 Hold the flowers with the bloom that is to occupy the lowest position first. If there is any difference in the size of the blooms, place the largest one at the base of the line.

2 Lay the other blooms on the first one, spacing them so that each is well displayed, none hiding another. If the flowers are in bud, or only partly opened, allow more space between each so that they can grow and expand fully, each in its own position. The smallest flowers or the youngest buds should always go at the tips, where stem length permits. This gives added grace and lightness as well as enabling all the flowers to be used.

3 Depending on the length of the tallest stem, or on the height of the finished flower line, cut all the stems level.

A daffodil crescent with aconites

Where the flowers are to make a vertical line, it should be possible simply to hold the prepared bunch and press the stem ends down onto a pinholder. Where the line is to curve, it is usually better to arrange the stems separately.

1 Begin with the tallest flower and set this well back on the holder, to leave room for the other stems and for any other materials which are to be used.

2 Try to mask the tallest stem so that its straight line does not detract from the curve. Here one of the tall, curving daffodil leaves is used for this purpose. Other leaves placed among the stems will also help to accentuate the curves. Only a few of these are required.

3 Green moss and a few winter aconites are used to hide the stem holder. Make sure that the water is deep enough to cover the holder.

*Never let moss hang
over the edge of a container,
for it will act as a siphon.
You will lose the water
and damage the furniture.*

For most arrangements, large mesh wire-netting is cut so that it is a little more than twice the depth of the vessel and a little wider. It is then folded into a U-shape and pushed down into the container. The cut ends of the mesh, now left uppermost, can be used in various ways. Some are hooked over the rim of the container to prevent the mesh from slipping on the smooth inner surface. Others can be used to grip a recalcitrant stem (right). Some of the sharp ends can even be used to pin a leaf or a fleshy stem into the desired position.

Right: When an attractive dish proves too shallow to take enough water to cover the pinholder and thus the base of the stems, use a smaller supplementary container which can be hidden from view. Fasten it so that it does not slide out of place if the arrangement is moved, using three or four small pills of plasticine or Oasisfix (see below). This should be done while both containers are dry.

Making arranging easy

Left: If pinholders are not securely anchored they tend to tip up when heavy stems are impaled on them. Fix three or four pea-sized pills of plasticine or Oasisfix on the dry pinholder base. Turn this back right way up and hold it above the spot where it is to stand. This must also be dry. Press it down firmly. Add water as usual.

Left: As long as the base of a block of Oasis is kept below water level, the rest can protrude well above the rim of the container. This is especially useful when a tall, slim vase is used for a spreading decoration. If some stems are inserted from below as well as from the sides and above, a greater depth of material can be assembled.

Oasis holds water well once it has been soaked and can be used without a container at all, though it will need moistening fairly frequently.

166

To prevent water being spilled, use a block of water-retentive foamed plastic instead of water. If it has been used several times already and is crumbled, use it with wire-netting.

1 Arrange the netting in the container and fill it with plastic. Bend the netting over the top to hold the plastic in a small parcel.

2 Arrange the first four stems of sweet peas to define the height, width and general style of the arrangement. When placing the horizontal stems, push them first across the rim and then slightly down into the stem holder package.

3 Fill in the spaces between the first stems, arranging some flowers to come out and over the rim in a three-dimensional manner.

4 Mass the shorter stemmed pansies low down among the sweet pea stems. See that the stem holder is completely hidden. Add water daily.

Sweet peas last longest
in shallow water
or in a water-soaked
foamed plastic.

Sweet peas and pansies
in a shallow vase

A Christmas arrangement in a cake tin

Decorations add colour to pussy willow, spruce, winter flowers and foliage.

1 Fill the tin with a mass of crumpled wire-netting. Raise this a little in the centre and insert the candle so that it stands on the floor of the tin. If necessary, hook a few cut ends of wire around it, but you should find the candle is soon firmly wedged by the interlocking stems.

2 Push the two longest stems of spruce into the netting. They should lie on the rim of the tin and define the length of the decoration.

3 Treat the candle as the centre stem and place everything else around it in such a way that all the stems appear to be radiating from a point at its base. This is done by pointing all stems towards the centre as you arrange them.

4 The flowers are cut from a long, branching stem. The willow twigs are side stems. Decorations are mounted on pipe cleaners. No sign of the tin shows when the decoration stands flat on a table surface. If it is raised on a stand, perhaps a comport or cake dish, any sign of the base will not be unsightly.

When you have to arrange different thicknesses and textures of stems, it helps to combine stem holders. Here a block of Oasis, to take firm, tall stems, is topped with a mass of wire-netting to hold the softer kinds and those that may not reach the vase bottom.

1 Pull up as many little cut ends of netting as you can. They will help to hold any frail, tall stems in place.

2 Arrange the central, tallest stem first. Even if its stem curves, the tip should be over the centre of the base of the container.

3 Arrange the side stems, parsley seed heads, to define the width and the intermediary stems, willow herb and poppy seed stems, to sketch the outline. Since the arrangement is to face one way, place these as near to the back of the vase as possible to leave plenty of room for the other materials.

You can anchor wire-netting securely by using adhesive tape passed over a strand of the wire and then fixed to the outside of the container.

Berries, leaves and grasses

There are many parts of familiar plants, even weeds, which, apart from their blooms, are lovely enough to be used as decorations. Even if you have no real flowers, you can still create beautiful colour harmonies and combine attractive and interesting textures.

Grasses, seed heads and satiny honesty moons, gleaming unripe bryony berries, cupped hazel nuts, green leaves of hedge lonicera, cow parsley, rose, ivy and sun spurge, the soft blue-grey and silvery foliage of rue, santolina and cineraria are some of the materials used here. Wherever possible, arrange the slim, tapering materials at the tips and edges of an arrangement and mass the largest at the centre.

Using long-lasting branches

If you have a framework of long-lived pussy willow stems, their catkins just beginning to show, you can vary the arrangement by using different kinds of other flowers with them each week. Choose similar shapes and follow the same basic pattern.

This arrangement uses
only a few actual flowers
but makes good use
of other simple materials.

1 Trim the willow to make several smooth single stems. Strip the stem ends. Fill a goblet with crumpled wire-netting, cut ends uppermost.

2 Arrange the tallest stem on the left. Hold it at the required angle and hook cut ends of wire-netting round it to secure it.

3 Balance this with a long stem on the opposite side to suggest a curve resting on the rim. Arrange the two longest flower stems to follow the lines indicated by the willow stems.

4 Cut each flower stem (here Poet's narcissi) a little shorter than the one arranged before it so that each bloom is well displayed.
As these are arranged, place their own leaves and some shorter willow stems among them to help wedge the stems in place and to make an attractive outline. See that all the stems appear to radiate from one central point.

170

Making use of foliage

Chrysanthemums are long-lasting but after a
week or two they tend to lose their leaves. It
is wise, therefore, to arrange them with
plenty of leafy or other well-covered material
which will disguise their loss.

1 Fill the vase from brim to brim with wire-
netting. Leave a few cut ends above the rim
at the back to hold any tall branches securely.

2 Prune side stems from the oak branches
and save them to arrange at lower levels.
Strip the stem ends so that the parts that go
under water are clear.

3 Arrange the tallest privet berry stem to
define the height of the arrangement. Plan
and then fill in the outline with the other
long berried and leaf stems. Arrange the
tallest flower back close to the tallest berried
stem.

4 Arrange the lowest flower, inserting its
stem through the wire-netting from the front
of the vase, pointing slightly downwards to
the back. Now arrange the flowers between
these two. Shorten the stems as you go,
gauging their length so that each bloom is
displayed to advantage.

Use left-over materials,
the leaf and berry side stems
to fill in any gaps
that remain. Try to avoid
making any straight lines
in the overall pattern.

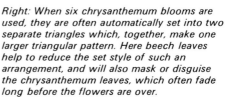

Arranging fruit and flowers

1 Fix a large pinholder to the floor of the bowl. The lilies vary in the number of blooms on each stem. Choose the fullest and set it in place first, in such a way that the flowers are all well displayed. Cut some from the large cluster and set them aside. Group the largest leaves round the stem to make a frame for the short flowers and the cherries.

2 Arrange the tallest stem behind these. Place some of the short blooms round the rim, impaling their stem ends on the very edge of the pinholder.

3 Arrange one or two tall stems at the back, their blooms below the first tall stem that was inserted.

4 Hosta leaves and cherries are massed to fill in the spaces between the short blooms. Cherries can be bunched together and tied to false stems.

Right: When six chrysanthemum blooms are used, they are often automatically set into two separate triangles which, together, make one larger triangular pattern. Here beech leaves help to reduce the set style of such an arrangement, and will also mask or disguise the chrysanthemum leaves, which often fade long before the flowers are over.

1 First fill the vase from base to rim with wire-netting. Keep some of the cut ends just above rim level. Arrange the flowers, beginning with the tallest at the back. If it is necessary to increase its height, lift this one up and secure its stem with the cut ends of the wire.

2 Remove the side stems from the lower portion of the branch in such a way that they retain a little of the main stem; even an inch will be useful. They will then flow easily and naturally to the left or the right to aid the design.

3 Arrange the tips of the branches between the flowers, spreading them well out. Short side stems should be used to flow forwards over the rim of the vase.

All branches will need some grooming and pruning. Cut away any damaged leaves first of all. Arrange the branch and then cut away any crossing leaves and remove any which seems to be making the foliage look too dense. Where possible place some of the leaves in front of the flower stems so that when their faded leaves are removed, no bare stem shows.

Be sure to
condition chrysanthemums
thoroughly
before arranging them.

Disguising a triangular outline

House plants can be used effectively
in winter and spring flower arrangements.
Begonia leaves, like this B. masoniana,
can be used time and time again. Later, if they have not
already rooted in the water, they can be used as leaf
cuttings. Mature leaves take water quickest and last
longest. Here they serve a dual purpose. With the
small pieces of gnarled driftwood they not only
complement the narcissi but also hide the heavy holder.
If you cut or buy narcissi in bud, you will be able
to watch them open. Buds also last much longer than
open blooms.

1 Fix a large pinholder to the base of the bowl and
arrange the begonia leaves well forward on it, leaving
plenty of room for the flower stems. You will then be
able to change them from time to time without
disturbing the leaves. If the holder still shows, recess
some knotty driftwood or a stone between the front
leaves to hide it.

2 Now arrange the flowers. You could make a vertical
crescent (see p. 165) but with smooth stemmed
flowers you can make a refreshingly simple design,
grouping them with their leaves together, just as you
might see them growing in the garden.

Using simple containers

Left: One way to make up for a lack of fresh flowers
is to use lots of leaves and bright or patterned
containers, like the coffee mug illustrated here. If you
use the container's colours as a theme and match the
plant materials to them, everything will be in harmony.

A design in a mug takes only a few minutes. You
need a tall stem of bright, glossy, variegated holly, a
shorter piece of the dark green kind for contrast, a
small side branch of spruce, two or three green ivy
trails, some holly berry sprigs and three flowers. The
blooms here were cut from a long stem of spray
chrysanthemums.

1 Strip the stem ends. Remove the side stems from
the holly. Snip the leaves from among the holly berries
for full colour value. Cut a downwards slice from the
back of the Oasis cylinder before putting it into the
mug, so that you can add water.

2 Arrange the tall stem of variegated holly against the
rim near the handle and let its curve, however slight,
follow the same line. Arrange the spruce tip so that it
flows over the opposite rim. These two define the
height, width and general shape of the arrangement.

3 Place the smaller pieces all around the rim so that
they flow over and hide it.

4 Add the dark green holly and let it curve down to
carry on the line of the first tall stem. Arrange the
berries in a cluster. Place the flowers at the foot of the
tall stem to act as a focal point.

174

Varying the arrangement

The same containers can often be used in different types of arrangements. On p. 174 the glass bowl (above) is used for an upright design. One problem with glass is to conceal the holder thoroughly. Here wire-netting has been used, but it is well hidden by the roses' own foliage.

1 Take a piece of large mesh wire-netting, to make a roll about 2in (5cm) long by 1in (2.5cm) deep.

2 Hook this to the rim of the bowl with a few of the projecting cut ends of wire. For extra security you can tape them to the outside of the bowl.

3 Arrange the longest stem so that it flows from the centre. Push it through the wire from the side, downwards into the water.

4 Arrange one opposite to balance. Let it flow out over the water. You will find that the stems lock and hold fast but if they seem insecure, wedge them in place with rose leaves. Top up the water daily.

On p. 169 a similarly shaped vase holds a symmetrical arrangement. Here the style captures the informality of the cup and saucer plant, Cobea scandens.

1 Stems are fine and blooms heavy, so use a mass of wire-netting.

2 Arrange the trails first. They are floppy, so fasten them near the rim with cut ends rising from the wire-netting.

3 Arrange the flowers so that they come below the trails. Begin at the back, then go to the sides, working to the centre.

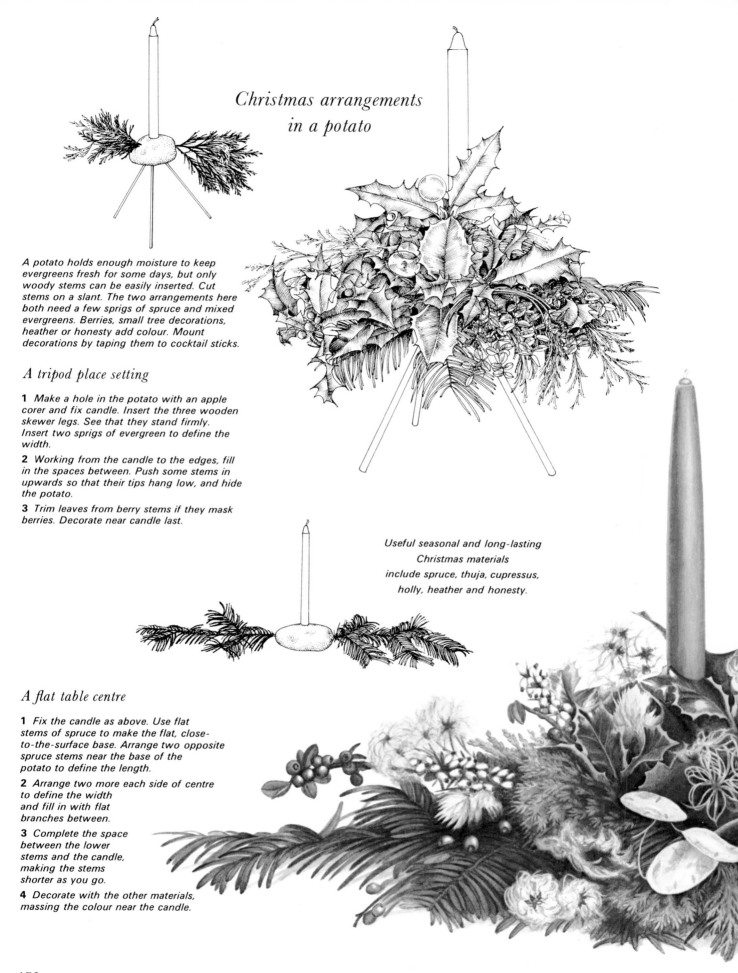

Christmas arrangements in a potato

A potato holds enough moisture to keep evergreens fresh for some days, but only woody stems can be easily inserted. Cut stems on a slant. The two arrangements here both need a few sprigs of spruce and mixed evergreens. Berries, small tree decorations, heather or honesty add colour. Mount decorations by taping them to cocktail sticks.

A tripod place setting

1 Make a hole in the potato with an apple corer and fix candle. Insert the three wooden skewer legs. See that they stand firmly. Insert two sprigs of evergreen to define the width.

2 Working from the candle to the edges, fill in the spaces between. Push some stems in upwards so that their tips hang low, and hide the potato.

3 Trim leaves from berry stems if they mask berries. Decorate near candle last.

Useful seasonal and long-lasting
Christmas materials
include spruce, thuja, cupressus,
holly, heather and honesty.

A flat table centre

1 Fix the candle as above. Use flat stems of spruce to make the flat, close-to-the-surface base. Arrange two opposite spruce stems near the base of the potato to define the length.

2 Arrange two more each side of centre to define the width and fill in with flat branches between.

3 Complete the space between the lower stems and the candle, making the stems shorter as you go.

4 Decorate with the other materials, massing the colour near the candle.

176

You can simplify arrangements considerably if you sometimes combine stem holders. Here a heavy metal pinholder is used for the heaviest material while a water-absorbent foamed plastic holds the soft, sappy coleus foliage.

It is essential always to hide stem holders. Fortunately the material used for this can be an integral part of the arrangement.

Driftwood with coleus

1 Fix a pinholder to the floor of the dish, using plasticine pills (p. 166). Tilt the driftwood to an attractive angle. Hold it firmly in place and press its base onto the pin-holder. It helps to cut wood on a slant.

2 Take a water-soaked cylinder of Oasis, tilt it slightly and press it on the front portion of the holder. Mask with a smaller piece of driftwood, arranging this so that it looks like a continuation of the taller piece. Leave a clear area of Oasis for the coleus stems.

3 Arrange coleus tips in Oasis so that they seem to be growing from the driftwood. Fill the dish with water and top up daily. If the coleus leaves droop they can easily be replaced.

A quick, easy and effective way of arranging roses of one variety is to use a tall, slim vase or glass and first bunch and tie the stems together before placing them in water. You can use this method with most uniform flowers.

1 Select the largest bloom, if you have a choice, and hold it in one hand to go at the bottom of the bunch. Grading the flowers as you go, place the stem of the next largest flower on this and proceed in this way until the last one is in position. Allow each bloom space to expand and be well displayed.

2 Tie the bunch just below the lowest bloom. Test it against the container so that you can see just how much stem to cut away. The tie should be just below the rim so that it does not show.

3 Strip the stem ends below this point. If you have to shorten the stems a lot, cut some leaves away with a little of the main stem so that you can arrange them at rim level. Use these also to wedge the bunch upright if necessary.

Below: When you have none of the flower's own foliage, you can add to the size and design of an arrangement by using stem ends of flowers you have shortened. Here red stalks of amaryllis add extra colour.

Formal flowers

A Byzantine cone

This ancient design looks well in a modern setting. This one, using lily-of-the-valley, roses, freesias, stephanotis and evergreens, was designed for a wedding but it can be copied using many other flowers and plant materials. It looks well as a Christmas decoration.
Sometimes it is possible to buy Oasis cones. If not, use cylindrical shapes.

1 Put one cylinder in the container and place two more on top. Then cut another in half and place it, cut side down, on top of the other three. Join all together by passing a fine cane or some florist wires down from the top centre to the base. Soak the plastic in water and keep it moist always.

2 Cover the whole surface lightly with short sprigs of evergreens. Longer stems arranged at the base, shortening gradually to the tip, define the cone shape.

3 Arrange the flowers, pushing stems tightly into the spaces between the evergreen materials. Let tapering forms follow the line of the cone.

179

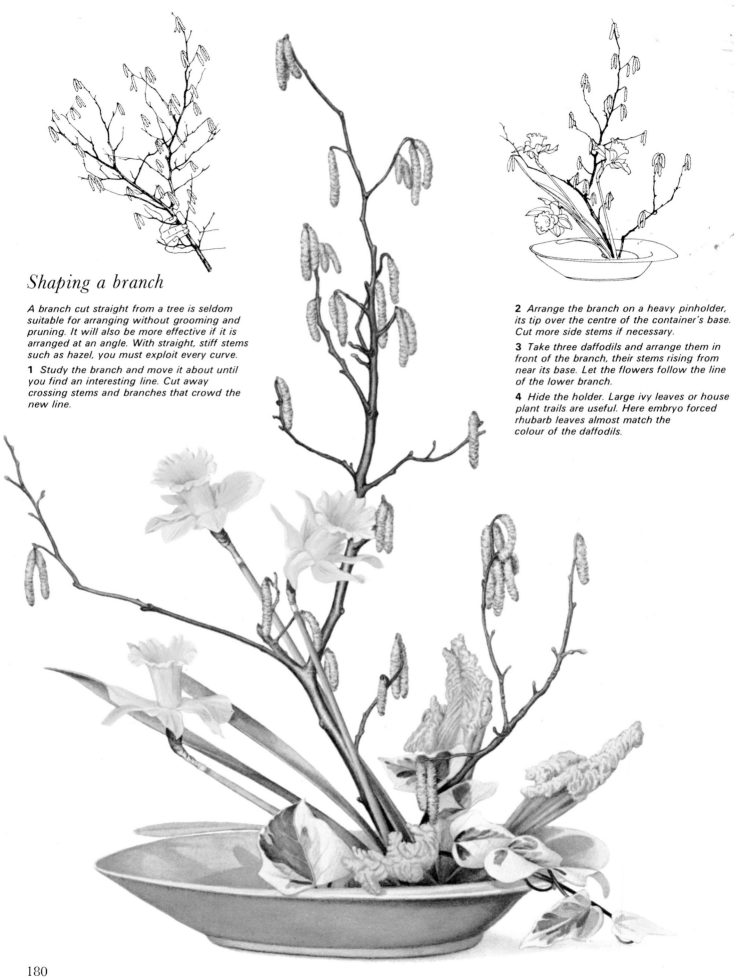

Shaping a branch

A branch cut straight from a tree is seldom suitable for arranging without grooming and pruning. It will also be more effective if it is arranged at an angle. With straight, stiff stems such as hazel, you must exploit every curve.

1 Study the branch and move it about until you find an interesting line. Cut away crossing stems and branches that crowd the new line.

2 Arrange the branch on a heavy pinholder, its tip over the centre of the container's base. Cut more side stems if necessary.

3 Take three daffodils and arrange them in front of the branch, their stems rising from near its base. Let the flowers follow the line of the lower branch.

4 Hide the holder. Large ivy leaves or house plant trails are useful. Here embryo forced rhubarb leaves almost match the colour of the daffodils.

Using a few flowers

Many natural materials can be used with flowers to make unusual, attractive designs — or even to save time. Shells and many kinds of marine objects are particularly useful when only a few flowers are available. Here five daffodils are arranged with a sea fan and scallop shells. The container, shaped like a clam, continues the theme.

1 Fix a large metal pinholder firmly in the centre of the dish. Arrange the sea fan well back on this, pushing it down between the points. If necessary, wedge it in one or two places with small portions of stem or with plasticine.

2 Bunch and cut the daffodils (p. 164).

3 Arrange them in a curve, placing their stem ends well back against the fan. A few leaves arranged among them in places will help to wedge them in the right position.

4 Hide the pinholder with scallop shells. Tilt them slightly so that you can push in the thin edge. The actual shell base is usually too thick to go between the points undamaged.

5 Fill the bowl with water and top it up daily.

It is worth while practising simple branch arrangements not only because they are attractive but also because they are economical and quick to do. Most branches are long lasting, so the framework of the arrangement can be left in place while the flowers are changed. When flowers are scarce or expensive, use small pot plants.

1 Strip the lowest side stems from a birch branch. Fix a long, rectangular pinholder to the dry base of a rectangular dish and arrange the birch in one corner.

2 Move the branch from the vertical by pressing on the base until the tip of the tallest curved twig appears to be over the centre of the base of the container.

3 Trim the branch. Begin by removing all damaged leaves and bare twigs. Try to accentuate the pendant curves.

4 Use some of the cut side stems to continue the line of the branch from its base outwards, giving a three-dimensional effect. These stems will help to hide the pinholder when the arrangement is complete.

Contrasting arrangements and containers

Many everyday vessels can be used for flower arrangement. Sometimes they even guide the arranger to a certain style. Here the formal shape of the pompon dahlias is repeated in the round oven dishes, and their concentric lines also reflect the floral crescent.

Adding height to short-stemmed flowers

A tablet tube in the container raises the central bunch of flowers and the whole arrangement is placed on a pedestal.

1 Secure the bowl to its pedestal with plasticine pills. Fill it with enough wire-netting to hold a tablet tube and flowers. Use cut ends of wire to keep this upright. Tie the flowers in the hand and place them in the tube.

2 Add the lowest side stems, bringing them down as low as possible, taking care not to snap any stems. To do this, wrap a wire end round the stem near the rim and exert gentle pressure on this.

3 Arrange more side stems to make a curve. These stem ends can go further into the bowl. Add flowers until the tube is completely hidden.

Two-tiered arrangements

This two-tier container was specially designed but you can build one by standing one bowl inside another. Fit the base of the top bowl into a jam jar or use a candlestick and cup. More than one tier can be made. Anchor with plasticine pills.

1 Fill the bowls with large mesh wire-netting, taking it round the support if necessary. Arrange the first flowers to define height, width and shape. Here roses, tulips, carnations, eucalyptus buds and foliage were used.

2 Following these lines add more, placing the lowest flowers in the upper bowl so that there are no separated zones.

Glossary

Index of Plants

General Index

Acknowledgements

Glossary

aroid A plant belonging to the **family** Araceae, e.g. an arum.

bigeneric Derived from two separate **genera**.

bract A modified leaf which grows near the **calyx** of a flower, often petal-like in appearance.

bulb An underground bud, covered in scales, from which the flower stems and leaves grow, e.g. an onion or daffodil.

calyx The outer envelope of the flower, consisting of sepals.

corm A thickened underground stem with a bud at its tip, e.g. a crocus.

corolla The inner envelope of the flower, usually consisting of petals.

crown Upper part of the root, enlarged in some plants.

cultivar A cultivated **variety**, not a natural one.

damp off A disease affecting seedlings. It is caused by a fungus and occurs when the seeds are over-watered.

dicotyledon A plant belonging to a large plant group, the Dicotyledons. Their most obvious characteristic is that the leaves have a network of veins.

ephemeral Lasting only for a short time.

epidermis The layer of cells covering the outer surface of plants.

epiphyte A non-parasitic plant that grows on another, generally on a tree.

family Group of animals or plants, subdivided into **genera**. For example the family Liliaceae includes chlorophytum, dracaena and sansevieria genera.

fern A large group of plants, differing greatly in appearance. They have fronds (leaves) that are often large and divided, a stem which is often a rhizome, and roots. They reproduce by spores, usually formed on the fronds.

floret Small flower head, usually in a group on a stem.

genus (pl. genera) Group of plants or animals, subdivision of **family** and in turn divided into related **species**.

glaucous Covered with a pale green bloom.

hybrid A plant grown from two different species.

lateral A stem growing from the side.

microclimate Climate in a very small area, such as inside a bottle garden. Usually different from the climate of the surrounding area.

monocotyledon Plant belonging to a large plant group, the Monocotyledons. Their leaves have parallel veins, e.g. grasses.

offset A root which develops a shoot and grows into a new plant.

palm A plant of the family Palmaceae. Palms are mainly unbranched shrubs or trees with large, persistent leaves in a terminal tuft, sometimes a rope-like trunk with scattered leaves and stout spines.

photosynthesis The process by which plants use light and carbon dioxide to produce sugar and other substances.

propagate To multiply, increase naturally.

rhizome A stem that creeps horizontally, usually partly covered in soil. Buds grow upwards from it, roots downwards.

runner A stem that runs along the ground and can develop roots of its own.

scape A naked flower stalk bearing one or more flowers.

to set (of flowers) To begin to form fruits.

spadix A succulent spike carrying male and female flowers.

spathe A large **bract** or modified leaf covering numerous flowers, usually on a **spadix**.

species A distinct group of plants or animals which are mutually fertile; a subdivision of **genus**.

spicate Forming a spike, spike-shaped.

staging Special shelves, used in greenhouses, with drainage spaces to allow for watering and spraying.

stamen Male organ of a flower.

stigma Female organ of a flower, which includes the ovary.

stipules Small growths, usually leafy, appearing at the base of the leaf. They are usually different in shape or texture from the main leaves.

stolon A sucker growing first in the air, then bending downwards towards the soil.

stomata Openings or pores in the **epidermis** of plants, either in leaves or roots.

succulents Plants, including cacti, that are specially adapted to withstand long periods of drought.

terrarium A completely contained indoor garden, sometimes sealed.

top dress To add fresh soil to a potted plant without re-potting.

tubes Part of a flower where the **calyx** and **corolla** are joined.

umbelliferous A plant that has umbels, several flower stalks springing from the same point with flower heads making a flat top together; a member of the family Umbelliferae.

tuber A thickened underground stem, e.g. a potato.

turgid Swollen, full of water.

variegation Having patches of different colours, usually green and white in plants.

variety A plant that is slightly different from other members of the same species, perhaps in colour only.

Index of Plants

Numbers in italics refer to illustrations.

INDEX OF PLANTS

continued

General Index

Numbers in italics refer to illustrations.

ACKNOWLEDGEMENTS

Colour photographs are by Leslie Johns with the following exceptions:

A–Z Botanical Collections Ltd: pp. 8, 28, 51 (l), 63, 64, 65, 67 (r), 71 (below), 72, 73, 75 (below), 76, 96, 101, 107, 108–9
Heather Angel: p. 31 (r)
Arup Associates: p. 81 (designed by Arup Associates, architects, engineers and quantity surveyors)
Ronald Boardman: p. 60
Harry Smith Photographic Collection: p. 99

Original illustrations in colour and line are by:
Norman Barber: pp. 59, 60–1, 71, 73, 85, 87, 95, 97, 98, 101, 104, 109, 110
Ian Garrard: pp. 14–17, 102, 115, 127, 131, 137, 157 and line illustrations on pp. 164–83
John Wilkinson: pp. 12–3, 52–3, 92–3 and colour illustrations on pp. 164–83

Index by Margaret Durst